What Did the Constitution Mean to Early Americans?

HISTORIANS AT WORK

Advisory Editor
Edward Countryman, Southern Methodist University

How Did American Slavery Begin?
Edward Countryman, Southern Methodist University

What Caused the Pueblo Revolt of 1680?
David J. Weber, Southern Methodist University

What Did the Declaration Declare?
Joseph J. Ellis, Mount Holyoke College

What Did the Constitution Mean to Early Americans?
Edward Countryman, Southern Methodist University

Does the Frontier Experience Make America Exceptional?
Richard W. Etulain, University of New Mexico
(forthcoming)

What Was Progressivism?
Glenda E. Gilmore, Yale University (forthcoming)

What Did the Constitution Mean to Early Americans?

Readings Selected and Introduced by

Edward Countryman
Southern Methodist University

Selections by

Isaac Kramnick

Stephen E. Patterson

Gordon S. Wood

Jan Lewis

Jack N. Rakove

Bedford/St. Martin's   *Boston* 🙖 *New York*

For Bedford / St. Martin's

History Editor: Katherine E. Kurzman
Developmental Editor: Charisse Kiino
Production Supervisor: Catherine Hetmansky
Marketing Manager: Charles Cavaliere
Editorial Assistant: Molly Kalkstein
Copyeditor: Barbara G. Flanagan
Text Design: Claire Seng-Niemoeller
Cover Design: Peter Blaiwas
Cover Art: U.S. Constitution, page one (detail). National Archives and Records Administration
Composition: ComCom
Printing and Binding: Haddon Craftsmen, Inc.

President: Charles H. Christensen
Editorial Director: Joan E. Feinberg
Director of Editing, Design, and Production: Marcia Cohen
Managing Editor: Elizabeth M. Schaaf

Library of Congress Catalog Card Number: 98–87526

Manufactured in the United States of America.

3   2   1   0   9   8

f   e   d   c   b   a

For information, write: Bedford / St. Martin's, 75 Arlington Street, Boston, MA 02116
(617-426-7440)

ISBN: 0–312–18262–7 (paperback)
0–312–21821–4 (hardcover)

Acknowledgments

Isaac Kramnick, "The 'Great National Discussion': The Discourse of Politics in 1787," *William and Mary Quarterly,* 3rd ser., 45 (January 1988): 3–32.

Jan Lewis, "'Of Every Age Sex & Condition': The Representation of Women in the Constitution," *Journal of the Early Republic* 15 (1995): 359–87. Reprinted with permission from the *Journal of the Early Republic.*

Stephen E. Patterson, "The Federalist Reaction to Shays's Rebellion," in *In Debt to Shays: The Bicentennial of an Agrarian Rebellion,* edited by Robert A. Gross. Reprinted with permission of the University Press of Virginia.

Jack N. Rakove, "The Perils of Originalism," in *Original Meanings: Politics and Ideas in the Making of the Constitution.* Copyright © 1996 by Jack N. Rakove. Reprinted by permission of Alfred A. Knopf, Inc.

Gordon S. Wood, from *The Creation of the American Republic, 1776–1787,* by Gordon S. Wood. Published by the Institute of Early American History and Culture. Copyright © 1969, 1998 by permission of the publisher and the author.

It is a violation of the law to reproduce these selections by any means whatsoever without the written permission of the copyright holder.

Foreword

The short, inexpensive, and tightly focused books in the Historians at Work series set out to show students what historians do by turning closed specialist debate into an open discussion about important and interesting historical problems. These volumes invite students to confront the issues historians grapple with while providing enough support so that students can form their own opinions and join the debate. The books convey the intellectual excitement of "doing history" that should be at the core of any undergraduate study of the discipline. Each volume starts with a contemporary historical question that is posed in the book's title. The question focuses on either an important historical document (the Declaration of Independence, the Emancipation Proclamation) or a major problem or event (the beginnings of American slavery, the Pueblo Revolt of 1680) in American history. An introduction supplies the basic historical context students need and then traces the ongoing debate among historians, showing both how old questions have yielded new answers and how new questions have arisen. Following this two-part introduction are four or five interpretive selections by top scholars, reprinted in their entirety from journals and books, including endnotes. Each selection is either a very recent piece or a classic argument that is still in play and is headed by a question that relates it to the book's core problem. Volumes that focus on a document reprint it in the opening materials so that students can read arguments alongside the evidence and reasoning on which they rest.

One purpose of these books is to show students that they *can* engage with sophisticated writing and arguments. To help them do so, each selection includes apparatus that provides context for engaged reading and critical thinking. An informative headnote introduces the angle of inquiry that the reading explores and closes with Questions for a Closer Reading, which invite students to probe the selection's assumptions, evidence, and argument. At the end of the book, Making Connections questions offer students ways to read the essays against one another, showing how interesting problems emerge from the debate. Suggestions for Further Reading conclude each book, pointing interested students toward relevant materials for extended study.

Historical discourse is rarely a matter of simple opposition. These volumes show how ideas develop and how answers change, as minor themes turn into major considerations. The Historians at Work volumes bring together thoughtful statements in an ongoing conversation about topics that continue to engender debate, drawing students into the historical discussion with enough context and support to participate themselves. These books aim to show how serious scholars have made sense of the past and why what they do is both enjoyable and worthwhile.

EDWARD COUNTRYMAN

Preface

There are very few moments when people make really fundamental decisions about the kind of future they want as a nation. When such a moment does come, it can be exhilarating but it can also be terrifying. Revolutionary Americans lived through two such moments. One came in 1776, when they declared that they had broken with Britain. The other came in 1787 and 1788, when they faced the question of what kind of place their independent America was going to be. Their answer was the federal Constitution, under which Americans still live.

The men responsible for writing the Constitution—whom we honor as "the Framers"—knew that they were making history. So did "the people of the United States," as they considered whether to accept or reject the document that the Framers offered. The fundamental issue at stake was establishing the terms of "being American." That issue has recurred again and again, as more and more people have claimed the title "American" and the Constitution's "blessings of liberty" for themselves.

This is one reason that the creation of the American Republic presents a historic occasion of the first order. Another reason is that what the Framers created has endured, while other governments and political systems around the globe have not. A third is that the United States has become the premier power of the modern world. All these have happened within the political framework that the Constitution established two hundred years ago.

The founding generation left behind an enormous amount of information about itself, what it thought, and what it did. Using that evidence, historians have probed deeply into the issues surrounding the creation of the American Republic. Hopes and fears, high-minded patriotism and mere self-interest, inspired creativity and reaction against a revolution "gone wrong": all these appear in the record. So does a great deal of conflict. Not all Americans agreed either with the Framers' diagnosis of America's ills or with the remedies they offered. Much of the argument took place in political theories among literate white males. But the issues at stake bore on every person and group within the Republic's boundaries. Recent historians have probed all these dimensions to discuss what the Constitution meant to the generation that created it; this collection of essays presents some of the highlights of what they have achieved. It shows historians at work on a subject of great complexity and enormous importance whose consequences we live with today.

Acknowledgments

This book is among the first volumes in the Historians at Work series. I owe thanks for help both in assembling the book itself and in working out the series template to my collaborators at Bedford/St. Martin's: Publisher Chuck Christensen, Associate Publisher Joan Feinberg, Sponsoring Editor Katherine Kurzman, Developmental Editor Charisse Kiino, Managing Editor Elizabeth Schaaf, Editorial Assistant Molly Kalkstein, Copyeditor Barbara Flanagan, and Art Director Donna Dennison. The series itself is Katherine's idea, and I'm very honored that she chose me to help her turn that idea into reality. Ross Murfin urged me to work with Bedford on the basis of his own good experience with the people there. Deep thanks go as well to historians Robert Allison, Lance Banning, Burton Kaufman, Rebecca Shoemaker, Melvin Yazawa, and Rosemarie Zagarri. They read my drafts with great care, told me honestly what they thought I was doing wrong, and encouraged me to keep at it until I finally got the book right.

EDWARD COUNTRYMAN

A Note for Students

Every piece of written history starts when somebody becomes curious and asks questions. The very first problem is who, or what, to study. A historian might ask an old question yet again, after deciding that existing answers are not good enough. But brand-new questions can emerge about old, familiar topics, particularly in light of new findings or directions in research, such as the rise of women's history in the late 1970s.

In one sense history is all that happened in the past. In another it is the universe of potential evidence that the past has bequeathed. But written history does not exist until a historian collects and probes that evidence *(research)*, makes sense of it *(interpretation)*, and shows to others what he or she has seen so that they can see it too *(writing)*. Good history begins with respecting people's complexity, not with any kind of preordained certainty. It might well mean using modern techniques that were unknown at the time, such as Freudian psychology or statistical assessment by computer. But good historians always approach the past on its own terms, taking careful stock of the period's cultural norms and people's assumptions or expectations, no matter how different from contemporary attitudes. Even a few decades can offer a surprisingly large gap to bridge, as each generation discovers when it evaluates the accomplishments of those who have come before.

To write history well requires three qualities. One is the courage to try to understand people whom we never can meet—unless our subject is very recent—and to explain events that no one can re-create. The second quality is the humility to realize that we can never entirely appreciate either the people or the events under study. However much evidence is compiled and however smart the questions posed, the past remains too large to contain. It will always continue to surprise.

The third quality historians need is the curiosity that turns sterile facts into clues about a world that once was just as alive, passionate, frightening, and exciting as our own, yet in different ways. Today we know how past events "turned out." But the people taking part had no such knowledge. Good history recaptures those people's fears, hopes, frustrations, failures, and achievements; it tells about people who faced the predicaments and choices that still confront us as we head into the twenty-first century.

All the essays collected in this volume bear on a single, shared problem that the authors agree is important, however differently they may choose to respond to it. On its own, each essay reveals a fine mind coming to grips with a worthwhile question. Taken together, the essays give a sense of just how complex the human situation can be. That point—that human situations are complex—applies just as much to life today as to the lives led in the past. History has no absolute "lessons" to teach; it follows no invariable "laws." But knowing about another time might be of some help as we struggle to live within our own.

EDWARD COUNTRYMAN

Contents

Foreword   *v*
Preface   *vii*
A Note for Students   *ix*

PART ONE   **The Document**   1

The Constitution of the United States   *3*

PART TWO   **Introduction**   15

The Creation of the United States   *17*
    From Revolution to Ratification   17
    Historians and the Constitution   24

PART THREE   **Some Current Questions**   31

1. What were the issues in 1787?   33

Isaac Kramnick

The "Great National Discussion": The Discourse of Politics in 1787

"The generations of Americans who lived through the founding and the framing have left us proof positive of their paradigmatic pluralism."

2. Were the framers counterrevolutionaries?   69

Stephen E. Patterson

The Federalist Reaction to Shays's Rebellion

"Shays's Rebellion, at least to certain leading men, was less a cause of Federalism than it was an opportunity to expand and popularize it."

3. What did the Federalists achieve?   89

Gordon S. Wood

The American Science of Politics, From *The Creation of the American Republic, 1776–1787*

"The Americans of the Revolutionary generation believed that they had made a momentous contribution to the history of politics."

4. Did the Constitution create a republic of white men?   113

Jan Lewis

"Of Every Age Sex & Condition": The Representation of Women in the Constitution

"As gender has been used to construct the political and social practices of race, and race to construct the practices of gender, the fleeting vision of a wide public sphere open to persons of every age, sex, race, and condition has faded, leaving barely a trace."

5. Can we know the original intent of the Framers?   141

Jack N. Rakove

The Perils of Originalism, From *Original Meanings: Politics and Ideas in the Making of the Constitution*

"By taking the problem of 'originalism' seriously, by considering the uses and potential misuses of different forms of evidence, it may be possible to advance a debate that is very much about a specific moment in history but is not about history alone."

Making Connections   165

Suggestions for Further Reading   167

What Did the Constitution Mean to Early Americans?

PART ONE

The Document

The Constitution of the United States

As Presented by the Federal Convention in 1787 and Adopted in 1788

The Constitution of the United States

As Presented by the Federal Convention in 1787 and Adopted in 1788

We the People of the United States, in Order to form a more perfect Union, establish Justice, insure domestic Tranquility, provide for the common defence, promote the general Welfare, and secure the Blessings of Liberty to ourselves and our Posterity, do ordain and establish this Constitution for the United States of America.

Article I

SECTION 1.   All legislative Powers herein granted shall be vested in a Congress of the United States, which shall consist of a Senate and House of Representatives.

SECTION 2.   The House of Representatives shall be composed of Members chosen every second Year by the People of the several States, and the Electors in each State shall have the Qualifications requisite for Electors of the most numerous Branch of the State Legislature.

No Person shall be a Representative who shall not have attained to the Age of twenty five Years, and been seven Years a Citizen of the United States, and who shall not, when elected, be an Inhabitant of that State in which he shall be chosen.

Representatives and direct Taxes shall be apportioned among the several States which may be included within this Union, according to their respective Numbers, which shall be determined by adding to the whole Number of free Persons, including those bound to Service for a Term of

The Constitution of the United States (1787), *American Testament: Fifty Great Documents of American History,* ed. Irwin Glusker and Richard M. Ketchum (New York: American Heritage, 1971), 45–56.

Years, and excluding Indians not taxed, three fifths of all other Persons. The actual Enumeration shall be made within three Years after the first Meeting of the Congress of the United States, and within every subsequent Term of ten Years, in such Manner as they shall by Law direct. The Number of Representatives shall not exceed one for every thirty Thousand, but each State shall have at Least one Representative; and until such enumeration shall be made, the State of New Hampshire shall be entitled to chuse three, Massachusetts eight, Rhode-Island and Providence Plantations one, Connecticut five, New-York six, New Jersey four, Pennsylvania eight, Delaware one, Maryland six, Virginia ten, North Carolina five, South Carolina five, and Georgia three.

When vacancies happen in the Representation from any State, the Executive Authority thereof shall issue Writs of Election to fill such Vacancies.

The House of Representatives shall chuse their Speaker and other Officers; and shall have the sole Power of Impeachment.

SECTION 3.   The Senate of the United States shall be composed of two Senators from each State, chosen by the Legislature thereof, for six Years; and each Senator shall have one Vote.

Immediately after they shall be assembled in Consequence of the first Election, they shall be divided as equally as may be into three Classes. The Seats of the Senators of the first Class shall be vacated at the Expiration of the second Year, of the second Class at the Expiration of the fourth Year, and of the third Class at the Expiration of the sixth Year, so that one third may be chosen every second Year; and if Vacancies happen by Resignation, or otherwise, during the Recess of the Legislature of any State, the Executive thereof may make temporary Appointments until the next Meeting of the Legislature, which shall then fill such Vacancies.

No Person shall be a Senator who shall not have attained to the Age of thirty Years, and been nine Years a Citizen of the United States, and who shall not, when elected, be an Inhabitant of that State for which he shall be chosen.

The Vice President of the United States shall be President of the Senate, but shall have no Vote, unless they be equally divided.

The Senate shall chuse their other Officers, and also a President pro tempore, in the Absence of the Vice President, or when he shall exercise the Office of President of the United States.

The Senate shall have the sole Power to try all Impeachments. When sitting for that Purpose, they shall be on Oath or Affirmation. When the President of the United States is tried, the Chief Justice shall preside: And no Person shall be convicted without the Concurrence of two thirds of the Members present.

Judgment in Cases of Impeachment shall not extend further than to removal from Office, and disqualification to hold and enjoy any Office of honor, Trust or Profit under the United States: but the Party convicted shall nevertheless be liable and subject to Indictment, Trial, Judgment and Punishment, according to Law.

SECTION 4.   The Times, Places and Manner of holding Elections for Senators and Representatives, shall be prescribed in each State by the Legislature thereof; but the Congress may at any time by Law make or alter such Regulations, except as to the Places of chusing Senators.

The Congress shall assemble at least once in every Year, and such Meeting shall be on the first Monday in December, unless they shall by Law appoint a different Day.

SECTION 5.   Each House shall be the Judge of the Elections, Returns and Qualifications of its own Members, and a Majority of each shall constitute a Quorum to do Business; but a smaller Number may adjourn from day to day, and may be authorized to compel the Attendance of absent Members, in such Manner, and under such Penalties as each House may provide.

Each House may determine the Rules of its Proceedings, punish its Members for disorderly Behaviour, and, with the Concurrence of two thirds, expel a Member.

Each House shall keep a Journal of its Proceedings, and from time to time publish the same, excepting such Parts as may in their Judgment require Secrecy; and the Yeas and Nays of the Members of either House on any question shall, at the Desire of one fifth of those Present, be entered on the Journal.

Neither House, during the Session of Congress, shall, without the Consent of the other, adjourn for more than three days, nor to any other Place than that in which the two Houses shall be sitting.

SECTION 6.   The Senators and Representatives shall receive a Compensation for their Services, to be ascertained by Law, and paid out of the Treasury of the United States. They shall in all Cases, except Treason, Felony and Breach of the Peace, be privileged from Arrest during their Attendance at the Session of their respective Houses, and in going to and returning from the same; and for any Speech or Debate in either House, they shall not be questioned in any other Place.

No Senator or Representative shall, during the Time for which he was elected, be appointed to any civil Office under the Authority of the United States which shall have been created, or the Emoluments whereof shall have been encreased during such time; and no Person holding any Office under the United States, shall be a Member of either House during his Continuance in Office.

SECTION 7.   All Bills for raising Revenue shall originate in the House of Representatives; but the Senate may propose or concur with Amendments as on other Bills.

Every Bill which shall have passed the House of Representatives and the Senate, shall, before it become a Law, be presented to the President of the United States; If he approve he shall sign it, but if not he shall return it, with his Objections to that House in which it shall have originated, who shall enter the Objections at large on their Journal, and proceed to reconsider it. If after such Reconsideration two thirds of that House shall agree to pass the Bill, it shall be sent, together with the Objections, to the other House, by which it shall likewise be reconsidered, and if approved by two thirds of that House, it shall become a Law. But in all such Cases the Votes of both Houses shall be determined by Yeas and Nays, and the Names of the Persons voting for and against the Bill shall be entered on the Journal of each House respectively. If any Bill shall not be returned by the President within ten Days (Sundays excepted) after it shall have been presented to him, the Same shall be a Law, in like Manner as if he had signed it, unless the Congress by their Adjournment prevent its Return, in which Case it shall not be a Law.

Every Order, Resolution, or Vote to which the Concurrence of the Senate and House of Representatives may be necessary (except on a question of Adjournment) shall be presented to the President of the United States; and before the Same shall take Effect, shall be approved by him, or being disapproved by him, shall be repassed by two thirds of the Senate and House of Representatives, according to the Rules and Limitations prescribed in the Case of a Bill.

SECTION 8.   The Congress shall have Power To lay and collect Taxes, Duties, Imposts and Excises, to pay the Debts and provide for the common Defence and general Welfare of the United States; but all Duties, Imposts and Excises shall be uniform throughout the United States;

To borrow Money on the credit of the United States;

To regulate Commerce with foreign Nations, and among the several States, and with the Indian Tribes;

To establish an uniform Rule of Naturalization, and uniform Laws on the subject of Bankruptcies throughout the United States;

To coin Money, regulate the Value thereof, and of foreign Coin, and fix the Standard of Weights and Measures;

To provide for the Punishment of counterfeiting the Securities and current Coin of the United States;

To establish Post Offices and post Roads;

To promote the Progress of Science and useful Arts, by securing for limited Times to Authors and Inventors the exclusive Right to their respective Writings and Discoveries;

To constitute Tribunals inferior to the supreme Court;

To define and punish Piracies and Felonies committed on the high Seas, and Offences against the Law of Nations;

To declare War, grant Letters of Marque and Reprisal, and make Rules concerning Captures on Land and Water;

To raise and support Armies, but no Appropriation of Money to that Use shall be for a longer Term than two Years;

To provide and maintain a Navy;

To make Rules for the Government and Regulation of the land and naval Forces;

To provide for calling forth the Militia to execute the Laws of the Union, suppress Insurrections and repel Invasions;

To provide for organizing, arming, and disciplining the Militia, and for governing such Part of them as may be employed in the Service of the United States, reserving to the States respectively, the Appointment of the Officers, and the Authority of training the Militia according to the discipline prescribed by Congress;

To exercise exclusive Legislation in all Cases whatsoever, over such District (not exceeding ten Miles square) as may, by Cession of particular States, and the Acceptance of Congress, become the Seat of the Government of the United States, and to exercise like Authority over all Places purchased by the Consent of the Legislature of the State in which the Same shall be, for the Erection of Forts, Magazines, Arsenals, dock-Yards, and other needful Buildings;—And

To make all Laws which shall be necessary and proper for carrying into Execution the foregoing Powers, and all other Powers vested by this Constitution in the Government of the United States, or in any Department or Officer thereof.

SECTION 9.   The Migration or Importation of such Persons as any of the States now existing shall think proper to admit, shall not be prohibited by the Congress prior to the Year one thousand eight hundred and eight, but a Tax or duty may be imposed on such Importation, not exceeding ten dollars for each Person.

The Privilege of the Writ of Habeas Corpus shall not be suspended, unless when in Cases of Rebellion or Invasion the public Safety may require it.

No Bill of Attainder or ex post facto Law shall be passed.

No Capitation, or other direct, Tax shall be laid, unless in Proportion to the Census or Enumeration herein before directed to be taken.

No Tax or Duty shall be laid on Articles exported from any State.

No Preference shall be given by any Regulation of Commerce or Revenue to the Ports of one State over those of another: nor shall Vessels bound to, or from, one State, be obliged to enter, clear, or pay Duties in another.

No Money shall be drawn from the Treasury, but in Consequence of Appropriations made by Law; and a regular Statement and Account of the Receipts and Expenditures of all public Money shall be published from time to time.

No Title of Nobility shall be granted by the United States: And no Person holding any Office of Profit or Trust under them, shall, without the Consent of the Congress, accept of any present, Emolument, Office, or Title, of any kind whatever, from any King, Prince or foreign State.

SECTION 10. No State shall enter into any Treaty, Alliance, or Confederation; grant Letters of Marque and Reprisal; coin Money; emit Bills of Credit; make any Thing but gold and silver Coin a Tender in Payment of Debts; pass any Bill of Attainder, ex post facto Law, or Law impairing the Obligation of Contracts, or grant any Title of Nobility.

No State shall, without the Consent of the Congress, lay any Imposts or Duties on Imports or Exports, except what may be absolutely necessary for executing it's inspection Laws: and the net Produce of all Duties and Imposts, laid by any State on Imports or Exports, shall be for the Use of the Treasury of the United States; and all such Laws shall be subject to the Revision and Controul of the Congress.

No State shall, without the Consent of Congress, lay any Duty of Tonnage, keep Troops, or Ships of War in time of Peace, enter into any Agreement or Compact with another State, or with a foreign Power, or engage in War, unless actually invaded, or in such imminent Danger as will not admit of delay.

Article II

SECTION 1. The executive Power shall be vested in a President of the United States of America. He shall hold his Office during the Term of four Years, and, together with the Vice President, chosen for the same Term, be elected, as follows

Each State shall appoint, in such Manner as the Legislature thereof may direct, a Number of Electors, equal to the whole Number of Senators and

Representatives to which the State may be entitled in the Congress: but no Senator or Representative, or Person holding an Office of Trust or Profit under the United States, shall be appointed an Elector.

The Electors shall meet in their respective States, and vote by Ballot for two Persons, of whom one at least shall not be an Inhabitant of the same State with themselves. And they shall make a List of all the Persons voted for, and of the Number of Votes for each; which List they shall sign and certify, and transmit sealed to the Seat of the Government of the United States, directed to the President of the Senate. The President of the Senate shall, in the Presence of the Senate and House of Representatives, open all the Certificates, and the Votes shall then be counted. The Person having the greatest Number of Votes shall be the President, if such Number be a Majority of the whole Number of Electors appointed; and if there be more than one who have such Majority, and have an equal Number of Votes, then the House of Representatives shall immediately chuse by Ballot one of them for President; and if no person have a Majority, then from the five highest on the List the said House shall in like Manner chuse the President. But in chusing the President, the Votes shall be taken by States, the Representation from each State having one Vote; A quorum for this Purpose shall consist of a Member or Members from two thirds of the States, and a Majority of all the States shall be necessary to a Choice. In every Case, after the Choice of the President, the Person having the greatest Number of Votes of the Electors shall be the Vice President. But if there should remain two or more who have equal Votes, the Senate shall chuse from them by Ballot the Vice President.

The Congress may determine the Time of chusing the Electors, and the Day on which they shall give their Votes; which Day shall be the same throughout the United States.

No Person except a natural born Citizen, or a Citizen of the United States, at the time of the Adoption of this Constitution, shall be eligible to the Office of President; neither shall any Person be eligible to that Office who shall not have attained to the Age of thirty five Years, and been fourteen Years a Resident within the United States.

In Case of the Removal of the President from Office, or of his Death, Resignation, or Inability to discharge the Powers and Duties of the said Office, the Same shall devolve on the Vice President, and the Congress may by Law provide for the Case of Removal, Death, Resignation or Inability, both of the President and Vice President, declaring what Officer shall then act as President, and such Officer shall act accordingly, until the Disability be removed, or a President shall be elected.

The President shall, at stated Times, receive for his Services, a Compensation, which shall neither be encreased nor diminished during the Period for which he shall have been elected, and he shall not receive within that Period any other Emolument from the United States, or any of them.

Before he enter on the Execution of his Office, he shall take the following Oath or Affirmation:—"I do solemnly swear (or affirm) that I will faithfully execute the Office of President of the United States, and will to the best of my Ability, preserve, protect and defend the Constitution of the United States."

SECTION 2.   The President shall be Commander in Chief of the Army and Navy of the United States, and of the Militia of the several States, when called into the actual Service of the United States; he may require the Opinion, in writing, of the principal Officer in each of the executive Departments, upon any Subject relating to the Duties of their respective Offices, and he shall have Power to grant Reprieves and Pardons for Offences against the United States, except in Cases of Impeachment.

He shall have Power, by and with the Advice and Consent of the Senate, to make Treaties, provided two thirds of the Senators present concur; and he shall nominate, and by and with the Advice and Consent of the Senate, shall appoint Ambassadors, other public Ministers and Consuls, Judges of the supreme Court, and all other Officers of the United States, whose Appointments are not herein otherwise provided for, and which shall be established by Law: but the Congress may by Law vest the Appointment of such inferior Officers, as they think proper, in the President alone, in the Courts of Law, or in the Heads of Departments.

The President shall have Power to fill up all Vacancies that may happen during the Recess of the Senate, by granting Commissions which shall expire at the End of their next Session.

SECTION 3.   He shall from time to time give to the Congress Information of the State of the Union, and recommend to their Consideration such Measures as he shall judge necessary and expedient; he may, on extraordinary Occasions, convene both Houses, or either of them, and in Case of Disagreement between them, with Respect to the Time of Adjournment, he may adjourn them to such Time as he shall think proper; he shall receive Ambassadors and other public Ministers; he shall take Care that the Laws be faithfully executed, and shall Commission all the Officers of the United States.

SECTION 4.   The President, Vice President and all civil Officers of the United States, shall be removed from Office on Impeachment for, and Conviction of, Treason, Bribery, or other high Crimes and Misdemeanors.

Article III

SECTION 1.   The judicial Power of the United States, shall be vested in one supreme Court, and in such inferior Courts as the Congress may from time to time ordain and establish. The Judges, both of the supreme and inferior Courts, shall hold their Offices during good Behaviour, and shall, at stated Times, receive for their Services, a Compensation, which shall not be diminished during their Continuance in Office.

SECTION 2.   The judicial Power shall extend to all Cases, in Law and Equity, arising under this Constitution, the Laws of the United States, and Treaties made, or which shall be made, under their Authority; — to all Cases affecting Ambassadors, other public Ministers and Consuls; — to all Cases of admiralty and maritime Jurisdiction; — to Controversies to which the United States shall be a Party; — to Controversies between two or more States; — between a State and Citizens of another State; — between Citizens of different States, — between Citizens of the same State claiming Lands under Grants of different States, and between a State, or the Citizens thereof, and foreign States, Citizens or Subjects.

In all Cases affecting Ambassadors, other public Ministers and Consuls, and those in which a State shall be Party, the supreme Court shall have original Jurisdiction. In all the other cases before mentioned, the supreme Court shall have appellate Jurisdiction, both as to Law and Fact, with such Exceptions, and under such Regulations as the Congress shall make.

The Trial of all Crimes, except in Cases of Impeachment, shall be by Jury; and such Trial shall be held in the State where the said Crimes shall have been committed; but when not committed within any State, the Trial shall be at such Place or Places as the Congress may by Law have directed.

SECTION 3.   Treason against the United States, shall consist only in levying War against them, or in adhering to their Enemies, giving them Aid and Comfort. No Person shall be convicted of Treason unless on the Testimony of two Witnesses to the same overt Act, or on Confession in open Court.

The Congress shall have Power to declare the Punishment of Treason, but no Attainder of Treason shall work Corruption of Blood, or Forfeiture except during the Life of the Person attainted.

Article IV

SECTION 1. Full Faith and Credit shall be given in each State to the Public Acts, Records, and judicial Proceedings of every other State. And the Congress may by general Laws prescribe the Manner in which such Acts, Records and Proceedings shall be proved, and the Effect thereof.

SECTION 2. The Citizens of each State shall be entitled to all Privileges and Immunities of Citizens in the Several States.

A Person charged in any State with Treason, Felony, or other Crime, who shall flee from Justice, and be found in another State, shall on Demand of the executive Authority of the State from which he fled, be delivered up, to be removed to the State having Jurisdiction of the Crime.

No Person held to Service or Labour in one State, under the Laws thereof, escaping into another, shall, in Consequence of any Law or Regulation therein, be discharged from such Service or Labour, but shall be delivered up on Claim of the Party to whom such Service or Labour may be due.

SECTION 3. New States may be admitted by the Congress into this Union; but no new States shall be formed or erected within the Jurisdiction of any other State; nor any State be formed by the Junction of two or more States, or Parts of States, without the Consent of the Legislatures of the States concerned as well as of the Congress.

The Congress shall have Power to dispose of and make all needful Rules and Regulations respecting the Territory or other Property belonging to the United States; and nothing in this Constitution shall be so construed as to Prejudice any Claims of the United States, or of any particular State.

SECTION 4. The United States shall guarantee to every State in this Union a Republican Form of Government, and shall protect each of them against Invasion; and on Application of the Legislature, or of the Executive (when the Legislature cannot be convened) against domestic Violence.

Article V

The Congress, whenever two thirds of both Houses shall deem it necessary, shall propose Amendments to this Constitution, or, on the Application of the Legislatures of two thirds of the several States, shall call a Convention for proposing Amendments, which, in either Case, shall be valid to all Intents and Purposes, as Part of this Constitution, when ratified by the Legislatures of three fourths of the several States, or by Conventions in three fourths thereof, as the one or the other Mode of Ratification may be proposed by the Congress; Provided that no Amendment which may be made prior to the Year One thousand eight hundred and eight shall in any Manner affect the first and fourth Clauses in the Ninth Section of the first Article; and that no State, without its Consent, shall be deprived of it's equal Suffrage in the Senate.

Article VI

All Debts contracted and Engagements entered into, before the Adoption of this Constitution, shall be as valid against the United States under this Constitution, as under the Confederation.

This Constitution, and the Laws of the United States which shall be made in Pursuance thereof; and all Treaties made, or which shall be made, under the Authority of the United States, shall be the supreme Law of the Land; and the Judges in every State shall be bound thereby, any Thing in the Constitution or Laws of any State to the Contrary notwithstanding.

The Senators and Representatives before mentioned, and the Members of the several State Legislatures, and all executive and judicial Officers, both of the United States and of the several States, shall be bound by Oath or Affirmation, to support this Constitution; but no religious Test shall ever be required as a Qualification to any Office or public Trust under the United States.

Article VII

The Ratification of the Conventions of nine States, shall be sufficient for the Establishment of this Constitution between the States so ratifying the Same.

Done in Convention by the Unanimous Consent of the States present the Seventeenth Day of September in the Year of our Lord one thousand seven hundred and Eighty seven and of the Independance of the United States of America the Twelfth. In witness whereof We have hereunto subscribed our Names,

G° WASHINGTON

President and Deputy from Virginia

Delaware	*Maryland*	*Virginia*
Richard Bassett	Dan^L Carroll	John Blair
Gunning Bedford Jun	Dan of St Thos Jenifer	James Madison Jr.
Jaco: Broom	James McHenry	
John Dickinson		
Geo: Read		

North Carolina
Wm Blount
Richd Dobbs Spaight
Hu Williamson

South Carolina
Pierce Butler
Charles Cotesworth
    Pinckney
Charles Pinckney
J. Rutledge

Georgia
Abr Baldwin
William Few

New Hampshire
Nicholas Gilman
John Langdon

Massachusetts
Nathaniel Gorham
Rufus King

Connecticut
Wm Saml Johnson
Roger Sherman

New York
Alexander Hamilton

New Jersey
David Brearley
Jona: Dayton
Wil: Livingston
Wm Paterson

Pennsylvania
Geo. Clymer
Thos FitzSimons
B Franklin
Jared Ingersoll
Thomas Mifflin
Gouv Morris
Robt Morris
James Wilson

PART TWO

Introduction

The Creation of the United States

The Creation of the United States

From Revolution to Ratification

When "the Framers" wrote the United States Constitution in the summer of 1787 and "the People" ratified it during the months that followed, they ended a long period of uncertainty about the fundamentals of public life. The crisis had begun more than two decades earlier, when Parliament tried to impose direct taxes on Britain's "dominions" in North America. That simple dispute escalated to a fierce ten-year quarrel about what powers the government of Britain could wield over people who called themselves British but who dwelt outside Britain. Argument flamed into the War of Independence, which completely destroyed British authority and British identity on the winning side. With those gone, and with most local institutions shattered or in disarray, a major vacuum of power, belonging, obligation, and belief needed to be filled.

Undoubtedly, there would be no new king to replace George III. In Americans' eyes the whole principle of monarchy, not just one king, had failed. Americans would be citizens rather than subjects. But every other political and social question seemed open. With the ancient, hallowed authority of monarchy gone, how could some people be justified in wielding power over others? What kind of persons should the new rulers be? How should they deal with the people they ruled? How could citizens protect themselves if the new rulers abused their power? How should the separate states relate to one another and to what little central government there was? Most fundamentally, if "all men" were "created equal," as the Declaration of Independence said, what became of the old gradations of status, age, gender, and race that had made nobody equal to anybody else while a king had reigned over them all? Every one of these questions was raised and disputed between independence and the adoption of the Constitution.

Beginning to address those problems, Congress named a committee to frame "Articles of Confederation and Perpetual Union" as it prepared to declare independence. The committee finished the Articles in 1777, but it took four more years to obtain the required consent of all thirteen founding states. Until then, there was no formal justification for the existence of "the United States in Congress Assembled," just the sheer necessity of conducting a long, difficult, and expensive war. During those same years, each separate state wrote a constitution for itself. In contrast to the Articles, the writing and implementation of these documents generated intense interest and dispute. Most likely this was because each state already was a historic entity, whereas the "United States" was little more than a brand-new idea. For the most part, the state constitutions were simply proclaimed to be in effect, once drafting was done. The problem of how to create a genuinely "higher" law remained unresolved. Not until 1780 did Massachusetts employ the twin devices of a special convention empowered to do nothing but write a constitution and a special process of submitting the document to "the people" for their approval. These are still the mechanisms by which Americans exercise the ultimate, final power that is called sovereignty.

Over the half dozen years that followed the adoption of the Articles of Confederation, problem upon problem appeared both in Congress and in the states. Once the war ended, Congress seemed impotent. It could not pay the enormous debts that the struggle for independence had incurred. It could not enforce the peace treaty that its own emissaries worked out in Paris in 1783. It could not persuade the states to modify the Articles, though it tried in 1782, 1784, and again in 1786. Each time the failure was due to just one state that refused to go along. Many times, Congress could not even muster a quorum so it could do business.

Matters in the states were different, but to the minds of the men who would become "the Framers," they were just as troubling. A host of "new men" who never would have enjoyed high office under the colonial order came to power. One way to understand those people is to see them as the products of a democratic transformation that brought ordinary citizens into the center of public affairs. Another way might be to see them as persons totally unfit to hold power, whether for lack of education, public experience, social position, or understanding about the issues of the day. This position was widespread among the Constitution's supporters. The same dilemma—are we looking at the fruits of democracy or at mere foolishness?—applies to the policies that every state except Massachusetts adopted. The most controversial were strong penalties on former loyalists and laws to protect a state's people against an economic depression that descended late in 1784.

All these issues—the fundamental basis of public authority, the weakness of the Articles, the place of the United States in an unfriendly world, the kind of people who wielded public power, and what those people were doing with the power they held—contributed to the movement that led to the Constitution. By 1782, Alexander Hamilton of New York was thinking and writing about these issues in essays bearing titles like "The Continentalist." After peace returned in 1783, George Washington's extensive correspondence shows him brooding about the situation in his retirement at Mount Vernon. Meanwhile, from their vantage points as representatives in Paris and London, Thomas Jefferson and John Adams watched America's international reputation plummet. Virginia's scholarly James Madison retreated from the frustrations of Congress to his study in order to consider political history and political theory, especially the writings of the Scottish philosopher David Hume. The eventual results were, first, Madison's astute analysis of the "vices" of the American political system and, second, the persuasive agenda that he prepared for the Constitutional Convention, known now as the "Virginia Plan." All these men had experienced the Revolution at the center and the top, as congressmen, generals, staff officers, and diplomats. Late in 1786, their sort and many others were horrified by the backcountry rebellion that erupted against tax and finance policies in Massachusetts, deriving its name from Captain Daniel Shays, the former officer in Washington's army who seemed to lead the rebellion.

Shays's Rebellion posed very compelling questions. From the Massachusetts farmers' point of view, their own government had adopted policies that threatened their welfare just as severely as Britain had done. The state's policies that all debts be paid in hard coin, which most rural Americans did not possess, seemed to open the way to lawsuits, court-ordered property seizures, and the danger that freeholders would be reduced to tenantry on land they and their ancestors had owned. Petitions and protests had no effect. Rising in arms to close the courts seemed the only answer, and their own history appeared to justify such action. It was just what they had done in 1774 to frustrate the severe punishments that Britain had imposed on Massachusetts after the Boston Tea Party. From the state government's perspective, however, its policies were necessary to secure the good name of Massachusetts in the world of commerce. Rather than supporting the uprising, the government moved to crush it, with strong support from Boston and other commercial towns.

Immediate issues were only part of the problem, however. The Revolutionary generation was attempting to establish a republican order in place of monarchy. People who knew the history of previous republics understood that republicanism had a dismal past. From the ancient world of Greece and Rome to seventeenth-century England, republics had collapsed into tyranny as their citizens proved literally unable to govern themselves. Did the Massachusetts uprising suggest that America was bound to produce its own Julius Caesar or Oliver Cromwell who would step into the turmoil and take over by sheer force?

The statesmen who responded to the crisis understood that they faced very deep problems. They also pose a problem for us. We might see them as farsighted patriots who saw what needed to be done. We might see them as creative intellectuals who worked out nothing less than a new theory of politics. We might also see them as opponents of democracy who were convinced that only their own sort of people should be in power. We might regard them as self-seekers, with their own eyes on the main chance. We might consider them visionaries. Or we might see them nearly paralyzed by fear that the Revolution was failing, as so many revolutions had failed before and have failed since. Historians have advanced every one of these possibilities for understanding the men we honor as "the Framers."

Whatever the worries of such men, there were many others who did not believe that things had gone fundamentally wrong. Except perhaps for Patrick Henry of Virginia, their names are not as famous. George Clinton, New York's very successful governor between 1777 and 1795, may have summed up their attitude in 1786, when he simply refused to call a special legislative session to consider a request to add to the power of Congress. The issue, he explained, was not pressing enough. Whatever his opponents thought of him, Clinton was no demagogue. His own state was doing quite well under his leadership. In fact, Henry and Clinton probably spoke for the vast majority of Americans in 1787. They understood that some problems needed solving. But they did not believe that radical change was needed. Most historians agree that had the finished Constitution been submitted at the very same moment to everybody qualified to vote in 1787, it would have been rejected.

It was not "the People" who clamored for a Constitution, but rather a small, elite group of men who began the movement by writing letters to one another, essays in newspapers, and legal opinions. The movement spilled into actual politics in 1785, when Maryland and Virginia sent "commissioners" to Mount Vernon to consider how to improve navigation on the Potomac River. George Washington merely acted as host, but his presence undoubtedly blessed their gathering. The commissioners proposed a general meeting of state delegates on the subject of commercial problems the next year at Annapolis, Maryland. Only five states sent representatives to that gathering; the host state was not among them. The Annapolis Convention had no formal standing at all, but it did propose a general gathering of state delegates the following year to consider amendments to the Articles of Confederation. Congress passed a resolution that made the call legal.

The result was the Constitutional Convention, which met in Philadelphia over the summer of 1787. Its fifty-five members came from every state except Rhode Island, which declined to participate. The Convention kept its proceedings completely secret, even to the extent of having the windows of its meeting room nailed shut. Not until decades later would it be possible for Americans to learn about such subjects as the Virginia Plan and the New Jersey Plan (which pitted the interests of large states against those of small ones), or Alexander Hamilton's call for a lifetime presidency, or the disputes that erupted about counting slaves in apportioning the House of Representatives. When it adjourned, the Convention presented its work simply as a finished product, which the people could approve or reject. Only a few men who had been members refused to sign the proposals, and even they did not break their promise not to reveal how the debates had gone.

Nonetheless, problems appeared as soon as the Constitution was published. "We the People . . . do ordain and establish this Constitution," declares the preamble. It sounds simple, but it posed one difficulty after another. Was there in fact a single, self-sovereign American people that could "ordain and establish" anything? Or were there simply thirteen separate states (fourteen, if we count unrecognized maverick Vermont), each sovereign unto itself in the sense of acknowledging no higher authority? It took an act of faith to say yes to the first question and declare that a single American people did exist, that it could express its collective will, and that it was doing so through the Constitution.

If "we the People" did exist, how could that be reconciled with the fact that each founding state's decision to ratify or reject the document was equal in political weight to every other state's? Given their different populations, the ratification process endowed a voter in tiny Delaware with a great deal more individual power to influence the large event than a Pennsylvanian or a Virginian. That made no difference if the states were "corporate" bodies, each of whose "people" acted as a whole. A state was a state, and all states were equal. But if the citizens of all the separate states were construed as "Americans," equal as individuals to one another, such a situation seemed manifestly unfair. It also left unresolved the problem of whether a state could withdraw from the Union once it had joined.

Finally, how the Constitution was adopted posed a real problem of legality. For all the weaknesses of the Articles of Confederation, the document was the law of the land, and it *specifically* required the unanimous consent of all thirteen state legislatures for any amendment to itself. The Convention had no other mandate than to propose such amendments. Yet the Constitution declared that it would take effect not upon unanimous legislative consent, but rather when specially called conventions in just *nine* states voted in its favor. Avoiding the unanimous-consent requirement was realistic; most likely, it was necessary. Perhaps by invoking the idea that only "the People" could be the source from which power flowed, the decision to bypass the legislatures expressed the fundamental spirit of the Revolution. But what the Convention proposed was at the very edge of legality, if not beyond it.

Two states, Rhode Island and North Carolina, just said no. Nonetheless, the Constitution's supporters enjoyed several large advantages. One was appropriating the enormously positive word "Federalist" to describe themselves, leaving their opponents to flounder among the difficulties of being merely "Antifederalist." Another was that the Federalists shared a single position: the Constitution should be adopted, exactly as the Convention had presented it, without any amendments. Two of the foremost Federalists, James Madison and Alexander Hamilton, in fact had grave doubts about what the Convention had produced. But they kept their thoughts entirely to themselves and publicly argued for unconditional ratification.

The Federalists' third advantage was sharp political strategy. Wanting to build momentum, they sought ratification quickly in the states most likely to grant it with little dispute: Delaware, Maryland, New Jersey, Connecticut, South Carolina, and Georgia. They added Pennsylvania by persuading its legislature to call an election so fast that the state's numerous Antifederalists had no time to organize. When New Hampshire voters elected a convention committed to rejecting the Constitution, the Federalist minority persuaded the convention to adjourn for months in order to consult the citizens, without making any decision at all.

The most difficult and most crucial states were Massachusetts and Virginia, where the balance in the ratifying conventions was roughly even and the decision could have gone either way, and New York, whose convention was Antifederalist by a count of forty-five to nineteen. Strong pressure on Massachusetts leaders Samuel Adams and John Hancock brought them to the Federalist side, and with their support Massachusetts ratified early in 1788. New Hampshire's convention changed its mind after it reconvened early in the summer, giving the requisite nine states and also transforming the issue. Now the problem was not whether there would be a United States as the Constitution set out but rather whether the remaining states would take part. Though the debates were extended in Virginia and New York, both states finally voted to ratify.

Three separate developments took place during the ratification struggle. One was an enormous outflow of creative, insightful writing on both sides. Historians, political scientists, and lawyers all assign the premier place in that flood of ink to the eighty-five essays that constitute *The Federalist*. Jointly written by Alexander Hamilton, John Jay, and James Madison under the pen name Publius, these essays were intended to persuade the "considerate citizens of the state of New York" to favor ratification. Two of Madison's contributions, number 10 and number 51, stand among the world classics of political theory. Justices of the Supreme Court still cite Publius as an authority in their opinions on constitutional questions. The collection of essays was recognized on both sides as the foremost Federalist statement and quoted in many debates. But for all its brilliance, *The Federalist* was not the only major piece of pro-Constitution writing. Moreover, hard politics rather than close argument won the day in New York, including a threat that New York City would secede from the state and ratify on its own.

Writers of real power also appeared among the Antifederalists, most notably Richard Henry Lee of Virginia, New York's George Clinton and Melancton Smith, and the Massachusetts playwright-historian Mercy Otis Warren. The most complete collection of their work fills seven sizable volumes. Taken together, the Federalist and Antifederalist writers were launching a vital public debate about the interplay among the federal government, the states, and the American people. That debate still goes on.

The second great consequence of the ratification period was to demonstrate that the Constitution did enjoy genuine popular support. That came not only in the states that ratified quickly, which tended to be places at the mercy of more powerful neighbors, but also and especially in the major cities. Every sizable town except Albany, New York, proved to be strongly Federalist. Beginning in Boston, these towns organized great parades to celebrate as their respective states ratified, the greatest taking place in Philadelphia on July 4, 1788.

A formula quickly developed. Each parade began with a celebration of American history and the Revolution. Then came the different groups that made up the town, some with floats, some with banners and slogans, all expressing pride both in themselves and in their larger sense of the Republic and its future. Judges, professors, cart men, whip makers, printers, bakers, blacksmiths, and many more took part. Generally the groups took their positions in the parades not by social standing but rather according to lot. The banner borne by Philadelphia's bricklayers summed up both their own separate pride and their sense of citizenship: "Both Buildings and Rulers Are the Work of Our Hands." Picking up on the assertion of fundamental human equality in the Declaration of Independence, these people were claiming their own equal places in the mosaic of American citizenship. American Indians, black people, and women took part in the processions of 1788 too. But it was as mute symbols, without either public voices or places of their own. Their place in the mosaic remained unsure.

The final consequence of the ratification controversy was the Bill of Rights, which the new federal Congress proposed almost as soon as it opened for business and which the states quickly ratified. Many amendments had been proposed during the ratification process. Federalist leaders feared that to deal with all the proposals the Convention would need to be reconvened, opening up the text of the document once again and perhaps with different delegates taking part. They also wanted to avoid any state giving "conditional" ratification; their greatest triumph came when New York's convention reversed its constituents' anti-Constitution instructions by ratifying "in full confidence" that there would be amendments to safeguard citizens' rights.

As with the text of the Constitution, James Madison was the main author of the first ten Amendments. The Bill of Rights was not an afterthought, but rather a continuation of the work of the Philadelphia Convention and the ratification debates. Its existence may be the Antifederalists' great contribution to American history. But it did address a different problem from the Constitution itself. The main document's concern was to establish firm conditions for the distribution and the exercise of national public power, over both the states and the people. The Bill of Rights, however, set out to establish the limits beyond which that power could not be used. We might regard the Bill as a segue from the revolutionary politics of disruption, confusion, and fundamental dispute to a search for acceptable policies based on electoral politics and national agendas. That is why none of the selections in this volume takes the Bill of Rights as its main topic.

When the Constitution took effect, most of the social, cultural, and economic implications of the American Revolution remained to be worked out. Some befuddle us still. Nonetheless, with the Constitution written and ratified, the American Republic as we know it appeared. The problems of justifying authority and of what public offices ought to exist both were resolved. Amendments that came later, after the initial Bill of Rights, generally were a response to pressing needs that nobody foresaw in 1787. But with the gross, bloody exception of the Civil War, there has been no absolute, fundamental, irreconcilable dispute about the structure of public authority in the United States during all that time. Governments have fallen and risen in country after country around the globe. The United States endures, under the terms that the Constitution and its amendments continue to set out.

Historians and the Constitution

One of the most surprising qualities of the ratification debate is that hardly any dissenting history emerged from it. Arch-Antifederalist Abraham Yates of Albany, New York, did write a history of the movement for the Constitution that he framed in terms of a conspiracy among men he scorned as "high-flyers." But he never published it. Mercy Otis Warren contributed to the Antifederalist side, writing as "Columbian Patriot," and went on to produce a highly partisan general history of the Revolution. Her zeal, however, was for the emergent political group that centered on Thomas Jefferson, not for what rapidly became the lost cause of antifederalism. The fact that prominent Antifederalists James Monroe and George Clinton became, respectively, president and vice president of the United States suggests how completely the disputes of 1787–88 died away.

For most of the century that followed, historical understanding of the Constitution was shaped by such writers as John Marshall and George Bancroft. Marshall had been an ardent Federalist during ratification, and he spent his three decades as chief justice of the United States Supreme Court solidifying and expanding the powers that he thought the Constitution outlined. Bancroft was on the other side of his own era's party disputes, adhering firmly to Marshall's enemy Andrew Jackson, but he agreed with Marshall about the fundamentals. His nine-volume *History of the United States of America from the Discovery of the Continent* (1834–74) told a story of freedom's triumph in which the Constitution represented the culmination.

Not until the beginning of the twentieth century did historians start to bring the Constitution into question rather than celebrate its eternal wisdom. One somewhat distant reason was the emergence in Europe and America of Marxist and other forms of critical social thought. Another was a clear pattern among the justices of the Supreme Court of using the Constitution to thwart attempts at social reform. A third, perhaps, was a shift among the sort of people who wrote history, as gentlemen-celebrants like Bancroft gave way to self-consciously analytical and "debunking" writers who regarded no cow as sacred. Although he did not stand alone, the most important of these was Charles A. Beard, who began his career at Columbia University but spent most of it as an independent scholar. For decades after its publication in 1913, most professional historical discussion of the Constitution centered around Beard's withering *Economic Interpretation of the Constitution of the United States*.

One of Beard's propositions was that the men who went to the federal Convention stood to gain considerably in financial terms from what they were doing. This was because giving the central government a secure taxing power would raise the value of depreciated certificates of public debt and of badly inflated paper currency. His research suggested that many of the Framers and their supporters had bought up that kind of paper at cheap rates and that when its value rose they would recoup losses that somebody else in fact had suffered. In modern parlance, a scam was under way.

Beard's other main argument was that rather than offering an abstract charter of human freedom, the Constitution was very much concerned with economics. In Beard's reading, the Constitution laid out the political and juridical framework that a developing capitalist society was going to need for its own protection and for the protection of its ruling class. Beard's suggestion that the Constitution did bear on the long-term future development of the American economy still commands attention, though whether that was *all* that the Framers intended is quite another matter. Partly because of its quasi indictment of the Framers and partly because of its general irreverence, Beard's book provoked a major storm, both among academics and in the popular press. Nonetheless, when the Constitution reached the age of 150, in 1937, Beard was among the contributors to the American Historical Association's celebratory volume *The Constitution Reconsidered.*

Three years later, Merrill Jensen published his positive reconsideration in *The Articles of Confederation,* and in 1950 the same author's *The New Nation* reinterpreted the 1780s. The first book argued that loose, disorganized democracy was what the revolutionaries wanted. The second proposed that the "critical" 1780s were a time of success rather than failure. Though Jensen's tone was less polemical than Beard's, his work bore out Beard's proposition that the origins of the Constitution had to be understood in terms of conflict among different kinds of self-interested Americans, rather than as an enlightened response to a general need.

Many of Jensen's graduate students at the University of Wisconsin continued to work in the tradition that Beard had begun. But in 1958 Forrest McDonald published a massively documented book that used Beard's own sources to disprove what Beard had asserted. In *We the People: The Economic Origins of the Constitution,* McDonald demonstrated that among Framers and ratifying-convention members alike, the ownership of depreciated paper had no generally demonstrable bearing on a person's being in favor of the Constitution or against it. McDonald did not attack alone. Other historians took Beard to task for his understanding of human motivation, suggesting that in moments of serious crisis people are likely to have other concerns than personal gain on their minds. By McDonald's own admission, he was destroying a mode of thinking without advancing an alternative. The time was ripe for that alternative to emerge. Beard's originality and intellectual power still deserve respect, and the problems of internal dispute that he raised are not at all dead. But we must turn to other scholars to appreciate how historians presently understand the original meaning of the Constitution.

For roughly the past quarter century, the prime subject has been how republicanism developed in the young United States. During the era of independence the modern American notion of democracy—majority rule, through the means of contested elections and political parties—as the best form of government was only beginning to take shape. But republicanism was well understood. Republicanism's first tenet was that citizens could govern themselves without aristocrats or monarchs above them. Its second tenet was that achieving self-government required general agreement about what made up the public good (in Latin, *res publica*), together with a willingness among citizens to sacrifice their own interests to that public good.

As a body of ideas, this so-called classical republicanism or civic humanism was immensely attractive. But, as already noted, attempts to put the idea into practice had a long history of failure. Federalist and Antifederalist alike, the people who debated whether to ratify the Constitution kept returning to the problem of whether America could do better and make republicanism actually work. One of the major tasks of the historians who followed upon McDonald's demolition of Beard has been to explore how the Revolutionary generation tried to deal with the problems that implementing the American Republic presented.

This involved a shift in the kind of evidence that needed to be considered. Scholars like Beard dismissed the enormous body of writing that the constitutional debates produced, on the ground that its high-flown language usually masked some baser and perhaps more sordid interest. Now, however, historians began to take that writing seriously, beginning with an understanding that the English language of two centuries ago differed in important ways from the English language of our time. Language ceased to be regarded as a transparent window opening on another world and turned into a historical problem in its own right. Consider one instance. Throughout the Revolutionary era Americans extolled the idea of liberty. The "liberties" that rebellious colonials set out to defend against Britain comprised a bundle of uneven privileges and customs that they had inherited from the past and that differed from place to place and person to person. The "liberty" that the Declaration of Independence proclaims as an "unalienable right" of "all men" seemed much more a blanket concept, though nobody could really say what it meant. "The blessings of liberty" that the Constitution proposed "to secure . . . to ourselves and our prosperity" were different again. Yet one word—*liberty*—was used in the era to describe them all. Not the least problem that historians began to confront was how people argued over what a word like *liberty* really meant.

Even as language opens possibilities for imagination and action, it also limits what can be thought. Historians found that taking political language seriously raised a number of problems in addition to the historical meaning of specific words. One of the most pressing and politically important problems is whether the Republic's latter-day citizens are bound not only by what the Constitution says, as we read it now, but also by what the Framers and the ratifiers meant when they agreed that the Constitution should say it. That problem has been the subject of great discussion among politicians, political scientists, and lawyers as well as among historians. The essays in this volume by the political scientist Isaac Kramnick and by historians Gordon S. Wood and Jack N. Rakove address both the issue of establishing what Rakove calls the Constitution's "original meaning" and the problems involved in applying that meaning now.

Yet the issue of material and social differences among the people who framed and adopted the Constitution refuses to go away. One reason is what historian J. G. A. Pocock has called the "politics" of language. A symbol, like liberty, might well be shared. What different kinds of people understand by that symbol can vary enormously. Though Gordon Wood's "take" on the debates about the Constitution is very different from Charles Beard's, his close analysis of language reveals just as much dispute as Beard found in his reading of economic evidence. Stephen Patterson's assertion of the importance of Shays's Rebellion in Massachusetts in spurring the Framers to do what they did turns back from problems of language to the questions of material interest and social power that had preoccupied Beard. Like Beard, Patterson sees the emergent Federalists as opportunistic politicians, seizing the issue of the rebellion to push their own program.

Social class inscribed only one area of stress among Americans of the Constitution era. Perhaps reflecting on the momentous change in race relations and in gender relations of the past half century, considerable discussion among recent historians has turned on the fact that being black or female cut off a person from liberty's blessings just as surely in 1787 as when a king reigned over America. How could the Framers possibly have been blind to the glaring inconsistency between what they preached and the continuing reality of American slavery? How could they have continued to treat the female half of the human species as condemned by birth to be lesser? Although Jan Lewis's essay deals more with the problems faced by women than with the crushing weight of enslavement, she does address the large issue of continuing inequality in an American Republic of free men.

It might seem that to ask questions about race and gender in the constitutional era is to be grossly anachronistic, inviting modern readers to condemn an earlier time according to standards and ideals that it could not have known. But such questions do flow directly from the fundamental assertions about human equality that the revolutionaries made. Even during the Revolution, some people were asking them. We need only look to the evidence that they left behind to learn what kind of place those people wanted their America to be. Their debate about the Constitution touched on the most fundamental issues that women and men of their time could imagine. Our own era's continuing debate does just the same.

As long as the Constitution remains in effect, as long as its authoritative language governs Americans' lives, and as long as Americans turn to the Constitution to resolve the problems that their own times give to them, debate about the Constitution will continue. No group within American society has a monopoly on what the Constitution can be taken to mean, though the women and men of the Supreme Court do have a monopoly on saying authoritatively what it shall mean in their own time. People reading this book now will face the task of deciding what the Constitution shall mean in a future that no more can be predicted in 1998 than the former future, which we now call history, could have been predicted two centuries ago. In the light of those problems, new constitutional history certainly will be made and new histories of the American Constitution will need to be written.

Some Current Questions

The selections that follow deal with some of the issues about the making and the ratification of the Constitution that now interest historians. Other questions and other selections could have been chosen, but these show the current state of the conversation. Each selection is preceded by a headnote that introduces both its specific subject and its author. After the headnote come Questions for a Closer Reading. The headnote and the questions offer signposts that will allow you to understand more readily what the author is saying. The selections are uncut and they include the original notes. The notes are also signposts for further exploration. If an issue that the author raises intrigues you, use the notes to follow it up. At the end of all the selections are more questions, under the heading Making Connections. Turn to these after you have read the selections, and use them to bring the whole discussion together. In order to answer them, you may find that you need to reread. But no historical source yields up all that is within it to a person content to read it just once.

Isaac Kramnick

The "Great National Discussion": The Discourse of Politics in 1787

Isaac Kramnick is a political scientist, holding the Richard J. Schwartz Professorship of Government at Cornell University. In this essay he writes like a historian, exploring the problems that the language of 1787 presents if we are to understand what the Framers sought and what they achieved. One argument that scholars have advanced suggests that only one "mode" of speech and writing was "available" in 1787. Kramnick rejects that. Central to his essay is an understanding that different sorts of people were capable of different ways of speaking and thinking, then as much as now.

He sees four paradigms at work. One is liberalism, the belief that the purpose of government is to set individuals free to make the most of themselves. This may be what Jefferson meant by "liberty and the pursuit of happiness" in the Declaration of Independence. The second is "civic republicanism," a pattern of thought that reached back from Revolutionary America to England in the seventeenth century and to Italy during the Renaissance, if not to ancient Greece and Rome. Its central point is that a good citizen finds the fullness of being human not by pursuing self-interest but rather by taking part in something much larger, even if that means self-sacrifice. The third pattern is "work-ethic Protestantism," which he also describes as a variant of "virtuous republicanism." This found virtue less in public political activity than in private qualities such as "industry, frugality, and economy." Kramnick's final pattern is the language of power and glory, an awareness among some Americans that the future looked very bright, if they and their progeny had the will to pursue it. Kramnick's central point is that all of these visions were in tension with one another rather than any single vision being the only one that people could see.

Questions for a Closer Reading

1. What does Kramnick mean by the concepts of "liberalism," "civic humanism," and "the language of power"? Why might it seem that accepting one of these ways of thought would make it impossible to accept the others?

2. Take any one of those three concepts and describe what it implied about being a good citizen within a good community.

3. If "liberalism" looked forward and "civic humanism" looked backward, was it the Federalists or the Antifederalists who were forward-looking during the ratification debates?

4. Liberalism, civic humanism, work-ethic Protestantism, and the language of power implied different understandings of what causes people to act. What was the "psychology" hidden within each of these concepts?

5. If all four of these concepts were "in the air" in 1787 and 1788, how can each of them be seen within the Constitution itself?

The "Great National Discussion": The Discourse of Politics in 1787

Americans, Alexander Hamilton wrote on October 27, 1787, in the New York *Independent Journal,* were "called upon to deliberate on a new Constitution." His essay, *The Federalist* No. 1, pointed out that in doing this Americans were proving that men could create their own governments "from reflection and choice," instead of forever having to depend on "accident and force." These deliberations on the Constitution would by no means be decorous and genteel. Much too much was at stake, and, as Hamilton predicted, "a torrent of angry and malignant passions" was let loose in the "great national discussion." His *Federalist* essays, Hamilton promised, would provide a different voice in the national debate; they would rise above "the loudness of [the opposition's] declamations, and the . . . bitterness of [its] invectives."

How does one read that "great national discussion" two centuries later? Most present-day scholars would follow the methodological guidelines offered by J. G. A. Pocock in this respect. The historian of political thought, Pocock suggests, is engaged in a quest for the "languages," "idioms," and "modes of discourse" that characterize an age. Certain "languages" are accredited at various moments in time "to take part" in the public speech of a country. These "distinguishable idioms" are paradigms that selectively encompass all information about politics and delimit appropriate usage. Pocock writes of the "continuum of discourse," which persists over time in terms of paradigms that both constrain and provide opportunities for authors with a language available for their use. To understand texts and "great national discussions," then, is to penetrate the "modes of discourse" and the meanings available to authors and speakers at particular moments in time. The scholar must know what the normal possibilities of language, the capacities for discourse, were. Paradigms change, to be sure, ever so

Isaac Kramnick, "The 'Great National Discussion': The Discourse of Politics in 1787," *William and Mary Quarterly,* 3rd ser., 45 (1988): 3–32.

slowly, and we recognize this subtle process through anomalies and innovations. But much more significant is the static and exclusive aspect of
"modes of discourse." Pocock cautions that one "cannot get out of a language that which was never in it." People only think "about what they have
the means of verbalizing." Anyone studying political texts, then, must use
"the languages in which the inhabitants . . . did in fact present their society
and cosmos to themselves and to each other."[1]

Problematic in this approach is the assumption that there is but one
language — one exclusive or even hegemonic paradigm — that characterizes the political discourse of a particular place or moment in time. This
was not the case in 1787. In the "great national discussion" of the Constitution Federalists and Antifederalists, in fact, tapped several languages of
politics, the terms of which they could easily verbalize. This article exam-
ines four such "distinguishable idioms," which coexisted in the discourse
of politics in 1787–1788. None dominated the field, and the use of one
was compatible with the use of another by the very same writer or speaker.
There was a profusion and confusion of political tongues among the
founders. They lived easily with that clatter; it is we two hundred years later
who chafe at their inconsistency. Reading the framers and the critics of the
Constitution, one discerns the languages of republicanism, of Lockean liberalism,* of work-ethic Protestantism, and of state-centered theories of
power and sovereignty.[2]

Civic Humanism and Liberalism in the Constitution and Its Critics

Contemporary scholarship seems obsessed with forever ridding the college curriculum of the baleful influence of Louis Hartz.† In place of the
"Liberal Tradition in America," it posits the omnipresence of neoclassical
civic humanism. Dominating eighteenth-century political thought in
Britain and America, it is insisted, was the language of republican virtue.
Man was a political being who realized his telos only when living in a *vivere
civile*‡ with other propertied, arms-bearing citizens, in a republic where
they ruled and were ruled in turn. Behind this republican discourse is a

---

Lockean liberalism: The set of political ideas derived from philosopher John Locke that
places the protection of private property and the pursuit of individual satisfaction as the foremost reasons that people enter political society and consent to be bound by its rules.

†*Louis Hartz:* American political scientist who argued in *The Liberal Tradition in America*
(1955) that Lockean liberalism has underpinned all American political thought.

‡*vivere civile:* Latin phrase meaning "to live in a civic manner." In the classical republican
or civic humanist tradition, the public activity that this phrase connotes enjoyed a higher
value than the individual pursuit of happiness or satisfaction that is central to Lockean liberalism.

tradition of political philosophy with roots in Aristotle's *Politics,* Cicero's *Res Publica,* Machiavelli, Harrington, Bolingbroke, and the nostalgic country's virtuous opposition to Walpole and the commercialization of English life.* The pursuit of public good is privileged over private interests, and freedom means participation in civic life rather than the protection of individual rights from interference. Central to the scholarly enterprise of republicanism has been the self-proclaimed "dethronement of the paradigm of liberalism and of the Lockean paradigm associated with it."[3]

In response to these republican imperial claims, a group whom Gordon S. Wood[†] has labeled "neo-Lockeans" has insisted that Locke and liberalism were alive and well in Anglo-American thought in the period of the founding.[4] Individualism, the moral legitimacy of private interest, and market society are privileged in this reading over community, public good, and the virtuous pursuit of civic fulfillment. For these "neo-Lockeans"[‡] it is not Machiavelli and Montesquieu who set the textual codes that dominated the "great national discussion," but Hobbes and Locke and the assumptions of possessive individualism.

Can we have it both ways? We certainly can if we take Federalist and Antifederalist views as representing a single text of political discourse at the founding. A persuasive case can be made for the Federalists as liberal modernists and the Antifederalists as nostalgic republican communitarians seeking desperately to hold on to a virtuous moral order threatened by commerce and market society. The Federalist tendency was to depict America in amoral terms as an enlarged nation that transcended local community and moral conviction as the focus of politics. The Federalists seemed to glory in an individualistic and competitive America, which was preoccupied with private rights and personal autonomy. This reading of America is associated with James Madison more than with anyone else, and with his writings in the *Federalist.*

Madison's adulation of heterogeneous factions and interests in an enlarged America, which he introduced into so many of his contributions to the *Federalist,* assumed that the only way to protect the rights of minorities was to enlarge the political sphere and thereby divide the community into so great a number of interests and parties, that

---

*"*Aristotle's* Politics . . . *commercialization of English life*"*: Kramnick is summarizing the major literary sources for the argument that Lockean liberalism was not the form of political thought with which the Revolutionary era was familiar. All the writers he cites advanced the notion that public life as citizens is a more satisfying way of being human than following self-interest.

†*Gordon S. Wood:* See pages 89–111 for the selection by Wood in this volume.

‡*neo-Lockeans:* Scholars of American political thought and practice who continue to work from the perspective that John Locke's writings and the pursuit of individual satisfaction are fundamental to the American idea of the good life.

in the 1st. place a majority will not be likely at the same moment to have a common interest separate from that of the whole or of the minority; and in the 2d. place, that in case they shd. have such an interest, they may not be apt to unite in the pursuit of it. It was incumbent on us then to try this remedy, and with that view to frame a republican system on such a scale & in such a form as will controul all the evils wch. have been experienced.[5]

In *Federalist* No. 10 Madison described the multiplication of regional, religious, and economic interests, factions, and parties as the guarantor of American freedom and justice. He put his case somewhat differently in a letter to Thomas Jefferson: "Divide et impera, the reprobated axiom of tyranny, is under certain conditions, the only policy, by which a republic can be administered on just principles."[6] Pride of place among "these clashing interests," so essential for a just order, went to the economic interests inevitable in a complex market society. They were described in the often-quoted passage from *Federalist* No. 10:

The most common and durable source of factions has been the various and unequal distribution of property. Those who hold and those who are without property have ever formed distinct interests in society. . . . creditors. . . debtors. . . . A landed interest, a manufacturing interest, a mercantile interest, a moneyed interest. . . . The regulation of these various and interfering interests forms the principal task of modern legislation.

Government for Madison, much as for Locke, was a neutral arbiter among competing interests. Indeed, in *Federalist* No. 43 Madison described the legislative task as providing "umpires"; and in a letter to George Washington he described government's role as a "disinterested & dispassionate umpire in disputes."[7] Sounding much like Locke in chapter 5, "Of Property," of the *Second Treatise,* Madison, in No. 10, attributed the differential possession of property to the "diversity in the faculties of man," to their "different and unequal faculties of acquiring property." It was "the protection of these faculties" that constituted "the first object of government." As it was for Locke—who wrote that "*justice* gives every Man a Title to the product of his honest Industry"—so, too, for Madison and the Federalists: justice effectively meant respecting private rights, especially property rights.[8]

Justice for the Federalists was less a matter of civic virtue, of public participation in politics, as emphasized by recent American historical scholarship, or of a neoplatonic ideal of a transcendent moral order, as argued by scholars such as Walter Berns, than it was a reflection of the Lockean liberal world of personal rights, and most dramatically of property rights. It was a substantive, not procedural or civic, ideal of justice that preoccupied the framers in 1787. It was much more often their content, not their violation of due process, that condemned state legislative actions as wicked. With striking frequency, the condemnation of state laws that interfered with private contracts or established paper money schemes was cast in the language of "unjust laws." In South Carolina such laws were called "open and outrageous . . . violations of every principle of Justice." In New Jersey debtor relief legislation was criticized as "founded not upon the principles of Justice, but upon the Right of the Sword." The Boston *Independent Chronicle* complained in May 1787 that the Massachusetts legislature lacked "a decided tone . . . in favor of the general principles of justice." A "virtuous legislature," wrote a New Jersey critic in 1786, "cannot listen to any proposition, however popular, that came within the description of being unjust, impolitic or unnecessary." In Massachusetts the legislation sought by the Shaysites was seen to be acts of "injustice," establishing "iniquity by Law" and violating "the most simple ties of common honesty." The linkage between the procedural and substantive objections to the state legislatures was made clearly by Noah Webster. They were, he wrote, guilty of "so many legal infractions of sacred right—so many public invasions of private property—so many wanton abuses of legislative powers!"[9]

Madison, too, read justice as the substantive protection of rights. In his argument before the convention on behalf of a council of revision he pleaded that the president and judges should have the power to veto "unwise & unjust measures" of the state legislatures "which constituted so great a portion of our calamities."[10] This is equally evident in the pages of the *Federalist*. In No. 10, state actions reflecting "a rage for paper money, for an abolition of debts, for an equal division of property" were "schemes of injustice" and "improper or wicked project[s]." The fruit of unjust and wicked laws was the "alarm for private rights" that is "echoed from one end of the continent to the other." In No. 44 Madison equated the "love of justice" with hatred of paper money. Such pestilential laws required, in turn, sacrifices on "the altar of justice." The end of government itself was justice, Madison wrote in No. 51, and in No. 54 he refined this further by noting that "government is instituted no less for protection of the property than of the persons of individuals." It was the same for Hamilton, who wrote in *Federalist* No. 70 of "the protection of property" constituting "the ordinary course of justice." In No. 78 Hamilton also described the "private rights of particular classes of citizens" injured "by unjust and partial laws."

The commitment in the preamble to the Constitution to "establish justice" meant for the framers that it would protect private rights, which would help it achieve the next objective—to "insure domestic tranquility." Should there be doubts about this, we have Madison as our guide to what "establish justice" meant. On June 6 he had risen at the convention to answer Roger Sherman's suggestion that the only objects of union were better relations with foreign powers and the prevention of conflicts and disputes among the states. What about justice? was the thrust of Madison's intervention. To Sherman's list of the Constitution's objectives Madison insisted that there be added "the necessity of providing more effectually for the security of private rights, and the steady dispensation of Justice. Interferences with these were evils which had more perhaps than any thing else produced this convention."[11]

The acceptance of modern liberal society in the Federalist camp went beyond a legitimization of the politics of interest and a conviction that government's purpose was to protect the fruits of honest industry. There was also an unabashed appreciation of modern commercial society. Secretary of Education William Bennett is quite right in his recent reminder that "commerce had a central place in the ideas of the Founders."[12] Hamilton, for example, in *Federalist* No. 12, insisted that

> the prosperity of commerce is now perceived and acknowledged by all enlightened statesmen to be the most useful as well as the most productive source of national wealth, and has accordingly become a primary object of their political cares. By multiplying the means of gratification, by promoting the introduction and circulation of the precious metals, those darling objects of human avarice and enterprise, it serves to vivify and invigorate the channels of industry and to make them flow with greater activity and copiousness.

Hamilton was perfectly aware that his praise of private gratification, avarice, and gain flew in the face of older ideals of civic virtue and public duty that emphasized the subordination of private interest to the public good. He turned this very rejection of the republican moral ideal into an argument for the need of a federal standing army. This was a further blow to the ideals of civic virtue, which had always seen professional armies as evil incarnate, undermining the citizen's self-sacrificial participation in the defense of the public realm, which was the premise of the militia. America as a market society could not rely on the militia, according to Hamilton. "The militia," he wrote in *Federalist* No. 24, "would not long, if at all, submit to be dragged from their occupations and families." He was writing of manning garrisons involved in protecting the frontiers: "And if they could be prevailed upon or compelled to do it, the increased expense of a frequent rotation of service, and the loss of labor and disconcertation of the industrious pursuits of individuals, would form conclusive objections to the scheme. It would be as burdensome and injurious to the public as ruinous to private citizens."

In *Federalist* No. 8, another defense of standing armies, Hamilton acknowledged the eclipse of older civic ideals of self-sacrifice and participatory citizenship in commercial America: "The industrious habits of the people of the present day, absorbed in the pursuit of gain and devoted to the improvements of agriculture and commerce, are incompatible with the condition of a nation of soldiers, which was the true condition of the people of those [ancient Greek] republics."

Many of the Antifederalists, on the other hand, were still wedded to a republican civic ideal, to the making of America into what Samuel Adams called "a Christian Sparta." The very feature of pluralist diversity in the new constitutional order that Madison saw as its great virtue, the Antifederalists saw as its major defect. For the Antifederalist "Brutus" it was absurd that the legislature "would be composed of such heterogeneous and discordant principles, as would constantly be contending with each other." A chorus of Antifederalists insisted that virtuous republican government required a small area and a homogeneous population. Patrick Henry noted that a republican form of government extending across the continent "contradicts all the experience of the world." Richard Henry Lee argued that "a free elective government cannot be extended over large territories." Robert Yates of New York saw liberty "swallowed up" because the new republic was too large.[13]

Montesquieu and others had taught Antifederalists "that so extensive a territory as that of the United States, including such a variety of climates, productions, interests, and so great differences of manners, habits, and customs" could never constitute a moral republic. This was the crucial issue for the minority members of the Pennsylvania ratifying convention: "We dissent, first, because it is the opinion of the most celebrated writers on government, and confirmed by uniform experience, that a very extensive territory cannot be governed on the principles of freedom, otherwise than by a confederation of republics."[14]

Antifederalists' fears over the absence of homogeneity in the enlarged republic were as important as the issue of size. In the course of arguing that a national government could not be trusted if it were to allow open immigration, "Agrippa," the popular Antifederalist pamphleteer assumed to be James Winthrop, contrasted the much more desirable situation in "the eastern states" with the sad plight of Pennsylvania, which for years had allowed open immigration and in which religious toleration and diversity flourished:

> Pennsylvania has chosen to receive all that would come there. Let any indifferent person judge whether that state in point of morals, education, energy is equal to any of the eastern states . . . [which,] by keeping separate from the

foreign mixtures, [have] acquired their present greatness in the course of a century and a half, and have preserved their religion and morals. . . . Reasons of equal weight may induce other states . . . to keep their blood pure.[15]

Most Antifederalists held that a republican system required similarity of religion, manners, sentiments, and interests. They were convinced that no such sense of community could exist in an enlarged republic, that no one set of laws could work within such diversity. "We see plainly that men who come from New England are different from us," wrote Joseph Taylor, a southern Antifederalist. "Agrippa," on the other hand, declared that "the inhabitants of warmer climates are more dissolute in their manners, and less industrious, than in colder countries. A degree of severity is, therefore, necessary with one which would cramp the spirit of the other. . . . It is impossible for one code of laws to suit Georgia and Massachusetts."[16]

A just society, for many Antifederalists, involved more than simply protecting property rights. Government had more responsibilities than merely to regulate "various and interfering interests." It was expected to promote morality, virtue, and religion. Many Antifederalists, for example, were shocked at the Constitution's totally secular tone and its general disregard of religion and morality. Equally upsetting was the lack of any religious content in Federalist arguments for the Constitution.

Some Antifederalists were angered that the Constitution, in Article VI, Section 3, prohibited religious tests for officeholders while giving no public support for religious institutions. Amos Singletary of Massachusetts was disturbed that it did not require men in power to be religious: "though he hoped to see Christians, yet, by the Constitution, a Papist, or an Infidel, was as eligible as they." Henry Abbot, an Antifederalist in North Carolina, wrote that "the exclusion of religious tests is by many thought dangerous and impolitic. They suppose . . . pagans, deists, and Mahometans might obtain offices among us." For David Caldwell of North Carolina, this prohibition of religious tests constituted "an invitation for Jews and pagans of every kind to come among us." Since Christianity was the best religion for producing "good members of society, . . . those gentlemen who formed this Constitution should not have given this invitation to Jews and heathens."[17]

Antifederalists held that religion was a crucial support of government. For Richard Henry Lee, "refiners may weave as fine a web of reason as they please, but the experience of all times shews Religion to be the guardian of morals." The state, according to some Antifederalists, had to be concerned with civic and religious education. Several made specific proposals for state-sponsored "seminaries of useful learning" to instill "the principles of free government" and "the science of morality." The state, they urged, should encourage "the people in favour of virtue by affording publick protection to religion."[18] Going a long step further, Charles Turner of Massachusetts insisted that "without the prevalence of *Christian piety and morals,* the best republican Constitution can never save us from slavery and ruin." He urged that the government institute some means of education "as shall be *adequate* to the *divine, patriotick purpose* of training up the children and youth at large, in that solid learning, and in those pious and moral principles, which are the *support,* the *life* and the SOUL of republican government and liberty, of which a free Constitution is the body."[19]

There was, not surprisingly, also a tendency in some Antifederalist circles to see the exchange principles of commercial society, so praised by the Federalists, as threats to civic and moral virtue. Would not the self-seeking activities "of a commercial society beget luxury, the parent of inequality, the foe to virtue, and the enemy to restraint"? The spread of commerce would undermine republican simplicity, for the more a people succumbed to luxury, the more incapable they became of governing themselves. As one Antifederalist put it, speaking critically of the silence of the Constitution on questions of morality, "whatever the refinement of modern politics may inculcate, it still is certain that some degree of virtue must exist, or freedom cannot live." Honest folk like himself, he went on, objected to "Mandevill[e]'s position . . . 'that private vices are public benefits.'" This was not an unfamiliar theme to the men who would oppose the Constitution. Richard Henry Lee singled out the same source of evil, "Mandevilles . . . who laugh at virtue, and with vain ostentatious display of words will deduce from vice, public good!"[20]

The problem with the Federalist position for many Antifederalists was the inadequacy of its vision of community based on mere interests and their protection. The Antifederalists suspected that such a community could not persist through what Madison called in *Federalist* No. 51 "the policy of supplying, by opposite and rival interests, the defect of better motives." A proper republican community, for these Antifederalists, required a moral consensus, which, in turn, required similarity, familiarity, and fraternity. How, they asked, could one govern oneself and prefer the common good over private interests outside a shared community small enough and homogeneous enough to allow one to know and sympathize with one's neighbors? The republican spirit of Rousseau* hovered over these

---

Rousseau: Jean-Jacques Rousseau (1712–1778), the French thinker whose book *The Social Contract* (1762) is regarded as one of the most influential pieces of Enlightenment political thinking.

Antifederalists as they identified with small, simple, face-to-face, uniform societies.

Madison and Hamilton understood full well that this communitarian sentiment lay at the core of much of the Antifederalist critique of the new constitutional order. In *Federalist* No. 35 Hamilton ridiculed the face-to-face politics of those "whose observation does not travel beyond the circle of his neighbors and his acquaintances." Madison in No. 10 described two alternative ways of eliminating the causes of factions and thus the politics of interest: one by "destroying the liberty which is essential to its existence; the other by giving to every citizen the same opinions, the same passions, and the same interests." These were both unacceptable. To do either would cut out the very heart of the liberal polity he championed.[21]

Can one go too far in making the case for the Antifederalists as anti-liberal communitarians or Rousseauean republicans? Some were, without doubt, but others responded to the enlargement of the federal government and the enhancement of executive power with a call for the protection of private and individual rights through a bill of rights. Even this, however, may be explained by their communitarian bias. If, after all, government was to be run from some city hundreds of miles away, by people superior, more learned, and more deliberative than they, by people with whom they had little in common, then individual rights needed specific protection. The basis for trust present in the small moral community where men shared what Madison disparagingly described as "the same opinions, the same passions, and the same interests" was extinguished.

An equally strong case can be made for the Federalists as republican theorists, and here we see full-blown the confusion of idioms, the overlapping of political languages, in 1787. There is, of course, Madison's redefinition of and identification with a republicanism that involved "the delegation of the government . . . to a small number of citizens elected by the rest" as opposed to a democracy "consisting of a small number of citizens who assemble and administer the government in person." But the crucial move in No. 10 that sets Madison firmly within the republican paradigm is his assumption that the representative function in an enlarged republic would produce officeholders who would sacrifice personal, private, and parochial interest to the public good and the public interest. What made the layers of filtration prescribed by the new constitutional order so welcome was their ultimate purpose — producing enlightened public-spirited men who found fulfillment in the quest for public good. It is this feature of Madison's No. 10 that Garry Wills has drawn attention to as the crowning inspiration of Madison's moral republicanism. Republican government over a large country would, according to Madison, refine and enlarge the public views by passing them through the medium of a chosen body of citizens whose wisdom may best discern the true interest of their country, and whose patriotism and love of justice will be least likely to sacrifice it to temporary or partial considerations. Under such a regulation it may well happen that the public voice pronounced by the representatives of the people will be more consonant to the public good than if pronounced by the people themselves, convened for the purpose.

The greater number of citizens choosing representatives in a larger republic would reject "unworthy candidates" and select "men who possess the most attractive merit." A large republic and a national government would lead to "the substitution of representatives whose enlightened views and virtuous sentiments render them superior to local prejudices and to schemes of injustice." We know, given Madison's candor, what this meant.[22]

Working out the mechanisms by which this filtration process would "refine" and "enlarge" public views and enhance the quality of the men chosen to express them preoccupied the delegates at Philadelphia. This explains their lengthy deliberations over how governing officials such as the president and senators should be selected. Indirect processes of selection would, Madison wrote in his notes, "extract from the mass of the Society the purest and noblest characters which it contains."[23] The people involved in choosing the president or senators would be, according to Jay in *Federalist* No. 64, "the most enlightened and respectable." The Senate, Madison wrote in *Federalist* No. 63, would then be made up of "temperate and respectable" men standing for "reason, justice and truth" in the face of the people's "errors and delusions."

Madison privileged public over private elsewhere in the *Federalist* as well. In No. 49 he envisioned public "reason" and "the true merits of the question" controlling and regulating government, not particular and private "passions." Similarly, in No. 55 he saw "the public interests" at risk in large legislative assemblies where "passion" always triumphed over "reason." The smaller House of Representatives constructed by the Federalists would better ensure the victory of public good over self-interest.

The class focus of the Federalists' republicanism is self-evident. Their vision was of an elite corps of men in whom civic spirit and love of the general good overcame particular and narrow interest. Such men were men of substance, independence, and fame who had the leisure to devote their time to public life and the wisdom to seek the true interests of the country as opposed to the wicked projects of local and particular interests. This republicanism of Madison and the Federalists was, of course, quite consistent with the general aristocratic orientation of classical republicanism, which was, after all, the ideal of the independent, propertied, and therefore leisured citizen with time and reason to find fulfillment as *homo civicus.**

Filtering out mediocrity for Madison went hand in hand with disinterested pursuit of the public good. Many Antifederalists, for their part, saw legislatures as most representative when their membership mirrored the complexity and diversity of society—when, in fact, each geographical unit and social rank was represented. In offering the mirror, not the filter, as the model for representation, Antifederalists seemed to be calling for the representation of every particular interest and thus appear to resemble interest-centered liberals. It was they, as well as Madison in his nonrepublican passages, who, it can be claimed, articulated the politics of interest, to be sure in a language much more democratic and participatory. The classic expression of this Antifederalist interest theory of representation came from Melancton Smith, the great antagonist of Hamilton at the New York ratification convention. He told the delegates that "the idea that naturally suggests itself to our minds, when we speak of representatives, is, that they resemble those they represent. They should be a true picture of the people, possess a knowledge of their circumstances and their wants, sympathize in all their distresses, and be disposed to seek their true interests." Directly refuting the filtration model, Smith insisted that a representative system ought not to seek "brilliant talents," but "a sameness, as to residence and interests, between the representative and his constituents."[24]

Hamilton repudiated the Antifederalist interest theory in *Federalist* No. 35. "The idea of an actual representation of all classes of the people, by persons of each class," so that the feelings and interests of all would be expressed, "is altogether visionary," he wrote. The national legislature, Hamilton recommended, should be composed only of "landholders, merchants, and men of the learned professions." Ordinary people, however much confidence "they may justly feel in their own good sense," should realize that "their interests can be more effectually promoted" by men from these three stations in life.

The confusion of paradigms is further evident when one analyzes in more detail these Federalist and Antifederalist theories of representation. The interest- and particularistic-oriented Antifederalists tended to espouse the traditional republican conviction, dominant in most states under the Articles of Confederation, that representatives should be directly responsible to their constituents and easily removable. This, of course, tapped a rich eighteenth-century republican tradition of demanding frequent elec-

---

**homo civicus:* Latin for "civic man," referring to the classical republican belief that citizenship is the highest human activity.

tions. Implicit in the Federalist notion of filtration, however, was a denial of the representative as mere delegate or servant of his constituents. In Madison's republicanism the representative was chosen for his superior ability to discern the public good, not as a mere spokesman for his town or region, or for the farmers or mechanics who elected him. It followed, then, that Federalists rejected the traditional republican ideal of annual or frequent elections, which was so bound to the more democratic ideal of the legislator as delegate. It is no surprise to find Madison, in *Federalist* Nos. 37, 52, and 53, critical of frequent elections and offering several arguments against them. The proposed federal government, he insisted, was less powerful than the British government had been; its servants, therefore, were less to be feared. State affairs, he contended, could be mastered in less than a year, but the complexity of national politics was such that more time was needed to grasp its details. More important than these arguments, however, was the basic ideological gulf that here separated Madison's republicanism from the Antifederalist republican proponents of annual elections. Madison's legislators of "refined and enlarged public views," seeking "the true interest of their country," ought not to be subject to yearly review by local farmers and small-town tradesmen.

The Language of Virtuous Republicanism

The meaning of virtue in the language of civic humanism is clear. It is the privileging of the public over the private. Samuel Adams persistently evoked the idioms of Aristotle and Cicero. "A Citizen," he wrote, "owes everything to the Commonwealth." He worried that Americans would so "forget their own generous Feelings for the Publick and for each other, as to set private Interest in Competition with that of the great Community." Benjamin Rush went so far in 1786 as to reject the very core belief of what in a later day would come to be called possessive individualism. Every young man in a true republic, he noted, must "be taught that he does not belong to himself, but that he is public property." All his time and effort throughout "his youth—his manhood—his old age—nay more, life, all belong to his country." For John Adams, "public Virtue is the only Foundation of Republics." Republican government required "a positive Passion for the public good, the public Interest.... Superiour to all private Passions."[25]

This is not all that virtue meant. Subtle changes were taking place during the founding of the American republic in the notion of virtue, and at their core was a transvaluation of public and private. Dramatic witness is given to these changes by Madison's *Federalist* No. 44 where he depicted paper money as a threat to the republican character and spirit of the American people. That spirit, however, was neither civic nor public in nature. The values at risk were apolitical and personal. Madison feared for the sobriety, the prudence, and the industry of Americans. His concern was "the industry and morals of the people." A similar concern appeared in William Livingston's worrying that his countrymen "do not exhibit the virtue that is necessary to support a republican government." John Jay agreed. "Too much," he wrote, "has been expected from the Virtue and good Sense of the People." But like Madison, when Americans became specific about exactly what the decline of virtue meant, their language was often noncivic and instead self-referential. Writing to Jefferson in 1787, friends told of "symptoms . . . truly alarming, which have tainted the faith of the most orthodox republicans." Americans lacked "industry, economy, temperance, and other republican virtues." Their fall from virtue was marked not by turning from public life (was there not, indeed, too much of that very republican value in the overheated state legislatures?) but by their becoming "a Luxurious Voluptuous indolent expensive people without Economy or Industry." Virtuous republican people could, in fact, be described in noncivic, personal terms by the very same men who used the language of civic humanism. John Adams could see the foundation of virtuous government in men who are "sober, industrious and frugal."[26]

One of the most striking aspects of political discourse in this era is the formulaic frequency with which this different sense of virtue is heard. For Joel Barlow in a 1787 Fourth of July oration at Hartford, the "noble republican virtues which constitute the chief excellency" of government were "industry, frugality, and economy." Richard Henry Lee described the virtuous as a "wise, attentive, sober, diligent & frugal" people who had established "the independence of America." A Virginian wondering whether America could sustain republican government asked, "Have we that Industry, Frugality, Economy, that Virtue which is necessary to constitute it?"[27] The constitutions of Pennsylvania and Vermont actually enlisted the Machiavellian republican notion of the return to original principles for their noncivic definition of a virtuous people. They specified that "a frequent recurrence to fundamental principles, and a firm adherence to justice, moderation, temperance, industry, and frugality are absolutely necessary to preserve the blessings of liberty and keep a government free."[28]

The Antifederalists, ostensible communitarian and public-oriented foils to Madisonian interest-based liberalism, could also use this more personal idiomatic notion of virtue. The Articles were not at fault, according to John Williams of New York. The great problem was the decline of virtue in the middle 1780s, "banishing all that economy, frugality, and industry, which had been exhibited during the war." For the Antifederalist pamphleteer "Candidus," it was not a new constitution that America needed but a return to the virtues of "industry and frugality."[29]

The republican tradition had, to be sure, always privileged economy over luxury. From Aristotle and Cicero through Harrington and the eighteenth-century opposition to Walpole, republican rhetoric linked a virtuous republican order to the frugal abstention from extravagance and luxury. But there is more than the all-pervasive paradigm of republicanism at work here. The inclusion of industry in the litany of virtue directs us to another inheritance, to another language in which Americans in the late eighteenth century conceptualized their personal and political universe. Americans also spoke the language of work-ethic Protestantism derived from Richard Baxter, John Bunyan, and the literature of the calling and of "industry." In the later decades of the eighteenth century this was the discourse that monopolized the texts of the English Dissenters, James Burgh, Richard Price, and Joseph Priestley, whose writings were so influential in the founding generation.[30]

Central in work-ethic Protestantism was the vision of a cosmic struggle between the forces of industry and idleness. Its texts vibrated less with the dialectic of civic virtue and self-centered commerce than with the dialectic of productive hardworking energy, on the one hand, and idle unproductive sloth, on the other. Its idiom was more personal and individualistic than public and communal. Work was a test of self-sufficiency and self-reliance, a battleground for personal salvation. All men were "called" to serve God by busying themselves in useful productive work that served both society and the individual. Daily labor was sanctified and thus was both a specific obligation and a positive moral value. The doctrine of the calling gave each man a sense of his unique self; work appropriate to each individual was imposed by God. After being called to a particular occupation, it was a man's duty to labor diligently and to avoid idleness and sloth.

The fruits of his labor were justly man's. There was for Baxter an "honest increase and provision which is the end of our labour." It was, therefore, "no sin, but a duty to choose a gainful calling rather than another, that we may be able to do good." Not only was working hard and seeking to prosper the mark of a just and virtuous man and idleness a sign of spiritual corruption, but work was also the anodyne for physical corruption. Hard work disciplined the wayward and sinful impulses that lay like Satan's traces within all men. Baxter wrote that "for want of *bodily* labour a multitude of the idle Gentry, and rich people, and young people that are slothful, do heap up in the secret receptacles of the body a dunghill of unconcocted excrementitious filth ... and dye by thousands of untimely deaths[.] ... [I]t is their own doing, and by their sloth they kill themselves."[31]

The Protestant language of work and the calling is, of course, complementary to the liberal language of Locke with its similar voluntaristic and individualistic emphasis. Locke's *Second Treatise* and its chapter "Of Property," with its very Protestant God enjoining industrious man to subdue the earth through work and thus to realize himself, is, as Quentin Skinner insists, "the classical text of radical Calvinist politics."[32] The kinship of work-ethic Protestant discourse to Locke has less to do with the juristic discourse of rights than with the Protestant theme of work. In the Protestant vocabulary there is much mention of virtue and corruption, but these have primarily nonclassical referents. Virtuous man is solitary and private man on his own, realizing himself and his talents through labor and achievement; corrupt man is unproductive, indolent, and in the devil's camp. He fails the test of individual responsibility. Few have captured the compatibility of the liberal and work-ethic Protestant paradigms as well as Tocqueville, albeit unintentionally. In *Democracy in America* he wrote of the American character in noncivic, individualistic terms that are at bottom central to both liberal and Protestant discourse. Americans, Tocqueville wrote, "owe nothing to any man, they expect nothing from any man; they acquire the habit of always considering themselves as standing alone, and they are apt to imagine that their whole destiny is in their own hands."[33]

Contemporary scholars such as Edmund S. Morgan, J. E. Crowley, Joyce Appleby, and John Patrick Diggins have described this alternative paradigm of Protestantism and the Protestant ethic in eighteenth-century America and with it a language quite congenial to individualistic liberalism and the capitalist spirit.[34] Next to the Bible, the texts of Protestant moralists like Baxter were the most likely to be found in the libraries of eighteenth-century Americans.[35] From them Americans came to know the virtuous man as productive, thrifty, and diligent. Morgan and Crowley, especially, have documented how the American response to English taxation centered on a dual policy of self-denial and commitment to industry. Richard Henry Lee, as early as 1764, when hearing of the Sugar Act, assumed it would "introduce a virtuous industry." The subsequent nonconsumption and nonimportation policy of colonial protestors led many a moralist, in fact, to applaud parliamentary taxation as a blessing in disguise, recalling America to simplicity and frugality. As Morgan notes, the boycott movements were seen by many as not simply negative and reactive. "They were also a positive end in themselves, a way of reaffirming and rehabilitating the virtues of the Puritan Ethic."[36]

In this vocabulary, industry, simplicity, and frugality were the signs not only of a virtuous people but also of a free people. As one Rhode Island writer put it, "the industrious and the frugal only will be free."[37] The Boston *Evening-Post* of November 16, 1767, noted that "by consuming *less* of what we are not really in want of, and by industriously cultivating and improving the natural advantages of our own country, we might save our *substance, even our lands,* from becoming the property of others, and we might effectually preserve our *virtue* and our *liberty,* to the latest posterity." Three weeks later the *Pennsylvania Journal* proclaimed: "SAVE YOUR MONEY AND YOU WILL SAVE YOUR COUNTRY." In one of her famous letters to her husband, John, away at the Continental Congress, Abigail Adams revealed how salient the Protestant virtues were in the political context of her day. Would, she wrote, that Americans "return a little more to their primitive Simplicity of Manners, and not sink into inglorious ease." They must "retrench their expenses. . . . Indeed their [*sic*] is occasion for all our industry and economy."[38]

From pulpit and pamphlet Americans had long heard praises of industry and denunciations of idleness. For Benjamin Colman, minister of Boston's Brattle Street Church, *"all Nature is Industrious and every Creature about us diligent in their proper Work."* Constant activity was the human telos for Ebenezer Pemberton, an end even after death. He complained of those who thought that "the happiness of Heaven consisted only in Enjoyment, and a stupid Indolence." This Protestant paradigm of restless and disciplined human activity also spoke in the idiomatic terms of life as a race. The life of the virtuous Christian was "compared to a *Race,* a *Warfare; Watching, Running, Fighting;* all which imply Activity, Earnestness, Speed, etc." The race, according to Nathaniel Henchman, called "for the utmost striving of the whole Man, unfainting Resolute perseverance."[39]

Idleness, on the other hand, was a denial of the human essence. To be idle was to neglect "Duty and lawful Employment . . . for Man is by Nature such an active Creature, that he cannot be wholly Idle." Idleness for Americans had specific class referents. It was the sinful mark of the poor or the great, those below and those above the virtuous man of the middle. Cotton Mather made it clear that the idle poor had no claims on society. *"We should let them Starve,"* he wrote. As for the idle rich, Nathaniel Clap expelled them from the very fold of Christendom. "If Persons Live upon the Labours of others," he wrote, "and spend their Time in Idleness, without any Imployment, for the Benefit of others, they cannot be numb[e]red among Christians. Yea, If Persons Labour, to get great Estates, with this design, chiefly, that they and theirs may live in Idleness, They cannot be Acknowledged for Christians."[40]

America in the 1780s, Drew R. McCoy tells us, may well have had one of the highest rates of population growth in her history. For many, this conjured up fears of vast increases in the numbers of the poor and idle. Only a cultivation of domestic manufacturers would keep these idle hordes from the devil's hands. Once again the marriage of necessity and virtue led

Americans to turn from foreign imports to local manufacture and domestic hard work. As Morgan noted of the pre-war boycott of the British, so McCoy characterizes similar promotion of native production in the 1780s "as the necessary means of making Americans into an active, industrious, republican people."[41] Indeed, in February 1787 one observer noted how absurd it was for Americans to support manufactures "at several thousand miles distance, while a great part of our own people are idle." American manufactures would "deliver them from the curse of idleness. We shall hold out . . . a new stimulus and encouragement to industry and every useful art."[42]

Communitarian critics of an individualistic interest-based politics could also speak the Protestant language of sobriety, frugality, and industry and also locate these virtues in the particularly virtuous middle ranks of life. The Antifederalists were in good company, then, when they enlisted that language to condemn what they saw as the aristocratic character of the new constitutional order. The Federal Farmer saw the new Constitution resulting from the conflict between leveling debtors "who want a share of the property of others" and men "called aristocrats" who "grasp at all power and property." Uninvolved and victimized were the larger number of "men of middling property" who worked hard and made up the "solid, free, and independent part of the community." It was Melancton Smith, the bearer of a proud Protestant name, who best made the Protestant case for the virtuous middle against Hamilton's aristocratic Constitution at the New York ratifying convention. It was an evil Constitution, Smith claimed, because it restricted representation to the idle few, excluding those who were morally superior. What is crucial to note is that virtue here is apolitical and non-civic:

> Those in middling circumstances, have less temptation — they are inclined by habit and the company with whom they associate, to set bounds to their passions and appetites — if this is not sufficient, the want of means to gratify them will be a restraint — they are obliged to employ their time in their respective callings — hence the substantial yeomanry of the country are more temperate, of better morals and less ambitious than the great.[43]

In his most recent collection of essays J. G. A. Pocock has suggested that in the eighteenth century "virtue was redefined," but he is wide of the mark in suggesting that "there are signs of an inclination to abandon the word" and in claiming that it was simply redefined "as the practice and refinement of manners." Virtue had for some time been part of the Protestant discourse with its nonrepublican image of virtuous man as productive, thrifty, and frugal. By the second half of the century this noncivic personal reading of virtue would be secularized, as in Adam Smith's negative assessment of the aristocrat who "shudders with horror at the thought of any situation which demands the continual and long exertion of patience, industry, fortitude, and application of thought. These virtues are hardly ever to be met with in men who are born to those high stations."[44]

Virtue was becoming privatized in the latter part of the eighteenth century. It was being moved from the realm of public activity to the sphere of personal character. The virtuous man partook less and less of that republican ideal that held sway from Aristotle to Harrington—the man whose landed property gave him the leisure necessary for civic commitment in the public arena, be its manifestations political or martial. Property was still important in the Protestant paradigm—not, however, as grantor of leisure but as the rightful fruit of industrious work.

Gordon Wood has noted that Carter Braxton more than any other in the founding generation of Americans sensed the tension between a republicanism based on public virtue—the "disinterested attachment to the public good, exclusive and independent of all private and selfish interest"—and an American polity where in reality most practiced a private virtue in which each man "acts for himself, and with a view of promoting his own particular welfare." Republican privileging of public over private had never been, according to Braxton, the politics of "the mass of the people in any state." In this observation lay Braxton's real insight. Republican virtue was historically the ideal of a circumscribed, privileged citizenry with an independent propertied base that provided the leisure and time for fulfillment in public life through the moral pursuit of public things, *res publica*. Americans, on the other hand, Braxton wrote, "who inhabit a country to which providence has been more bountiful," live lives of hard work and private virtue, and their industry, frugality, and economy produce the fruits of honest labor.[45] From our perspective, we can credit Braxton with perceiving the decline of republican hegemony in the face of the alternative worlds of Lockean liberalism and the Protestant ethic. What we now know is that one hears more and more in the course of the late eighteenth century a different language of virtue, one that rejects the assumptions of civic humanism. Citizenship and the public quest for the common good were for some replaced by economic productivity and industrious work as the criteria of virtue. It is a mistake, however, to see this simply as a withdrawal from public activity to a private, self-centered realm. The transformation also involved a changed emphasis on the nature of public behavior. The moral and virtuous man was no longer defined by his civic activity but by his economic activity. One's duty was still to contribute to the public good, but this was best done through economic activity, which actually aimed at private gain. Self-centered economic productivity, not public citizenship, would become a badge of the

virtuous man. At the heart of this shift from republican to Protestant notions of virtue was also a transvaluation of work and leisure. Many Americans in 1787 would have dissented vigorously from the centuries-old republican paradigm set forth in Aristotle's *Politics:* "In the state with the
finest constitution, which possesses just men who are just absolutely and
not relatively to the assumed situation, the citizens must not live a me-
chanical or commercial life. Such a life is not noble, and it militates
against virtue. Nor must those who are to be citizens be agricultural work-
ers, for they must have leisure to develop their virtue, and for the activities
of a citizen."[46]

The Language of Power and the State

Lost today in the legitimate characterization of the Constitution as bent on
setting limits to the power exercised by less than angelic men is the extent
to which the Constitution is a grant of power to a centralized nation-state.
This loss reflects a persistent privileging of Madison over Hamilton in
reading the text. While posterity emphasizes the Constitution's complex
web of checks and balances and the many institutionalized separations of
powers, the participants in the "great national discussion," on whichever
side they stood, agreed with Hamilton that the Constitution intended a victory for power, for the "principle of *strength* and *stability* in the organization
of our government, and *vigor* in its operations."[47]

A pro-Constitution newspaper, the *Pennsylvania Packet,* declared in September 1787: "The year 1776 is celebrated . . . for a revolution in favor of
liberty. The year 1787, it is expected, will be celebrated with equal joy, for a
revolution in favor of Government." The theme was repeated by Benjamin
Rush, also a defender of the Constitution. Rush wrote in June 1787 to his
English friend Richard Price that "the same enthusiasm *now* pervades all
classes in favor of *government* that actuated us in favor of *liberty* in the years
1774 and 1775."[10]

Critics of the Constitution saw the same forces at work. For Patrick
Henry, "the tyranny of Philadelphia" was little different from "the tyranny
of George III." An Antifederalist told the Virginia ratification convention
that "had the Constitution been presented to our view ten years ago, . . . it
would have been considered as containing principles incompatible with
republican liberty, and, therefore, doomed to infamy." But the real foil to
Hamilton, using the very same whig language, was Richard Henry Lee,
who wrote in 1788: "It will be considered, I believe, as a most extraordinary epoch in the history of mankind, that in a few years there should be
so essential a change in the minds of men. 'Tis really astonishing that the

same people, who have just emerged from a long and cruel war in defense of liberty, should now agree to fix an elective despotism upon themselves and their posterity."[49]

But always there were other and louder voices using this same language in defense of the Constitution. Benjamin Franklin wrote that "we have been guarding against an evil that old States are most liable to, *excess of power* in the rulers; but our present danger seems to be *defect of obedience* in the subjects." For the *Connecticut Courant* it was all quite simple. The principles of 1776 had produced a glaring problem, "a want of energy in the administration of government."[50]

In the political discourse of 1787 there was thus a fourth paradigm at work, the state-centered language of power. It, too, reached back into the classical world, to the great lawgivers and founders Solon and Lycurgus, and to the imperial ideal of Alexander and Julius Caesar. Not republican city states but empire and, much later, the nation-state were its institutional units. Its doctrines and commitments were captured less by *zöon politicon, vivere civilere, res publica,* and *virtú* than by *imperium, potestas, gubernaculum,* prerogative, and sovereignty. Its prophets were Dante, Marsilio, Bodin, Richelieu, Hobbes, Machiavelli (of *The Prince,* not the *Discourses*), and James I.* This language of politics was focused on the moral, heroic, and self-realizing dimensions of the exercise and use of power.

For Charles Howard McIlwain the recurring answer to this power-centered language of politics was the discourse of "jurisdictio";† for contemporary scholars it would be the law-centered paradigm or the language of jurisprudence and rights.[51] For our purposes, it is important to recognize how the discourse of power and sovereignty renders problematic the reading of the "great national discussion" as simply a dialogue between republicanism and liberalism. To be sure, as the language of Protestantism was complementary to and supportive of liberalism, so the state-centered language of power was closer to and more easily compatible with the discourse of republicanism. Hamilton was fascinated by the nation-state builders in early modern Europe, but his power-centered politics still touched base with much of the older republican ideal. It shared the reading of man as a political animal, as a community-building creature. It, too, privileged public life and public pursuits over a reading of politics that

---

Solon . . . James I: Kramnick is referring to a long tradition of thinkers who have placed the creation and exercise of power over both active citizenship and individual satisfaction as central to political life. Note that he classed the Italian thinker Niccolò Machiavelli as a major influence on both the republican and state-centered traditions that he describes.

†*jurisdictio:* Literally, the "speaking" of law by legislators and judges as superior to the exercise of power by rulers and politicians.

stressed the private context of self-regarding lives of individuals. It did not, however, share the participatory ideals of moral citizenship, basic to much of the republican tradition, and this difference dramatically sets it off as a separate discourse.

In *Federalist* No. 1 Hamilton proclaimed his "enlightened zeal" for "the energy" and "vigor of government." His achievement, and that of the other young men at Philadelphia, was the creation of the American state. Some decades later, Hegel could find nothing in America that he recognized as the "state."[52] But that was in comparison with established European states, and in that sense he was quite right. What little there was of an American state, however, was crafted by Hamilton, Madison, and the framers of the Constitution, who began their work *de nouveau,* from nothing. There was no royal household whose offices would become state bureaus, no royal army from a feudal past to be transformed into an expression of the state's reality.

It was the experience of war that shaped the vision of America's state-builders. The war against Britain provided them with a continental and national experience that replaced the states-centered focus of the pre-1776 generation. A remarkable number of framers of the Constitution either served in the Continental army or were diplomats or administrative officials for the Confederation or members of the Continental Congress. Indeed, thirty-nine of the fifty-five delegates to the Constitutional Convention had sat in the Congress. This is where the generational issue, so brilliantly described by Stanley Elkins and Eric McKitrick, was so crucial.[53] Most of the principal Federalists had forged their identity in service to the war and the national cause and in dealing with the individual states' reluctance to assist that continental effort. Washington, Knox, and Hamilton were key figures in military affairs. Robert Morris was superintendent of finance, whose unhappy task it was to try to finance the war. John Jay had been president of the Confederation Congress for a short while and a central actor in trying to implement a common foreign policy for the thirteen states. While most of the Antifederalists were states-centered politicians whose heroics took place before 1776, most of the Federalists were shaped by the need to realize the national interest in an international war. Their common bond was an experience that transcended and dissolved state boundaries.

Madison and Hamilton had sat on the same committee of the Continental Congress in 1782–1783, working on the funding of the war and the maintenance of the French alliance. From experiences like this they and their state-building colleagues came to view the thirteen states collectively as a "country," a country among countries. If their country were going to live in a world of nation-states, it needed to become, like the others, a centralized nation-state with sovereign power to tax, regulate trade, coin money, fund a debt, conduct a foreign policy, and organize a standing army.

The lack of such an American state was profoundly dispiriting to Hamilton. In *Federalist* No. 85 he declared that "a nation without a national government is, in my view, a sad spectacle." In No. 15 he was even more distraught: "We have neither troops, nor treasury, nor government for the Union . . . our ambassadors abroad are the mere pageants of mimic sovereignty." One can, in fact, construct a theory of the origin and development of the state in *The Federalist,* all from Hamilton's contributions. The state is defined in No. 15 as a coercive agent having the power to make laws. To perform this function, a state requires a stable and predictable system of taxation (Nos. 30, 36) and agencies of force, that is, armies and police (Nos. 6, 34). Especially important for Hamilton's theory of state development are Nos. 16 and 17. In the former he insisted that "the majesty of the national authority" cannot work if impeded by intermediate bodies: "It must carry its agency to the persons of the citizens." Independent and sovereign nations do not govern or coerce states; they rule over individuals.

Hamilton's preoccupation with money and arms as essential for state-building, and his zeal to push aside any intermediate bodies between the state and individuals, while directly relevant for the case he was making on behalf of the Constitution, were also heavily influenced by his perceptive reading of the pattern of state-building in Europe. This is revealed in the all-important *Federalist* No. 17, where Hamilton compares America under the Articles of Confederation to the "feudal anarchy" of medieval Europe. Clearly, for Hamilton, the separate American states were intermediate "political bodies" like "principal vassals" and "feudal baronies," each "a kind of sovereign within . . . particular demesnes." Equally evident is his sense that the pattern of European development, with the triumph of coercive centralized nation-states, should be reproduced in America under the Constitution. On both sides of the Atlantic, then, the state will have "subdued" the "fierce and ungovernable spirit and reduced it within those rules of subordination" that characterize "a more rational and more energetic system of civil polity." Nor is this state-building scenario unrelated to liberal ideological concerns. Hamilton in *Federalist* No. 26 sounds very much like the liberal theorists of state, Hobbes and Locke, when he writes of the role that the "energy of government" plays in ensuring "the security of private rights." However, Hamilton was interested less in the limited liberal state than in the heroic state; heroic state-builders like him cannot fear power, for power is the essence of the state. That power is so often abused does not rule out its creative and useful role. This was the message of a Hamilton speech to the New York legislature in early 1787:

We are told it is dangerous to trust power any where; that *power* is liable to *abuse* with a variety of trite maxims of the same kind. General propositions of this nature are easily framed, the truth of which cannot be denied, but they rarely convey any precise idea. To these we might oppose other propositions equally true and equally indefinite. It might be said that too little power is as dangerous as too much, that it leads to anarchy, and from anarchy to despotism. . . . Powers must be granted, or civil Society cannot exist; the possibility of abuse is no argument against the *thing*.[54]

All of the power-centered paradigm's euphemisms for power — "strength," "vigor," "energy" — come together in Hamilton's conception of the presidential office. The presidency was the heart of the new American state for Hamilton, just as the monarch or chief magistrate was for older European nation-states. In Hamilton's president could be heard the echoes of *potestas* and *gubernaculum*.* Had he not argued at Philadelphia for a life term for presidents? Short of that, in *Federalist* No. 72 he supported the president's eligibility for indefinite reelection. How else, he asked, would a president be able to "plan and undertake extensive and arduous enterprises for the public benefit"? The president was the energetic builder of an energetic state. In *Federalist* No. 70 Hamilton argued: "Energy in the executive is a leading character in the definition of good government. . . . A feeble executive implies a feeble execution of the government. A feeble execution is but another phrase for a bad execution; and a government ill executed, whatever it may be in theory, must be in practice, a bad government."

Hamilton saw a close relationship between a state with energy and power at home and a powerful state in the world of states. At the Constitutional Convention he angrily replied to Charles Pinckney's suggestion that republican governments should be uninterested in being respected abroad and concerned only with achieving domestic happiness: "It had been said that respectability in the eyes of foreign Nations was not the object at which we aimed; that the proper object of republican government was domestic tranquillity & happiness. This was an ideal distinction. No governmt. could give us tranquillity & happiness at home, which did not possess sufficient stability and strength to make us respectable abroad."[55]

Hamilton was preoccupied with the interrelationship between commerce, state power, and international politics. A powerful state in his vision was a commercial state. In the competitive international system, nation-states sought to improve or protect their commercial strength, which led inevitably to wars. Powerful states therefore needed standing

potestas . . . gubernaculum: Latin terms referring to the power of a state over its citizens or subjects.

armies and strong navies. In *Federalist* No. 24 Hamilton insisted that "if we mean to be a commercial people, it must form a part of our policy, to be able to defend that commerce." In contrast to Paine and many isolationist Antifederalists, he rejected the notion that wars were fought only "by ambitious princes" or that republican government necessarily led to peace. Hamilton, the realist, ridiculed in *Federalist* No. 6 "visionary or designing men," who thought republics or trading nations immune from the natural conflicts of nation-states, who talked "of perpetual peace between the states," or who claimed that "the genius of republics is pacific."

> Have republics in practice been less addicted to war than monarchies? Are not the former administered by men as well as the latter? Are there not aversions, predilections, rivalships and desires of unjust acquisitions that affect nations as well as kings? Are not popular assemblies frequently subject to the impulses of rage, resentment, jealousy, avarice and of other irregular and violent propensities?

But Hamilton did not want to build an American state with all that statehood required — a financial and commercial infrastructure, energetic leadership, and powerful military forces — merely to allow America to hold its own in a world system characterized by conflict, competition, and clashing power. He had a grander vision for the American state, a call to greatness. In *Federalist* No. 11 Hamilton wrote of "what this country is capable of becoming," of a future glory for America of "a striking and animating kind." Under a properly "vigorous national government, the natural strength and resources of the country, directed to a common interest, would baffle all the combinations of European jealousy to restrain our growth." If Americans would only "concur in erecting one great American system," the American state would be "superior to the control of all transatlantic force or influence, and able to dictate the terms of the connection between the old and the new world." In the face of a vigorous American state Europe would cease to be "mistress of the world." America would become ascendant in the Western Hemisphere.

Hamilton's horizons were dazzling. His internationalism transcended the cosmopolitan vision of his fellow Federalists as it transcended the localism of the Antifederalists. The victory of the state center over the American periphery would in Hamilton's fertile imagination catapult America from the periphery of nations to the center of the world system.

It would be a heroic achievement for Hamilton and his colleagues in Philadelphia to create such a powerful American state. It would bring them everlasting fame, and, as Douglass Adair has told us, that may well have been the ultimate motive that prompted their state-building. In *Feder-*

alist No. 72 Hamilton suggested that political leaders who undertake "extensive and arduous enterprises for the public benefit" are activated by "the love of fame, the ruling passion of the noblest minds." He was describing his ideal of an energetic president, the subject of the paper, and the heroic enterprise of constitutional state-building embarked on by him and his fellow Federalists. It would bring them the fame and immortality of a Lycurgus as described by Madison in *Federalist* No. 38. The classical and Renaissance discourse of power was replete with praise for creative wielders of *potestas*. Literate men in the eighteenth century, like Hamilton and Madison, knew that Plutarch in his *Lives of the Noble Greeks and Romans* reserved the greatest historical glory for the "law giver" and the "founder of commonwealth." In a text equally well known in this period, Francis Bacon's *Essays,* the top of a fivefold scale of "fame and honour" was occupied by "Conditores Imperium, Founders of States and Commonwealths." David Hume, who was well read by both Hamilton and Madison, echoed this theme. He wrote that "of all men that distinguish themselves by memorable achievements, the first place of honour seems due to legislators and founders of states who transmit a system of laws and institutions to secure the peace, happiness and liberty of future generations." Hamilton must have seen himself and his fellow state-builders as achieving such everlasting fame. Ten years earlier, in a pamphlet attacking congressmen for not better realizing the potential of their position, he had written of true greatness and fame. He signed the pamphlet with the pseudonym "Publius," a fabled figure in Plutarch's *Lives* and the name later used by the authors of the *Federalist.* Hamilton's vision transcended the walls of Congress in the infant nation and spoke to the historic discourse of power.

> The station of a member of C——ss, is the most illustrious and important of any I am able to conceive. He is to be regarded not only as a legislator, but as the founder of an empire. A man of virtue and ability, dignified with so precious a trust, would rejoice that fortune had given him birth at a time, and placed him in circumstances so favourable for promoting human happiness. He would esteem it not more the duty, than the privilege and ornament of his office, to do good to mankind.[56]

We must not lose sight of the other side in the "great national discussion," however. Hamilton's discourse of power with its vision of an imperial American state attracted the fire of Antifederalists like one of Franklin's lightning rods. It was Patrick Henry who most angrily and most movingly repudiated the Federalist state. Henry's American spirit was Tom Paine's. With the Federalist state America would lose its innocence, and "splendid government" would become its badge, its dress. On the ruins of paradise would be built, if not the palaces of kings, then armies and navies and mighty empires. At the Virginia ratifying convention Henry evoked a different language of politics.

> The American spirit has fled from hence; it has gone to regions where it has never been expected; it has gone to the people of France, in search of a splendid government, a strong, energetic government. Shall we imitate the example of those nations who have gone from a simple to a splendid government? Are those nations more worthy of our imitation? What can make an adequate satisfaction to them for the loss they have suffered in attaining such a government, for the loss of their liberty? If we admit this consolidated government, it will be because we like a great, splendid one. Some way or other we must be a great and mighty empire; we must have an army, and a navy, and a number of things. When the American spirit was in its youth, the language of America was different; liberty, sir, was then the primary object.[57]

What was Madison's relationship to the discourse of power and the Hamiltonian state? Madison was a state-builder, too, but his state was quite different from Hamilton's, and upon these differences a good deal of American politics in the next two decades, as well as to this day, would turn. Madison and Hamilton were in agreement on many things. They agreed on the need to establish an effective unified national government. They agreed on the serious threats to personal property rights posed by the state legislatures and on the role that a central government would play in protecting these rights. They agreed on the need to have the central government run by worthy, enlightened, and deliberative men. They agreed on the Constitution as necessary to provide the essential framework for commercial development through the creation of a national market, public credit, uniform currency, and the protection of contract. To be sure, Madison's vision tilted toward agrarian capitalism and Hamilton's toward manufactures and commerce. Where they markedly disagreed, however, was in giving positive, assertive power, "energy," and "vigor" to the state.

Hamilton held the new American state valuable for its own sake as assertive power. He saw the nation-state with its historic and heroic goals, seeking power in a competitive international system of other power-hungry states. Madison saw the nation-state as necessary only to protect private rights and thus ensure justice. Like Locke he saw the need for a grant of power to the state, but a grant of limited power. Madison saw the central government providing an arena for competitive power, where the private bargaining of free men, groups, and interests would take place, and the state would define no goals of its own other than ensuring the framework for orderly economic life. All the state would do was regulate "the various and interfering interests" or, as Madison put it to Washington in straightforward Lockean terms, be an impartial umpire in disputes. Energy in politics for Madison would come from individuals and groups seeking their own immediate goals, not from an energetic state seeking its own heroic ends.

What about Madison's governing elite of "enlightened views and virtuous sentiments," "whose wisdom may best discern the true interest of their country," of which he wrote in *Federalist* No. 10? Madison's "true interest" was not the "national interest" of Hamilton's realism. Nor was it some ideal transcending purpose or goal to which wise leadership would lead the state and those still in the shadows. Madison's enlightened leaders would demonstrate their wisdom and virtue more by what they did not do than by what they did. Being men of cool and deliberate judgment, they would not pass unjust laws that interfered with private rights. They would respect liberty, justice, and property, and run a limited government that did little else than preside over and adjudicate conflicts in a basically self-regulating social order. Did not Madison criticize in *Federalist* No. 62 the "excess of law-making" and the voluminousness of laws as the twin "diseases to which our governments are most liable"?

If the state legislators of the Confederation period had acted with self-restraint, there would have been no need for the institutions of the central state, but among generally fallen men they were an even more inferior lot, fired by local prejudices and warm passions. Should the unexpected happen and cooler men of enlightened views seek to do too much, that is, undertake what is described in *Federalist* No. 10 as "improper or wicked projects," then Madison's new constitutional government would rapidly cut them down as its multiplicity of built-in checks and balances preserved the Lockean limited state.

Madison's limited Federalist state might well appear meek and tame set next to Hamilton's energetic and vigorous state, but it was a matter of perspective. To the Antifederalists, even Madison's state, limited as it was by checks and balances and its cool men resisting the temptations of lawmaking, seemed a monstrous betrayal of the Revolution and its spirit. The Constitution could be seen, then, as the last, albeit Thermidorean,* act of the American Revolution. Like most revolutions, the American began as a repudiation of the state, of power, and of authority in the name of liberty.

Thermidorean: The reference is to the point when the French Revolution supposedly shifted from radicalism to reaction with the fall from power of Maximilien Robespierre (9–10 Thermidor, Year II [July 16–17, 1794]).

Like most revolutions, it ended with a stronger state, the revival of authority, and the taming of liberty's excesses.

The American state would never be quite as bad, however, as the Antifederalists' worst fears. They had assumed, for example, that "Congress will be vested with more extensive powers than ever Great Britain exercised over us." They worried that "after we have given them all our money, established them in a federal town, given them the power of coining money and raising a standing *army* . . . what resources have the people left?"[58] The reason the results would not be quite that bad is that the new American state created by that "triple headed monster" of a Constitution was much closer to Madison's state than to Hamilton's—at least, that is, for the rest of the eighteenth century and through most of the nineteenth. The twentieth century would be another matter and another story.

Conclusion

The Federalists triumphed in the "great national discussion" that was the debate over the ratification of the Constitution. But posterity has not remembered simply the victorious advocates of the Constitution in 1787 and 1788. The Antifederalists have lived on in the American imagination as well. Their worst fears were never realized, which proves the glaring exception in a comparison of the American Revolution with other revolutions. The Antifederalists, while losers in 1788, were neither liquidated nor forced to flee. Nor, more significantly, were their ideas extinguished. Their values lived on in America, as they themselves did, and have been absorbed into the larger pattern of American political culture. The states have endured as vital parts of the American political scene and in the unique configuration that is American federalism have retained tremendous power in numerous areas of public policy. In celebrating the bicentennial of its Constitution America celebrates both the Federalists and the Antifederalists, for the living American Constitution is by now a blend of the positions both sides took during the "great national discussion," however untidy that may seem to constitutional purists.

Just as there ultimately was no decisive victor in the political and pamphlet battle, so, too, there was none in the paradigm battle. No one paradigm cleared the field in 1788 and obtained exclusive dominance in the American political discourse. There was no watershed victory of liberalism over republicanism. These languages were heard on both sides during the "great national discussion." So, too, were the two other paradigms available to the framers' generation, the Protestant ethic and the ideals of sovereignty and power. So it has remained. American political discourse to this day tends to be articulated in one or another of these distinguishable idioms, however untidy that may seem to professors of history or political philosophy.

The generations of Americans who lived through the founding and the framing have left us proof positive of their paradigmatic pluralism. They imprinted on the landscape of their experience place names by which future generations would know them and their frames of reference. They took the physical world as their text and wrote on it with the conceptual structures of their political language. My corner of the American text, Upstate New York, was settled by Revolutionary War veterans in the last decades of the eighteenth century. When they named their parcels of American landscape, they knew in what tongues to speak.

There is a Rome, New York, and an Ithaca and a Syracuse. There is a Locke, New York, a mere ten miles from Ithaca. There is a Geneva, New York, at the top of Cayuga Lake. And for the state builders fascinated with founders of states, there is even a Romulus, New York. Such is the archaeology of paradigms far above Cayuga's waters.

Notes

1. Pocock, *Virtue, Commerce, and History: Essays on Political Thought and History, Chiefly in the Eighteenth Century* (Cambridge, 1985), 7–8, 12–13, 58, 290.

2. Even this list is not exhaustive. I leave to colleagues the explication of several other less discernible idioms of politics in the discourse of 1787, for example, the "language of jurisprudence," "scientific whiggism," and the "moral sentiment" schools of the Scottish Enlightenment.

3. J. G. A. Pocock, "An Appeal from the New to the Old Whigs? A Note on Joyce Appleby's Ideology and the History of Political Thought," Intellectual History Group, *Newsletter* (Spring, 1981), 47. Republican revisionism, often read as a critique from the right of hegemonic liberal scholarship, has been taken up by an unlikely ally, Critical Legal Studies, which from the left has embraced its communitarian focus and potential as an alternative to liberal possessive individualism. See, for example, Andrew Fraser, "Legal Amnesia: Modernism vs. the Republican Tradition in American Legal Theory," *Telos*, No. 60 (1984), 18, and Mark Tushnet, "The Constitution of Religion," *Connecticut Law Review*, XVIII (1986), 701.

4. Wood, "Hellfire Politics," *New York Review of Books*, XXXII, No. 3 (1985), 30. Wood's magisterial *The Creation of the American Republic, 1776–1787* (Chapel Hill, N.C., 1969), remains the most brilliant guide to the American founding. The pages that follow should make apparent the debt I (and all who write on this era) owe Wood.

5. Max Farrand, ed., *The Records of the Federal Convention of 1787* (New Haven, Conn., 1911), I, 136.

6. Madison to Jefferson, Oct. 24, 1787, in Gaillard Hunt, ed., *The Writings of James Madison . . .* (New York, 1900–1910), V, 31.

7. Madison to Washington, Apr. 16, 1787, ibid., II, 346.

8. John Locke, "First Treatise of Civil Government," in *Two Treatises of Government . . .* (1689), ed. Peter Laslett (Cambridge, 1960), chap. 4, sect. 42.

9. Berns, *Freedom, Virtue, and the First Amendment* (Baton Rouge, La., 1957). *State Gazette of South-Carolina* (Charleston), Mar. 5, 1787; quotation for New Jersey is in Wood, *Creation of the American Republic*, 406; *Independent Chronicle: and the Universal Advertiser* (Boston), May 31, 1787; *Political Intelligencer* (Elizabeth Town, N.J.), Jan. 4, 1786; quotation for Massachusetts is in Wood, *Creation of the American Republic*, 465; Webster quoted ibid., 411.

10. Farrand, ed., *Records of the Federal Convention*, II, 73–74.

11. Ibid., I, 134.

12. Bennett, "How Should Americans Celebrate the Bicentennial of the Constitution?" *National Forum*, LXIV (1984), 60.

13. Adams to John Scollay, Dec. 30, 1780, in Harry Alonzo Cushing, ed., *The Writings of Samuel Adams* (New York, 1904–1908), IV, 238; "Brutus," quoted in Herbert J. Storing, *What the Anti-Federalists Were* For (Chicago, 1981), 47; Henry, Lee, and Yates quoted in Leonard W. Levy, ed., *Essays on the Making of the Constitution* (New York, 1969), ix.

14. Montesquieu quoted in Wood, *Creation of the American Republic*, 499; quotation for Pennsylvania is in Levy, ed., *Essays on the Constitution*, x.

15. "Letters of Agrippa," Dec. 28, 1787, in Herbert J. Storing, ed., *The Complete Anti-Federalist* (Chicago, 1981), IV, 86.

16. Jonathan Elliot, ed., *The Debates of the Several State Conventions, on the Adoption of the Federal Constitution . . .* , 2d ed. (Philadelphia, 1863), IV, 24; "Letters of Agrippa," Dec. 3, 1787, in Storing, ed., *Complete Anti-Federalist*, IV, 76.

17. Elliot, ed., *Debates*, II, 44, IV, 192, 199.

18. Lee to Madison, Nov. 26, 1784, in James Curtis Ballagh, ed., *Letters of Richard Henry Lee* (New York, 1911–1914), II, 304; Storing, *Anti-Federalists*, 21.

19. Storing, *Anti-Federalists*, 23.

20. Ibid., 73; Ballagh, ed., *Letters of R. H. Lee*, II, 62–63.

21. Cf. Walter Berns, "Does the Constitution Secure These Rights?" in Robert A. Goldwin and William A. Schambra, eds., *How Democratic Is the Constitution?* (Washington, D.C., 1980), 73.

22. See Garry Wills, *Explaining America: The Federalist* (Garden City, N.Y., 1981).

23. Madison, "Vices of the Political System of the United States," in William T. Hutchinson et al., eds., *The Papers of James Madison* (Chicago, 1962–), IV, 357.

24. Elliot, ed., *Debates*, II, 245; *Letters from the Federal Farmer*, in Storing, ed., *Complete Anti-Federalist*, II, 298. For Smith as author of the *Federal Farmer* see Robert H. Webking, "Melancton Smith and the *Letters from the Federal Farmer,*" *William and Mary Quarterly*, 3d Ser., XLIV (1987), 510–28.

25. Adams to Caleb Davis, Apr. 3, 1781, in Cushing, ed., *Writings of Samuel Adams*, IV, 255, Adams to Scollay, Mar. 20, 1777, ibid., III, 365; Rush quoted in Wood, *Creation of the American Republic*, 427, and Dagobert D. Runes, ed., *Selected Writings of Benjamin Rush* (New York, 1947), 31; J. Adams, in [Worthington Chauncey Ford, ed.], *Warren-Adams Letters* (Massachusetts Historical Society, *Collections*, LXXII–LXXIII [Boston, 1917–1925]), I, 201–02, 222.

26. Theodore Sedgwick, *A Memoir of the Life of William Livingston . . .* (New York, 1833), 403; Jay to Jefferson, Feb. 9, 1787, in Julian P. Boyd et al., eds., *The Papers of Thomas Jefferson* (Princeton, N.J., 1950–), XI, 129; letters to Jefferson are quoted in

Wood, *Creation of the American Republic,* 424; J. Adams, "Thoughts on Government," in Charles Francis Adams, *The Works of John Adams . . . ,* IV (Boston, 1851), 199.

27. Barlow quoted in Wood, *Creation of the American Republic,* 418; Lee to Arthur Lee, Feb. 11, 1779, in Ballagh, ed., *Letters of R. H Lee,* II, 33; quotation for Virginian is in Wood, *Creation of the American Republic,* 95.

28. Cited in O. G. Hatch, "Civic Virtue: Wellspring of Liberty," *National Forum,* LXIV (1984), 35.

29. Elliot, ed., *Debates,* II, 240; "Essays by Candidus," in Storing, ed., *Complete Anti-Federalist,* IV, 129.

30. See my "Republican Revisionism Revisited," *American Historical Review,* LXXXVII (1982), 629–54, and "Children's Literature and Bourgeois Ideology: Observations on Culture and Industrial Capitalism in the Later Eighteenth Century," in Harry C. Payne, ed., *Studies in Eighteenth-Century Culture,* XII (Madison, Wis., 1983), 11–44. Burgh is cited in *Federalist* No. 56.

31. Baxter quoted in J. E. Crowley, *This Sheba, Self: The Conceptualization of Economic Life in Eighteenth-Century America* (Baltimore, 1974), 51, 17–18.

32. Skinner, *The Foundations of Modern Political Thought* (Cambridge, 1978), II, 239.

33. Alexis de Tocqueville, *Democracy in America* (1835), ed. Richard D. Heffner (New York, 1956), 194.

34. Morgan, "The Puritan Ethic and the American Revolution," *William and Mary Quarterly,* 3d Ser., XXIV (1967), 3–43; Crowley, *This Sheba, Self;* Appleby, "Liberalism and the American Revolution," *New England Quarterly,* XLIX (1976), 3–26, and *Capitalism and a New Social Order: The Republican Vision of the 1790s* (New York, 1984); Diggins, *The Lost Soul of American Politics: Virtue, Self-Interest, and the Foundations of Liberalism* (New York, 1984).

35. Crowley, *This Sheba, Self,* 50.

36. Lee to ———, May 31, 1764, in Ballagh, ed., *Letters of R. H. Lee,* I, 7; Morgan, "Puritan Ethic," *WMQ,* 3d Ser., XXIV (1967), 8.

37. *Newport Mercury,* Feb. 28, 1774.

38. *Pennsylvania Journal* (Philadelphia), Dec. 10, 1767; Abigail Adams to John Adams, Oct. 16, 1774, in L. H. Butterfield et al., eds., *Adams Family Correspondence* (Cambridge, Mass., 1963), I, 173.

39. Colman, Pemberton, and Henchman quoted in Crowley, *This Sheba, Self,* 56, 57.

40. Mather quoted ibid., 59; Clap, *The Duty of All Christians . . .* (New London, Conn., 1720), 8.

41. McCoy, *The Elusive Republic: Political Economy in Jeffersonian America* (Chapel Hill, N.C., 1980), 116.

42. *American Museum,* I (1787), 116, 119.

43. *Letters from the Federal Farmer,* in Storing, ed., *Complete Anti-Federalist,* II, 253; Smith, ibid., VI, 158.

44. Pocock, *Virtue, Commerce, and History,* 48, 50; Smith, *The Theory of Moral Sentiments* (1759), ed. D. D. Raphael and A. L. Macfie (Oxford, 1976), I, iii, 24.

45. [Braxton], *An Address to the Convention of . . . Virginia, on the Subject of Government . . .* (Philadelphia, 1776), 15, 17. For Wood's discussion of this text see *Creation of the American Republic,* 96–97.

46. Aristotle, *The Politics,* bk. VII, chap. 9.

47. Elliot, ed., *Debates,* II, 301.

48. *Pennsylvania Packet, and Daily Advertiser* (Philadelphia), Sept. 6, 1787; Rush to Price, June 2, 1787, in L. H. Butterfield, ed., *Letters of Benjamin Rush* (Princeton, N.J., 1951), I, 418–19.

49. Elliot, ed., *Debates,* III, 436, 607; Lee to John Lamb, June 27, 1788, in Ballagh, ed., *Letters of R. H. Lee,* II, 475.

50. Franklin to Charles Carroll, May 25, 1789, in Albert Henry Smyth, ed., *The Writings of Benjamin Franklin* (New York, 1907), X, 7; *Connecticut Courant,* quoted in Wood, *Creation of the American Republic,* 432.

51. McIlwain, *Constitutionalism: Ancient and Modern* (Ithaca, N.Y., 1947). For a discussion of these other paradigms and languages see the essays in Istvan Hont and Michael Ignatieff, eds., *Wealth and Virtue: The Shaping of Political Economy in the Scottish Enlightenment* (Cambridge, 1983), and Pocock, *Virtue, Commerce, and History.*

52. Georg Wilhelm Friedrich Hegel, *The Philosophy of History,* trans. J. Sibree (New York, 1956), 84–87.

53. Elkins and McKitrick, "The Founding Fathers: Young Men of the Revolution," *Political Science Quarterly,* LXXVI (1961), 181–216.

54. Harold C. Syrett et al., eds., *The Papers of Alexander Hamilton* (New York, 1961–1979), IV, 11.

55. Farrand, ed., *Records of the Federal Convention,* I, 466–67.

56. *Plutarch's Lives in Six Volumes* (London, 1758), I, 96; Bacon, "Of Honour and Reputation," in Richard Whatley, ed., *Bacon's Essays: With Annotations* (London, 1886); Hume, "Of Parties in General," in *The Philosophical Works of David Hume* (Edinburgh, 1826), III, 57; "Publius Letter, III," in Syrett et al., eds., *Hamilton Papers,* I, 580–81.

57. Elliot, ed., *Debates,* III, 53.

58. Ibid., II, 159, 62.

2. Were the framers counter-revolutionaries?

Stephen E. Patterson

The Federalist Reaction to Shays's Rebellion

Stephen Patterson teaches history at the University of New Brunswick, Canada. His book *Political Parties in Revolutionary Massachusetts* (1973) explored that state's revolutionary history from the point of view of conflict among its people rather than of unified patriotism. This essay continues that theme. It was written for a gathering to commemorate the rebellion that western Massachusetts farmers attempted in 1786 against their state government's firm policy of permitting no paper currency and requiring that both taxes and personal debts be paid in hard coin. (See p. 19 in this volume for a brief sketch of Shays's Rebellion.)

The rebellion demonstrated many important points, perhaps foremost of which was the rebels' belief that they could not make the political system of Massachusetts meet their needs. Their greatest immediate worry was that they would lose their land because they could not get the money to pay their debts and their taxes. Unlike virtually every other state, Massachusetts refused to adopt paper currency, which probably would have depreciated in value but which the country people could have offered in payment. One way to think about the dilemma is to see the farmers' problems as the result of their own economic foolishness. Another is in the class and regional interests that were developing well before the actual rebellion broke out. Different understandings about how the American economy should work and what the government should do in a time of crisis were certainly in play. People on both sides thought that they stood for what the Revolution had been about and what it symbolized. For the rebels' part, their tactic of closing the courts so that judgments could not be issued against them was exactly what they had done in 1774 in response to Britain's harsh punishments for the Boston Tea Party. Then they had enjoyed Boston's ardent support. Now, however, Bostonians and others in eastern Massachusetts portrayed them as dupes of malevolent British agents who were bent on destroying what the former colonists had achieved and who sent an army to put them down.

Questions for a Closer Reading

1. Did the farmers of western Massachusetts find themselves in trouble because of their own mistaken choices or because the economic system had entrapped them?

2. Why were backcountry people unable to make the Massachusetts political system work on their behalf once it became clear that they had different needs from townspeople?

3. Were the Shaysite rebels enemies of what the Revolution had achieved? Or were they acting in its true spirit?

4. Did the rebellion frighten the Federalist leadership? Or did it offer them an opportunity to achieve what they wanted?

5. Why did the seeming failure of the government of Massachusetts lead to the Federalist conclusion that only a national solution could solve America's problems?

The Federalist Reaction
to Shays's Rebellion

Early in this century, Massachusetts judge Jonathan Smith wisely remarked to his fellow amateur historians at the Clinton Historical Society that their understanding of Shays's Rebellion was laden with bias. For over a century, he said, the story had been told by men who had no sympathy with rebellious farmers. They were conservatives who had taken part in suppression of the rebellion or who, subsequently in the nineteenth century, were never able to rise above the limitations of the original conservative analysis. What was needed, he concluded—quite disingenuously—was an impartial examination of both sides.

Yet before this reasonable entreaty had scarcely passed his lips, Smith went on to propose that the first and presumably chief cause of the rebellion was "the absence of a strong national government, commanding the confidence and the obedience of the people." With the best will in the world, he obviously could not escape from the Federalist frame of reference: the structure of government under the Confederation was the problem. Congress and the states had issued "worthless and hopelessly irredeemable paper currency," and the economy was in a shambles characterized by a ruined commerce and "the crushing burdens of public and private indebtedness."[1]

What Smith illustrated, even better than he knew, was the very considerable difficulty in separating Shays's Rebellion from the Federalist analysis of it. This Federalist analysis merits examination. Granted, it tells us more about the men who suppressed the Shaysites than about the Shaysites themselves. But on the other hand, there are important questions about the Shaysites that can never really be abstracted from the perceptions of their opponents. Were the Shaysites a serious threat to the government

Stephen E. Patterson, "The Federalist Reaction to Shays's Rebellion," in *In Debt to Shays: The Bicentennial of an Agrarian Rebellion,* ed. Robert A. Gross (Charlottesville: University Press of Virginia, 1993), 101–18.

and constitution of Massachusetts? Was the rebellion a significant cause of the movement for a federal constitution? Massachusetts Federalists thought so. In fact, many of them agreed with Henry Knox, who later said that the Massachusetts Antifederalists were all Shaysites; in his mind the rebellion, the subsequent Philadelphia convention, and the ratification struggle were of a piece, one long continuous story. This view is what Judge Smith confronted ninety or so years ago. The mistake he made was in assuming he could get a clear picture of a farmer uprising through this Federalist lens. He would have done better to settle for the interesting reflected image of the Federalists themselves.

To get at the farmers' side, Smith should have focused on the changing scene in the rural west, noting that the American Revolutionary War had made western Massachusetts a much different place from what it had once been. From 1775 to 1780 farmers had a tremendous opportunity to sell their surplus production to feed the Continental army. Men who had once been subsistence farmers were encouraged to grow vegetables, grain, and livestock for commercial purposes and with the cash they received in return, even if it was paper, to invest in more agricultural land to expand production. Paper money was so plentiful down to 1780 that even those who might still be called subsistence farmers got used to having cash to pay taxes and to buy consumer items. The demand for French and West Indian imports was intense.[2]

The period after 1780 was not nearly so good for farmers. The vigorous deflationary program of the commercially dominated legislature drastically reduced the available money supply. The state began to exercise a much stronger centralizing pull on the lives of its people through commercial regulation, high taxes, and an energized court system.[3] The legal system became an omnipresent factor in the lives of rural people, given the almost phenomenal increase of lawyers—from thirty-four in 1780, according to one source, to a total of ninety-two in 1785—many of whom took up residence in the rural towns of the interior.[4] And other vocational pursuits opened up, such as in Springfield, where the federal arsenal continued to employ artisans after the war. Newspapers in Worcester, Springfield, and, by 1786, Northampton brought news of the world westward. Perhaps more important, the newspapers kept alive people's perceived need for cash by advertising commercial wares available at retail stores in market towns. In a tangible way, the war and postwar experiences of western farmers substantially changed their values and their expectations.[5] If only gradually and incompletely, rural people began moving away from the static and timeless patterns of traditional culture. In the search for causes, surely any objective historical interpretation of Shays's Rebellion would want to take account of this transformation.

In political terms, this change was observable in the dramatic increase in interest and participation of small rural towns in the legislature of the state. Here the elected representatives of hundreds of small farmers — often farmers themselves whose attendance at the General Court in Boston had to be fitted around the tilling, planting, and harvesting — adopted positions that reflected the concerns of their constituents. They favored paper currency and resisted when an eastern majority voted to end the legal tender provision of the state paper still in circulation after 1780. They sided with thousands of veterans in their demands that vouchers, given them during the war instead of pay, be accepted in payment of state taxes. They resisted impost and excise taxes that fell heavily on consumers, and they balked at the notion of a half-pay settlement with Continental officers when nothing had yet been done for the rank-and-file veterans. In House votes, they usually lost; but they were close enough in some votes to frighten the conservative majority, and along with the odd victory, they convinced their opponents that they represented a serious threat to the commercial and propertied interests of the state.[6]

It was these commercial and propertied interests which, of course, produced the Federalists in Massachusetts.[7] They enjoyed enormous advantages in the factional contests that took place in the legislature during the 1780s. They came from the larger towns of the state, they were better educated, they found it easier to attend the General Court and to remain through summer sessions, and they enjoyed the support of the newspapers, the courts, and the political system in general. When they occasionally lost votes in the House, they counted on the Senate to represent property, and they were not disappointed. But whatever their advantages, they rarely felt comfortably in command and anxiously observed the spreading populist tide. The extralegislative political activity of farmers fed their anxiety. During the Revolution, rural towns began organizing county conventions to state their grievances and to concert their political actions.[8] In 1782 an angry crowd of rural debtors attempted to disrupt the court in Northampton, and the old Revolutionary leader Joseph Hawley warned that law-abiding westerners were considering going over to the "mob" unless there was prompt legislative action to solve agrarian grievances.[9] By 1784 conventions in rural counties were commonplace, and conservative critics were condemning them as threats to property and a danger to the constitution of the state.[10] The divisions of Shays's Rebellion, in other words, were in evidence long before the insurrection broke out in 1786.

Thus, when Federalists came to write about the rebellion, they saw its causes in the political discord of the previous several years. They viewed the Shaysites as one and the same with the large number of inland farmers with whom they had been arguing for most of the 1780s: mad, distracted husbandmen who wanted to cheat their creditors with worthless paper money and who had no understanding of how a state must protect the property of its citizens by maintaining a stable monetary and financial system. Moreover, the Federalist analysis suggested that the insurrection had its roots in anarchic or democratic ideas—the two were interchangeable—all of which were let loose at dangerous and unconstitutional county conventions. They claimed that farmers were "ignorant" and easily manipulated by unscrupulous "gentlemen." When the Federalist George Richards Minot summed up this analysis in his *History of the Insurrections,* published in Worcester in 1788, he claimed that the society which produced the rebellion was characterized by what he called "a distinction of interests" at the root of which, as he interpreted it, lay a natural propensity for man to behave as his social and economic condition dictated. Sounding very much like the James Madison of *Federalist No. 10,* Minot suggested that the clash of interests was an inevitable feature of civil society. "These classes of people," he said of creditors or "men of property," "will ever be opposed by debtors and persons otherwise interested against them." Only the state and its constitution could stand between them and protect the few against the many.[11]

Without subscribing to the social biases of the Federalists, one can agree that it makes sense to look for the causes of Shays's Rebellion in the political turmoil of the 1780s. But if the political clashes of the decade explain the insurrection, did the insurrection cause the Federalist movement? Historians have reasonably seen a connection, arguing that the social threat posed by the Shaysites drove conservative merchants and other men of wealth to seek refuge in a stronger central government, capable of providing the security and financial stability they perceived to be lacking at the state level.[12] The public claims of Federalists at the time seem to lend weight to the theory, for mixed into their "interest-based" analysis of the causes of rebellion, they frequently added their certainty that only a strong national government could prevent such uprisings in the future.[13] Such assertions suggest that Shays's Rebellion was one cause among many leading to the calling of the federal convention and the writing of a new constitution, yet the pertinent fact about Massachusetts is that political battle lines had already been drawn before the insurrection ever broke out. Well before 1786 many conservatives, including most of Boston's merchants and traders, had already turned their back on the state and set their sights on the creation of a strong national government. For them, Shays's Rebellion tended not to shape or alter their outlook on the world so much as it simply confirmed them in their beliefs.

There was, however, yet another "cause" of Shays's Rebellion frequently mentioned by pseudonymous Federalist newspaper writers in 1786 and

1787, which showed that they feared not only an internal enemy but also an external one. This was the fairly widespread Federalist or proto-Federalist notion that the British were behind Shays, that the insurrection was an attempt to undo the American Revolution and discredit the new nation.[14] Here lies a clue to the origins of organized Federalism in Massachusetts. On the face of it, a Federalist suspicion of the British does not seem in character given what we know of the later Federalist party preference for things British. Nor does it seem to square with the past of many Massachusetts merchants who became Federalists. Various studies have shown that Boston merchants were deeply divided by Revolutionary events, and many, perhaps even a majority of them, if not always in agreement with British measures of the 1760s and early '70s, accepted the Patriot cause most reluctantly: they had resisted commercial boycotts of British manufactures at the time of the Stamp and Townshend acts and again after the tea crisis, and by June 1774 they had openly split with the more radical Revolutionary leaders.[15] Even many who were not openly Tory resisted Independence and, once it had been declared, adopted moderate if not conservative positions on most political and constitutional issues. Moreover, both during the war and after, merchants and their conservative allies resisted all attempts to deprive known Tories of their properties and rights and were poised at war's end to welcome Tories back into their midst.[16] In fact, Timothy Pickering of Essex County went so far as to claim that the country would be better off if some of the Patriots could be shipped out in exchange for some of the Tory refugees.[17]

This seemingly pro-British attitude, moreover, appeared to fit with the commercial expectations of Massachusetts merchants at war's end. Even before hostilities were formally concluded, merchants were looking optimistically to a future in which they would revive their trade with Britain and the West Indies, reestablish credit connections, and restock their shelves with the latest in British fashions and conveniences. Some even decided to go off to England themselves to conduct their own personal diplomacy and to select new stock.[18]

It did not take long, however, for optimism to give way to frustration and anger. British houses were willing enough to ship goods to America and to do so on credit, but the prospects looked good enough also to send dozens of British factors over to collect debts, as the peace treaty permitted, and also to carry on their own direct trade with inland shopkeepers and others on the wholesale market. Boston merchants blamed the British factors for their unfair intrusion, and the first postwar feeling of hostility began to develop.[19] Merchants are competitive by nature, however, and they recognized that there were things they could do to hold on to their fair share of the import trade. First and foremost, they could expand their domestic market far beyond its limited prewar size. They could aim to do more than satiate the pent-up demand of their former customers by making consumers of people who had heretofore perhaps only nibbled at the fringe of the consumer market. This they hoped to accomplish by stimulating demand among farmers in the rural interior; the means to this end was weekly newspaper advertisements which offered every conceivable article of British manufacture on such generous terms as to convince almost any reader that such items were affordable. At hand to help were not only the several newspapers in Boston but also the more recently established weeklies in Worcester and Springfield, eager to spread the gospel of consumerism for a small advertising fee.

There was nothing new about advertisements in American newspapers; what we must recognize are the new marketing techniques of the 1780s and the powerful transformation they wrought on rural values. The British historian Neil McKendrick has written brilliantly about the commercialization of eighteenth-century England and what he correctly calls *The Birth of a Consumer Society*.[20] It is easy to see that the same techniques that were rapidly expanding consumerism into provincial England were used by American merchants in the last quarter of the eighteenth century, and with tremendous impact in the immediate postwar period. The trick was not simply to stimulate people's appetite for more or to convince people that what were once considered luxuries were now necessities or, at the least, decencies, although these, too, were essential ingredients in the sales pitch. What was strikingly new was the trader's concern to put himself in the buyer's shoes and to explain how one could actually afford to pay for these things.

The short-lived first approach was to sell "very cheap for cash." But by the spring of 1784, tantalizing lists of imported goods were being offered in exchange for "furs, bees-wax, old pewter, and all kinds of grain [which] will be received as cash." Ebenezer Storer would sell for "cash, continental Loan certificates, Massachusetts state notes, or Good Pot-Ash" at his store in Union Street, Boston. Shopkeepers White and Clap of Rutland would give both cash and goods for pot and pearl ashes, but they were also looking for "salts, furs, Massachusetts state securities, continental certificates, and New York new emission money." It was only in late summer 1784 that traders began to admit openly in their ads that the buyer did not need money or goods at all. William Moore warned that all of his fellow traders were advertising goods on credit "at the lowest terms"; he urged his "impartial Customers" to compare before they bought and "to call and judge for themselves."

Since money was no object, who could resist reading the long lists of goods that now made up the typical advertisement? The variety in some was mind-boggling. Where once merchants had simply offered English dry goods as their stock in trade, now they followed the lead of such Boston importers as S. and S. Salisbury, whose itemized lists had something for everyone, but especially for women: "broad cloths, plains, serges, rateens, frizes, flannels, shalloons, tammies, poplins, crapes, quality bindings, variety of knee straps, men's worsted and cotton caps, corduroys, milliner's needles, Sattins, modes, calicoes, Irish linens, Cambricks, Lawns, Dutch Lace, Catgut, Silk handerchiefs, Muffs and Tippets, Bonnet Paper, Italian Sprigs, Ribbons, Fans, Silk thread and Cotton ditto, Silk and Cotton jacket patterns, Jacket buttons, blankets, Diapers, Sheetings, etc." Add to this the hardwares: "window glass, nails, shot, powder, smith's anvils and vices, mill saws, steel and iron plate hand saws, holsters and pocket pistols, coffee mills, wool cards, fox and rat traps, shovels, an elegant assortment of looking glasses, frying pans, chafing dishes, bellows, best London pewter, flat irons, knives and forks, an assortment of brass handles and escutcheons, hinges, locks, English glue, white lead, red lead." And if the reader was not already hooked, there were "West India goods, groceries, crockery ware, bibles, psalters, primers, writing paper, and a large assortment of Tin Ware."[21] Life would never be the same again.

What was happening was that Massachusetts merchants were attempting to expand their home market by transforming tastes and by drawing new consumers into the retail market. We have no direct knowledge of the extent to which they succeeded with the participants in Shays's Rebellion, although it might be possible to find sufficient estate inventories in the probate records to show that Shaysites included English manufactures among their valued possessions. What we do know, of course, is that whatever they were buying, Shaysites became heavily indebted and a substantial percentage of them ended up in court because they were unable to meet their obligations.[22] One way or another, these men who may have started life as subsistence farmers had, by this time, left the simple imperatives of subsistence behind them; their tastes were changing, their perceived needs were growing, they willingly risked indebtedness to expand their store of material possessions, and they now needed cash or a cash substitute to pay their debts and their taxes and perhaps also to maintain their new life-styles. Merchants would later claim that farmers bought luxuries they could not afford, but the fact is that merchants used advertising to blur the distinction between luxuries and necessities.

The newspaper advertisements, however, chart both the rise and the fall of the consumer boom. By the fall of 1784, notices of a new kind were beginning to appear. They were placed by brokers eager to buy and sell the bewildering array of paper still around at a time when hard money was fast disappearing. Joseph Ward of Boston dealt in "state notes, Continental certificates, Treasurers orders, New Emission money, and every other kind of State and Continental Securities." John Cunningham, Jr., of Boston wanted "New York and this State New Emission money, State notes payable in the next Tax, Orders from this State Treasurer, payable in Tax No. 2 and 3, and all other kinds of Publick securities." Even the post-rider between Worcester and Concord, New Hampshire, carried on a paper exchange on the side and advertised for "New York Emission money and Consolidated State Notes."[23] Money men were beginning to hedge and to hoard.

By 1785, when British credit had completely dried up and cash was as scarce in the city as in the country, merchants abandoned their effort to expand the domestic market for British manufactures, turned their backs on the problems of indebted farmers, and embarked upon a single-minded course to solve their commercial difficulties. If they could do nothing further to expand the domestic market or the demand side, then they must reduce the number of suppliers to bring the two sides of the equation back into balance. Some merchants knew that they simply were best off to get out of the business. The firm of J. and J. Amory, which ideally fits the earlier description of reluctant Revolutionaries who hoped to revive the British commercial connection, announced firmly in 1785 that it was closing out its trade in British goods and would sell off its supply at cost or even below cost.[24] But a substantial number of other merchants believed that the best solution was to eliminate the competition of the British factors.[25]

In mid-April 1785 Boston merchants and traders crowded into the long room of Colonel John Marston to "consider what discouragement should be given to the British Factors, who were residing here and monopolizing to themselves the benefits of commerce." Tempers were short. Even the once radical *Boston Gazette* observed of the meeting that "in every collection of men where the redress of any grievance is the object, there are some whose passions out run their reason." At an adjournment at Faneuil Hall, however, cooler heads urged the adoption of resolutions pledging not to purchase goods from British merchants, factors, or agents, nor to let or sell them warehouses, shops, houses, or ships. Moreover, in their anger they were willing to "encourage the manufacture & produce of this country," a clear offer of political alliance with the artisans of the town. But most important was their determination to get congressional action: they wanted a federal regulation of trade, blocking British exploitation of the American market and reserving it to Americans. To this end they instructed their committee to write to merchants everywhere in the nation "recommending to them an immediate application to the legislatures of their respective states, to vest such powers in Congress (if not already done) as shall be competent to the interesting purposes aforesaid, and also to petition Congress to make such regulations as shall have the desired effect."[26]

Boston's merchants committed themselves to what they called "federal policy," which was in effect an American mercantilism. Congress must be given the power to regulate trade. And with a blind eye and a deaf ear to farmers calling for paper money or cash substitutes, they went about building a political alliance that could accomplish their purpose. Their April offer to cut off British trade and encourage American manufactures immediately attracted the support of a number of Boston's tradesmen and artisans. The latter organized a committee of their own and then exchanged letters with the merchant committee in which they celebrated their new-found unity and unanimity.[27] Within weeks merchants and artisans together opened a lobbying campaign to win over the new governor, Bowdoin, and the legislature to their proposition that a convention of all the states must be called to revise the Confederation by vesting it with the power to regulate trade.[28] When the legislature responded with a favorable resolution, Nathan Dane explained to Rufus King off in Congress that the "mercantile interest," as he called it, knew exactly what it wanted and had got its way.[29] What he might have added is that the organization of this mercantile interest, or coalition of merchants and manufacturers, represented a new plateau in the development of nationalist sentiment in Massachusetts. Where before there had been legislative and limited public support for granting an impost to Congress, to create a national revenue, there was now an organized Federalist movement in Massachusetts committed to political action and to popularizing its approach in the press.[30] Its rallying cry for the next two years was the need to create a national commercial policy. Writers like "Americanus," writing in Worcester's *Massachusetts Spy*, spread the gospel, urging even the farmers to believe that the shortage of cash was not the fundamental problem. Americans would one day be a wealthy people, and they must hasten that day by "encouraging manufactures, discouraging the importation of superfluities, but especially by instructing our constitutional guardians to unite our commercial interest, by committing it to the care of the grand council of these states. Under the direction of that august body," he concluded confidently, "our trade will soon be wisely regulated, and our manufactures will encrease."[31]

The frustrated attempt to restore the British import trade was an important factor in creating the Federalist movement in Massachusetts, but it was not the only factor, nor even the only commercial factor. Eighteenth-century Massachusetts merchants were a diversified lot, as much so after the Revolutionary War as before. Many eagerly sought to return to the British West Indies with fish and lumber to exchange for sugar and molasses. Besides looking to the revival of British trade links, others with equal optimism looked outside the traditional patterns of imperial trade to new opportunities afforded by Independence: Some expected to profit from the carrying trade, especially in the southern states. They looked to new markets for American staples in France, Holland, Spain, and elsewhere in Europe. Merchants of Hingham and Salem eagerly planned risky voyages to China, hoping to be the first to open that potentially lucrative trade for the United States.[32] Meanwhile, American diplomats were ordered by Congress to help facilitate the economic development of the new nation by seeking most-favored-nation commercial treaties with European powers.

Yet by 1785, almost all of these endeavors were meeting with frustration. Within a year of the peace treaty, Britain closed its West Indies to American merchants in order to favor merchants in its loyal colonies north of the United States. America's ally, France, seemed suddenly to become jealous of reviving American trade and especially resented New England's exploitation of the Atlantic fisheries and the fish trade with the Caribbean. Spain and Portugal were reluctant to grant the United States most-favored-nation status, while the American envoys sent to arrange such treaties in several European countries lamented their lack of negotiating leverage. Merchants looking to the Mediterranean soon backed off because of the risks of seizure by Barbary pirates, while congressmen expressed frustration at their total inability to do anything about it.[33] Moreover, within Congress, the sectional interests of New England and the southern states clashed over whether the treaty with Spain should allow trade with the American west through the mouth of the Mississippi.[34] The New Englanders bitterly opposed this, perhaps, as southerners said, because they did not want to see development of the interior and a trade they could not control. And finally, New Englanders discovered to their dismay that their own countrymen in the southern states were unwilling to give Yankee merchants any privileges whatever in the carrying trade. Southerners liked free trade: whoever offered them the best deal, regardless of nationality, could carry their staples to European markets.[35]

There had been times during the American Revolution when New England merchants had also sounded like free traders, or at least they longed for the removal of the many British restrictions of the 1760s.[36] But an important aspect of their change of mind in the 1780s was their growing conviction—shared by both merchants and artisans—that free trade was not in their economic interest. Southerners maintained an interest in free trade because they had a ready staple for export and were convinced that free trade would give them the best deal with respect to freight, export prices, and import prices. They accepted the most-favored-nation approach to commercial treaties with foreign countries. But northern merchants, recognizing that free trade gave privileges to their foreign competitors—especially the British—were turning to protection through trade regulations, especially the mercantilist idea of confining the nation's trade to ships of the nation.

Even as late as the fall of 1785, however, the Federalist movement in Massachusetts was still largely confined to the alliance of merchants and artisans; many of the state's leading politicians feared what might happen were there to be a convention for the complete overhaul of the Articles of Confederation. They were agreed that Congress must have an independent revenue such as would be provided by a 5 percent impost, and they saw merit in a uniform regulation of trade. But these must be accomplished piecemeal by amendment, and national trade regulation, at least, should be limited to a fifteen-year period, after which the states could resume their regulatory powers if they so chose.[37] Rufus King was firmly convinced that a tight regulatory power exercised by Congress was the only answer, but he recognized that the issue would split the states into North and South.[38] Others who were soon to make their reputations as leading Federalists, such as Theodore Sedgwick, Caleb Strong, and Nathan Dane, tended to believe that caution was essential and that the merchants demanding a constitutional convention were acting only out of self-interest. Their caution is to be explained, in part, as a persistence of the New England suspicion of Robert Morris and the other Philadelphia-centered nationalists who had dominated Congress in the early 1780s. A wholesale revision of the Articles, they feared, could produce a significant power shift to the wrong kind of men.

But a series of developments in early 1786 brought them, too, into the growing Federalist coalition. Many of these men were lawyers. During the four months or so before spring elections in 1786, Massachusetts newspapers were filled with letters denouncing lawyers as parasites on poor debt-ridden farmers, gougers whose exorbitant fees should be reduced and regulated by law, and a budding group of aristocrats growing rich on the suffering of others. Spokesmen for debtors argued that small claims should be dealt with summarily without lawyers or that honest men might represent themselves in court. Others insisted that, since so many cases went to appeal, the lower courts should be abolished as an unnecessary additional expense. The more radical even insisted that the profession of law should be abolished along with the remnants of English common law by which lawyers practiced their sophistry.[39] The opportunity was ready-made for Federalist merchants to espouse the cause of their legal brethren and draw them into their conservative analysis of events. Significantly, before the election for representatives took place in Boston, a writer calling himself "A Barber" proposed that Boston would be best served in the legislature by two merchants, two lawyers, two tradesmen, and one other. The "two good lawyers" were needed, the "Barber" argued, "to outtalk the countrymen."[40] There was a natural congruity of interests that had brought merchants and lawyers together before; by the summer of 1786, lawyers were sounding much friendlier toward the merchants' plea for a strengthened federal system.[41]

All of this shows us that the Federalist movement was growing incrementally: from a core of merchants the movement expanded outward, absorbing the interests of artisans and lawyers and—although the story cannot be developed completely here—of bankers and financiers, of holders of public securities, and of army officers. But despite its dynamic growth, the Federalist movement in Massachusetts lacked the essential backing of a clear-minded majority of the voters of the state determined to rectify the shortcomings in the Articles of Confederation by establishing a strong, regulatory national government. The reluctance of some Massachusetts Federalists to send delegates off to James Madison's Annapolis convention to discuss trade regulation must also indicate that many were not yet convinced that there was anything like a sufficient body of opinion in America sympathetic to wholesale revision of the Articles.[42] Moreover there was the growing conviction among some leading men in the state—a conviction amounting almost to paranoia—that antagonism to national commercial regulation was concentrated in the southern states and that the achievement of a truly consolidated national government could come about only after the South was eliminated from the Union.[43] Secretive talk about dismembering the nation surely indicated the depths of their desperation. What they needed, if we may interpret the state of affairs in the fall of 1786, was a dramatic demonstration of the need for a stronger national government, something that would galvanize public sentiment in favor of immediate political action, something with a broader appeal than commercial policy.[44] Enter Shays's Rebellion.

The scattered county conventions and armed actions against the courts of law in 1786 provided the Federalists with exactly what they wanted, although events needed interpretation and perhaps even "improvement." The protest was widespread, but it was also disorganized, unconcerted, mostly verbal, and largely nonrebellious. Daniel Shay and his followers gave the protest its short-lived violent edge, yet the governor's ablest informers correctly assessed the demands as modest and the threat as lacking in broad-based support.[45] But whatever the inadequacies of the protest movement, shrill hyperbole filled the eastern newspapers expressing exaggerated fears of imminent invasion by barbaric hordes of ignorant farmers.[46] Boston raised new military regiments including an expensive artillery unit. Elaborate signals were worked out as part of a defensive strategy to protect the town from the thousands of rebels who were daily expected to descend on neighboring Cambridge. And eventually thousands of dollars were voluntarily collected from Boston merchants to pay for Benjamin Lincoln's army. Nervous easterners classified all rural protest, whether armed and violent or passive and verbal, as insurrectionary; the farmers' demands for paper money and other things anathema to conservatives were rolled together with the armed action of defiant Shaysites as evidence of widespread rebellion. By any measure, Federalists overreacted. They inflated the seriousness of the threat, and at least some of their exaggeration must have had a conscious purpose. For in their public utterances, they rarely missed the chance to explain with direct simplicity their conviction that this rebellion was occurring because the United States lacked a national government capable of regulating trade and rationalizing the public debt. It was a political analysis that repeated the articles of faith in what by now was a Federalist creed.

The polemical character of the Federalist analysis, however, was best typified by the now frequent claim that the regulation was more than a farmer uprising: British agents were at work attempting to undo the Revolution and destroy the republic. Did Federalists believe this, or were they simply interpolating into their analysis of the uprising their own frustrations and changes of heart? There had, after all, been British agents, but they were commercial agents or factors who had, so it was believed, ruined the import trade for the indigenous commercial community. Even as late as the spring of 1786, Federalist newspaper writers were tracing all of Massachusetts's problems, both the "public poverty" and the "general discontent," to the inability of Congress to regulate trade on the one hand and the British menace in their midst on the other.[47] Federalists simply rolled this interpretation into their analysis of the insurrection. Perhaps for some Federalists who had been reluctant Revolutionaries, soft on independence, or forgiving of Tories, this was a chance to get right with history: they now were ready to condemn Britain and wrap themselves in the flag if that could aid their pursuit of a strong national government. Whatever their motivations, there can be no doubting their frustration over the postwar failure to renew profitable economic ties with Britain.

Shays's Rebellion, at least to certain leading men, was less a cause of Federalism than it was an opportunity to expand and popularize it. Stephen Higginson, himself a recent convert to the nationalist solution, seemed almost delighted with the turn of events in the fall of 1786. Just at a time when he had given up on the General Court as reasoned directors of public affairs, "some new event turns up to avert the evil & show us the necessity of abridging the power of the states." The Shaysite action he looked at as a godsend because of its impact on public opinion. "I never saw so great a change in the public mind on any occasion as has lately appeared in this state as to the expediency of increasing the powers of Congress, not merely to commercial objects but generally." And with amazing perspicacity, he predicted that "by the next summer I expect we shall have been prepared for anything that is wise & fitting. Congress should be making the necessary arrangements for improving this disposition, when sufficiently increased, to right & valuable purposes. They must be prepared not only to support a proper force in the field, but to consolidate the several governments into one, general & efficient."[48] When Henry Knox wrote from the capital of the Confederation, he congratulated his friends as if both the rebellion and its suppression had been a Federalist accomplishment. "The energy of Massachusetts places it in an honorable point of view," he said, adding with obvious enthusiasm, "the strongest arguments possible may be drawn from the events that have happened in that state in order to effect a strong general government."[49] In short, if Shays's Rebellion had not occurred, the Federalists would have had to invent it.

At the least, Federalist leaders who had been searching for the way to convince fellow Americans of the need to create a strong central government astutely saw the potential in exploiting the rebellion. Their task was made easier, however, by the political culture in which they operated. In Massachusetts there already was a natural audience for the Federalist message among the population of the most commercial-cosmopolitan towns.[50] Over a decade of legislative conflict with farmers over courts, paper money, taxation, and management of the public debt had sharpened the competitive attitudes of such people and accustomed them to analyzing events in terms of self-interest. For most of those who became rank-and-file Federalists, the threat of armed popular insurrection was by itself convincing proof of the need for drastic measures, and they quickly concluded where their own interest lay. It was "we" versus "they," rich against poor, or creditor against debtor, just as George Minot said. Limited by their frame of reference, moreover, Federalists—leaders and followers alike—mistakenly attributed to rural protestors a similar level of solidarity on the basis of interest. The Federalist analysis of rural discontent shows that they neither understood the problems of western farmers nor sought to do so. They did not even see through a glass darkly. For them, Shays's Rebellion symbolized their worst fears about the democratic element in their society, and beyond that it simply mirrored their anxieties: it reflected familiar images of a Massachusetts that had failed to develop economic self-reliance, was unlikely to produce an agricultural surplus for export, and the trade of which was in danger of slipping into the hands of British competitors unless a faltering state economy was absorbed at once into a national one. It was ironic that the Federalists—the new nation's first political nationalists—included merchants who had once been tepid Patriots at best, many of whom at war's end had with great anticipation invested in renewed British ties. Yet, whatever the ironies, merchants and their associates stood converted to the national cause by a series of events of which Shays's Rebellion was only the last.

Notes

1. Jonathan Smith, "The Depression of 1785 and Daniel Shays' Rebellion," *William and Mary Quarterly (WMQ)*, 3rd ser., 5 (1948): 77–94, esp. 77–78. First published as a pamphlet in 1905, this article was republished by the *WMQ* because it was, in the view of the editor, "the best single article on the causes for the rebellion" (77).

2. William B. Weeden, *Economic and Social History of New England, 1620–1789,* 2 vols. (Boston: Houghton, Mifflin, 1890), 2:779–81; Ralph Volney Harlow, "Economic Conditions in Massachusetts during the American Revolution," Colonial Society of Massachusetts *Publications* 20 (1920): 163–90.

3. Van Beck Hall, *Politics without Parties: Massachusetts, 1780–1791* (Pittsburgh: Univ. of Pittsburgh Press, 1972), 96–110, 122–27, 192.

4. Gerald W. Gawalt, *The Promise of Power: The Emergence of the Legal Profession in Massachusetts, 1760–1840* (Westport, Conn.: Greenwood Press, 1979), 45.

5. For a slightly later period and in different ways, Richard D. Brown has written about similar changes in "The Emergence of Urban Society in Rural Massachusetts, 1790–1820," *Journal of American History* 61 (1974): 29–51.

6. Stephen E. Patterson, *Political Parties in Revolutionary Massachusetts* (Madison: Univ. of Wisconsin Press, 1973), 249; Hall, 166–89; James Sullivan to Benjamin Lincoln, Jan. 16, 1782, in Thomas C. Amory, *Life of James Sullivan, with Selections from His Writings,* 2 vols. (Boston: Phillips, Sampson, 1859), 2:384; *Massachusetts Spy,* Jan. 31, 1782; Joseph Hawley to Ephraim Wright, Apr. 16, 1782, "Documents: Shays's Rebellion," *American Historical Review* 36 (1931): 776–78.

7. Hall, 256, 263–65, 286–93; Jackson Turner Main, *Political Parties before the Constitution* (Chapel Hill: Univ. of North Carolina Press, 1973), 111–13, 119, 366, 396–97; Merrill Jensen, *The Making of the American Constitution* (New York: D. Van Nostrand, 1964), 142.

8. Stephen E. Patterson, "The Roots of Massachusetts Federalism: Conservative Politics and Political Culture before 1787," in Ronald Hoffman and Peter J. Albert, eds., *Sovereign States in an Age of Uncertainty* (Charlottesville: Univ. Press of Virginia, 1981), 31–61, 44–45, 48–50; Robert A. East, "The Massachusetts Conservatives in the Critical Period," in Richard B. Morris, ed., *The Era of the American Revolution* (New York: Columbia Univ. Press, 1939), 359–60.

9. Hawley to Ephraim Wright, Apr. 16, 1782, "Documents: Shays's Rebellion," 776–78.

10. *Independent Chronicle,* Apr. 5, 1784; *Massachusetts Spy,* Feb. 26, Mar. 25, 1784; [*Thirty-First*] *Report of the Records Commissioners of the City of Boston Containing the Boston Town Records, 1784–96* 31 (1903): 3, 12–14.

11. George Richards Minot, *History of the Insurrections in Massachusetts,* 2nd ed. (Boston: James W. Burditt, 1810), 9–10, 20–22; "An Honest and Chearful Citizen"

and a column headed "Boston," *Independent Chronicle,* Sept. 7, 1786; Circular Letter of the Town of Boston, Sept. 8, 11, 1786, *Boston Gazette,* Sept. 18, 1786; "Charge of the Chief Justice to the Grand Jury of the County of Middlesex," *Independent Chronicle,* Nov. 16, 1786; William Plumer to John Hale, Sept. 18, 1786, "Letters of William Plumer, 1786–1787," Colonial Society of Massachusetts *Publications* 11 (1910): 387–90.

12. See, for example, Alden Vaughan, "Shays' Rebellion," in John A. Garraty, ed., *Historical Viewpoints,* 2 vols. (New York: Harper & Row, 1970), 1:152–65; E. James Ferguson, *The American Revolution: A General History, 1763–1790* (Homewood, Ill.: Dorsey Press, 1979), 284–85.

13. "An American," *Boston Gazette,* June 19, 1786; "Seneca," *Independent Chronicle,* June 29, 1786; "An Honest and Chearful Citizen," *Independent Chronicle,* Sept. 7, 1786; "Political Paragraphs," *Boston Gazette,* Dec. 4, 1786.

14. See, for example, "A Letter Signed N.T.," *Independent Chronicle,* June 29, 1786, which purports to be "an extract of a letter from a gentleman at W[es]t S[pringfiel]d, to his friend in a remote part of the country." The letter discusses the plot in which both the author and correspondent are presumably engaged to restore British control of America. See also "Publicus" and "Boston," *Independent Chronicle,* Sept. 7, 1786; Boston Circular Letter, *Boston Gazette,* Sept. 18, 1786; "Justice," *Boston Gazette,* Oct. 9, 1786.

15. Arthur Meier Schlesinger, *Colonial Merchants and the American Revolution, 1763–1776* (1918; rept. New York: Frederick Ungar, 1957), 308–09, 311–25, 359, 604; Robert A. East, *Business Enterprise in the American Revolutionary Era* (New York: Columbia Univ. Press, 1938), 219–20; Patterson, *Political Parties,* 65–70, 75–86.

16. Patterson, *Political Parties,* 148–50, 158–61, 162, 179–80; Patterson, "The Roots of Massachusetts Federalism," 45–46.

17. Pickering to Mrs. Mehitible Higginson, June 15, 1783, Pickering Papers, MHS, as quoted by Merrill Jensen, *The New Nation: A History of the United States during the Confederation, 1781–1789* (New York: Knopf, 1950), 267.

18. See, for example, the advertisement of Samuel Eliot of Boston, *Massachusetts Spy,* July 19, 1784.

19. Weeden, *Economic and Social History* 2:819–20; Edmund C. Burnett, ed., *Letters of Members of the Continental Congress,* 8 vols. (Washington, D.C.: Carnegie Institution, 1921–36), 8:xv.

20. Neil McKendrick, John Brewer, and J. H. Plumb, *The Birth of a Consumer Society: The Commercialization of Eighteenth-Century England* (London: Europa Publications, 1982), pt. 1: Neil McKendrick, "Commercialization and the Economy," 9–194.

21. *Massachusetts Spy,* May 20, June 3, July 1, Aug. 26, Sept. 2, 9, 1784.

22. David A. Szatmary, *Shays' Rebellion: The Making of an Agrarian Insurrection* (Amherst: Univ. of Massachusetts Press, 1980), esp. 29–36.

23. *Massachusetts Spy,* Oct. 7, 14, 1784.

24. Ibid., Mar. 31, 1785.

25. Typical of the attacks on British factors in the Massachusetts press was one appearing under the heading "Worcester," ibid., June 16, 1785.

26. *Boston Gazette,* Apr. 18, 1785. See also "To All Whom It May Concern," ibid., Apr. 11, 1785.

27. Ibid., May 9, 1785.

28. Merchants & Traders of Boston to Gov. Bowdoin, June 4, 1785, Committee of Tradesmen & Manufacturers to Gov. Bowdoin, June 7, 1785, Bowdoin-Temple Papers, MHS.

29. Nathan Dane to Rufus King, Oct. 8, 1785, in Charles R. King, ed., *Life and Correspondence of Rufus King; Comprising His Letters, Private and Official, His Public Documents, and His Speeches,* 6 vols. (New York: Putnam, 1894–1900), 1:67–69.

30. Stephen E. Patterson, "After Newburgh: The Struggle for the Impost in Massachusetts," in James Kirby Martin, ed., *The Human Dimensions of Nation Making* (Madison: State Historical Society of Wisconsin, 1976), 218–42.

31. *Massachusetts Spy,* Nov. 24, 1785.

32. Samuel Eliot Morison, *The Maritime History of Massachusetts, 1783–1860* (1921; rept. Boston: Houghton Mifflin, 1961), 44–46.

33. Theodore Sedgwick to Caleb Strong, Aug. 6, 1786, *Letters of Members of Continental Congress* 8:415.

34. James Monroe to Thomas Jefferson, July 16, 1786, Charles Thomson's Minutes of Congress, Aug. 16, 1786 (Rufus King's speech), ibid., 8:403–4, 427–30.

35. James Monroe to James Madison, July 26, 1785, Richard Henry Lee to Madison, Aug. 11, 1785, David Howell to Gov. William Greene of Rhode Island, Aug. 23, 1785, ibid., 8:171–72, 180–81, 198–200.

36. John W. Tyler, *Smugglers and Patriots: Boston Merchants and the Advent of the American Revolution* (Boston: Northeastern Univ. Press, 1986), 100–07, 230–31, 238.

37. Massachusetts delegates to Gov. Bowdoin, Sept. 3, 1785, Rufus King to Nathan Dane, Sept. 17, 1785, Massachusetts delegates to Gov. Bowdoin, Nov. 2, 1785, *Letters of Members of Continental Congress,* 8:206–10, 218–19, 245–46.

38. King to John Adams, Nov. 2, Dec. 4, 1785, ibid., 8:247–48, 268–69.

39. Among the most vociferous antilawyer spokesmen was "Honestus," Boston ropemaker Benjamin Austin, Jr., who wrote in Boston's *Independent Chronicle,* Mar. 9, 30, May 25, 1786. See also "An Elector," "One of the People," and "Agrippa," *Boston Gazette,* Apr. 3, June 12, 19, 1786, and "Equity," *Independent Chronicle,* Apr. 27, 1786. For a full discussion of the antilawyer campaign, and especially of Austin, see Sidney Kaplan, "'Honestus' and the Annihilation of the Lawyers," *South Atlantic Quarterly* 48 (1949): 401–20.

40. *Boston Gazette,* May 1, 1786. For the prolawyer view, see "Zenas," *Independent Chronicle,* Apr. 27, 1786.

41. Caleb Strong to Theodore Sedgwick, June 24, 1786, Theodore Sedgwick Papers, MHS.

42. Rufus King warned Jonathan Jackson that the persons organizing the convention were opposed to a general regulation of trade and sought only to promote new state regulations (King to Jackson, June 11, 1786, *Letters of Members of Continental Congress* 8:389–90).

43. Theodore Sedgwick to Caleb Strong, Aug. 6, 1785, James Monroe to Gov. Patrick Henry, Aug. 12, 1786, ibid., 8:415, 421–25.

44. The mood of Federalists is indicated in Nathan Dane to Theodore Sedgwick and [Timothy?] Dwight, Feb. 11, 1786, Nathan Dane Papers, Library of Congress; Theodore Sedgwick to Nathan Dane, Feb. 24, 1786, Livingston Papers, ser. 2, box 2 (1784–87), New-York Historical Society.

45. Artemas Ward wrote Gov. James Bowdoin that the insurgents' demands could be easily satisfied, while most of the inhabitants of the interior were not very

sympathetic to the Shaysites (Ward to Bowdoin, Dec. 7, 1786, Shays' Rebellion Papers, MHS).

46. The material in this paragraph derives from a reading of the *Boston Gazette* and the *Independent Chronicle* for the fall and winter of 1786–87.

47. "Consideration," *Boston Gazette*, Apr. 17, 1786.

48. Stephen Higginson to [Henry Knox], Nov. 25, 1786, Henry Knox Papers, MHS.

49. Knox to Stephen Higginson, Feb. 25, 1787, ibid.

50. Patterson, "Roots of Massachusetts Federalism," 44–45.

Gordon S. Wood

The American Science of Politics

From *The Creation of the American Republic,
1776–1787*

Gordon S. Wood is University Professor at Brown University.
Wood sees the Federalists as very creative political thinkers
who changed the whole direction of republican thought.
This selection is the concluding chapter of his *The Creation
of the American Republic, 1776–1787,* which has replaced
Beard's *Economic Interpretation of the Constitution* as the study
that poses the central questions. Wood's main source of evidence is the vast amount of writing on political and institutional questions that Americans produced during the twelve
years that his book covers. Wood uses this material to show
literate Americans arguing with one another and, perhaps,
making up their country's collective mind. By the end of
those years of intense debate, they had abandoned almost
all the ideas that republican thinkers had been developing
since ancient Greece and Rome, except for the fundamental
point that in a republic citizens must rule themselves.

Wood's book also presents evidence of a great deal of social
conflict and transformation among Americans. As much as
Beard, Wood is interested in the historical relationship between American political culture and the development of
American capitalism. Perhaps the biggest difference between the two books is not the contrast between Beard's now
discredited use of financial records and Wood's search for
nuance and inflection within literary sources. Instead it is
the contrast between Beard's acerbic conclusion that "the
Constitution was . . . the work of a consolidated group whose
interests knew no state boundaries" and Wood's final argu-

ment that "the American system of government" emerged from political theorizing so creative that it is "worthy of a prominent place in the history of Western thought."

Questions for a Closer Reading

1. Why was the notion of "Democratic Republics" difficult to grasp when Federalist writers began using the term in 1787?

2. With its presidency, Senate, and House of Representatives, the American government looks very much like its British counterpart of monarch, lords, and commons. But Wood sees the two as not at all the same. What are the differences?

3. How did the Constitution solve the problem of creating fundamental authority that arose when Americans abandoned the idea of monarchy?

4. How in the new American system were all public officials in some sense representatives of "the sovereign people"?

5. What is the difference between the "classical politics" of "basic social forces" that the Constitution abandoned and the "American politics" of "various social interests" that it embodied?

The American Science of Politics

Democratic Republics

Undoubtedly John Taylor was right about the source of the new principles of politics discovered during the Revolutionary era. The creation of a new political theory was not as much a matter of deliberation as it was a matter of necessity. The blending of diverse views and clashing interests into the new federal system, Madison told Jefferson in October 1787, was nothing "less than a miracle." Although no one person had done so much to create the Constitution, Madison generously but rightly stressed to the end of his life that it was not "the offspring of a single brain" but "the work of many heads and many hands." The formation of the new government, as Franklin observed to a European correspondent in 1788, was not like a game of chess, methodically and consciously played. It was more like a game of dice, with so many players, "their ideas so different, their prejudices so strong and so various, and their particular interests, independent of the general, seeming so opposite, that not a move can be made that is not contested." Yet somehow out of all these various moves the Constitution had emerged, and with it had emerged not only "a wonder and admiration" among the members of the Convention themselves, but also a growing awareness among all Americans that the Constitution had actually created a political system "so novel, so complex, and intricate" that writing about it would never cease.[1] The Constitution had become the climax of a great revolution. "Till this period," declared Aaron Hall of New Hampshire in a 1788 oration, "the revolution in America has never appeared to me to be completed; but this is laying on the cap-stone of the great American Empire." It was not the revolution that had been intended but it was a real revolution nonetheless, marked by a momentous upheaval in the understanding of politics where the "collected wisdom of ages" was

Gordon S. Wood, "The American Science of Politics," in *The Creation of the American Republic, 1776–1787* (Chapel Hill: University of North Carolina Press, 1969), 593–618.

"interwoven in this form of government." "The independence of America considered merely as a separation from England, would have been a matter but of little importance," remarked Thomas Paine, "had it not been accompanied by a revolution in the principles and practise of governments." "There are some great eras," said James Wilson, "when important and very perceptible alterations take place in the situation of men and things." And America, added David Ramsay, was in the midst of one of those great eras.[2]

Americans now told themselves with greater assurance than ever that they had created something remarkable in the history of politics. "The different constitutions which have been adopted by these states," observed John Stevens in 1787, "are experiments in government entirely new; they are founded upon principles peculiar to themselves." Admittedly they had not fully understood politics at the outset of the Revolution; but within a decade they believed that most of the defects of their early state constitutions had been discovered and were on the way to being remedied. And the new federal Constitution expressed all they had learned. "The government of the United States," wrote Nathaniel Chipman of Vermont in 1793, "exhibits a new scene in the political history of the world, . . . exhibits, in theory, the most beautiful system, which has yet been devised by the wisdom of man." With their governments the Americans had placed the science of politics on a footing with the other great scientific discoveries of the previous century. Their governments, said William Vans Murray, represented "the most finished political forms" in history and had "deservedly attracted the attention of all speculative minds." It was therefore important for "the cause of liberty all over the world, that they should be understood." And by the end of the 1780's and the early nineties Americans increasingly felt compelled to explain to themselves and to the world the uniqueness of what they had discovered.[3]

Their governments were so new and so distinctive that they groped for political terms adequate to describe them. By the late 1780's Americans generally were calling their governments democracies, but peculiar kinds of democracies. America, said Murray, had established governments which were "in their principles, structure, and whole mass, purely and unalterably Democratic." The American republics, remarked John Stevens, approached "nearer to perfect democracies" than any other governments in the world. Yet democracy, as eighteenth-century political scientists generally understood the term, was not, they realized, a wholly accurate description of their new governments. They were "Democratic Republics," as Chipman called them, by which was "meant, a Representative Democracy." In *The Federalist,* Number 10, Madison called the American governments republics, as distinct from a "pure democracy" in which a small number of citizens assembled and administered the government in person. For Madison a republic had become a species of government to be classed along-side aristocracy or democracy, a distinctive form of government "in which the scheme of representation takes place." Representation—that was the key conception in unlocking an understanding of the American political system. America was, as Hamilton said, "a *representative democracy.*" Only the American scheme, wrote Thomas Paine, was based "wholly on the system of representation," and thus it was "the only real republic in character and practise, that now exists." The American polity was "representation in-grafted upon democracy," creating "a system of government capable of embracing and confederating all the various interests and every extent of territory and population."[4]

The Pervasiveness of Representation

It was representation then—"the delegation of the government . . . ," said Madison, "to a small number of citizens elected by the rest"—that ex-plained the uniqueness of the American polities. "The *principle* on which all the American governments are founded," wrote Samuel Williams of Vermont, "is *representation.*" No other nation, said Charles Pinckney of South Carolina, so enjoyed the right of self-government, "where the true principles of representation are understood and practised, and where all authority flows from and returns at stated periods to, the people." Repre-sentation, said Edmund Randolph, was "a thing not understood in its full extent till very lately." Neither the Israelites nor the ancients had properly comprehended the uses of representation—"a very excellent modern im-provement in the management of republics," said Samuel Langdon of New Hampshire. "It is surprising, indeed," said Wilson, "how very imper-fectly, at this day, the doctrine of representation is understood in Europe. Even Great Britain, which boasts a superior knowledge of the subject, and is generally supposed to have carried it into practice, falls far short of its true and genuine principles." Representation, remarked Wilson, barely touched the English constitution, since it was not immediately or remotely the source of executive or judicial power. Even in the legislature represen-tation was not "a pervading principle," but actually was only a check, con-fined to the Commons. The Lords acted either under hereditary right or under an authority granted by the prerogative of the Crown and hence were "not the representatives of the people." The world, it seemed, had "left to America the glory and happiness of forming a government where representation shall at once supply the basis and the cement of the super-structure."[5] "In America," said Williams, "every thing tended to introduce, and to complete the system of representation." America, wrote Madison, had created the first example of "a government wholly popular, and founded at the same time, wholly on that principle [of representation]." Americans had made their entire system from top to bottom representative, "diffusing," in Wilson's words, "this vital principle throughout all the different divisions and departments of the government." Since Americans, influenced by the implications of the developing conception of actual representation, now clearly believed that "the right of representing is conferred by the act of electing," every part of the elective governments had become representative of the people. In truth, said Madison, representation was "the pivot" on which the whole American system moved.[6]

Although the members of the houses of representatives were perhaps the more "immediate representatives," no longer were they the full and exclusive representatives of the people. "The Senators," said Nathaniel Chipman, "are to be representatives of the people, no less, in fact, than the members of the other house." Foreigners, noted William Vans Murray, had mistaken the division of the legislatures in America as some sort of an embodiment of an aristocracy. Even in Maryland and in the federal Constitution where the senates were indirectly elected, the upper house was derived mediately from the people. "It represents the people. It represents no particular order of men or of ranks." To those who sought to comprehend fully the integrity of the new system the senate could only be a weight in the powers of legislative deliberation, not a weight of property, of privileges, or of interests. Election by the people, not the number of chambers in the legislature, declared John Stevens, had made "our governments the most democratic that ever existed anywhere." "With us," concluded Wilson, "the power of magistrates, call them by whatever name you please, are the grants of the people."[7]

Therefore all governmental officials, including even the executive and judicial parts of the government, were agents of the people, not fundamentally different from the people's nominal representatives in the lower houses of the legislatures. The Americans of 1776, observed Wilson, had not clearly understood the nature of their executives and judiciaries. Although the authority of their governors and judges became in 1776 as much "the child of the people" as that of the legislatures, the people could not forget their traditional colonial aversion to the executive and judiciary, and their fondness for their legislatures, which under the British monarchy had been the guardians of their rights and the anchor of their political hopes. "Even at this time," Wilson noted with annoyance, "people can scarcely devest themselves of those opposite prepossessions." The legislatures often were still called "the *people's representatives*," implying, "though probably, not avowed upon reflection," that the executive and judicial powers were not so strongly or closely connected with the people. "But it is high time," said Wilson, "that we should chastise our prejudices." The dif-

ferent parts of the government were functionally but not substantively different. "The executive and judicial powers are now drawn from the same
source, are now animated by the same principles, and are now directed to
the same ends, with the legislative authority: they who execute, and they
who administer the laws, are so much the servants, and therefore as much
the friends of the people, as those who make them." The entire government had become the limited agency of the sovereign people.[8]

The pervasive Whig mistrust of power had in the years since Independence been increasingly directed not only against the traditional rulers,
but also against the supposed representatives of the people, who now
seemed to many to be often as distant and unrepresentative of the people's
interests as Parliament once had been. "The representatives of the people,
in a popular assembly," said Hamilton, "seem sometimes to fancy that
they are the people themselves." The constitutional reformers seized on
the people's growing suspicion of their own representatives and reversed the perspective: the houses of representatives, now no more
trusted than other parts of the government, seemed to be also no more
representative of the people than the other parts of the government.
They had lost their exclusive role of embodying the people in the government. In fact the people did not actually participate in the government
any more, as they did, for example, in the English House of Commons.
The Americans had taken the people out of the government altogether.
The "true distinction" of the American governments, wrote Madison in *The
Federalist*, "lies *in the total exclusion of the people, in their collective capacity,
from any share*" in the government. Or from a different point of view the
Americans could now argue that the people participated in all branches
of the government and not merely in their houses of representatives.
"The whole powers of the proposed government," said Hamilton in *The
Federalist*, "is to be in the hands of the representatives of the people." All
parts of the government were equally responsible but limited spokesmen
for the people, who remained as the absolute and perpetual sovereign,
distributing bits and pieces of power to their various agents.[9]

Confrontation with the Blackstonian* concept of legal sovereignty had
forced American theorists to relocate it in the people-at-large, a transfer-
ence that was comprehensible only because of the peculiar experience of
American politics. "Sovereignty," said James Sullivan, "must in its nature,
be absolute and uncontrolable by any civil authority. . . . A subordinate sovereignty is nonsense: A subordinate, uncontrolable power is a contradiction in terms." In America this kind of sovereignty could only exist in the

---

Blackstonian: Sir William Blackstone (1723–1780), the English jurist and legal scholar
who developed the idea of the absolute sovereignty of the "King-in-Parliament."

people themselves, who "may invest the exercise of it in whom they please; but where the power delegated by them is subordinate, or controlable by any other delegated civil power, it is not a sovereign power." Thus it was obvious that in America "there is no supreme power but what the people themselves hold." "The supreme power," said Wilson, "is in them; and in them, even when a constitution is formed, and government is in operation, the supreme power still remains." The powers of the people were thus never alienated or surrendered to a legislature. Representation, in other words, never eclipsed the people-at-large, as apparently it did in the English House of Commons. In America the people were never really represented in the English sense of the term. "A portion of their authority they, indeed, delegate; but they delegate that portion in whatever manner, in whatever measure, for whatever time, to whatever persons, and on whatever conditions they choose to fix." Such a delegation, said Sullivan, was necessarily fragmentary and provisional; "it may extend to some things and not to others or be vested for some purposes, and not for others." Only a proper understanding of this vital principle of the sovereignty of the people could make federalism intelligible. The representation of the people, as American politics in the Revolutionary era had made glaringly evident, could never be virtual, never inclusive; it was acutely actual, and always tentative and partial. "All power whatever," said John Stevens, "is vested in, and immediately derived from, the people only; the rulers are their deputies merely, and at certain short periods are removable by them: nay," he added, "the very government itself is a creature formed by themselves, and may, whenever they think it necessary, be at any time new modelled."[10]

The Equation of Rulers and Ruled

This conception of the sovereignty of the people used to create the new federal government had at last clarified the peculiar American idea of a constitution. A constitution, as James Iredell said, was "a declaration of particular powers by the people to their representatives, for particular purposes. It may be considered as a great power of attorney, under which no power can be exercised but what is expressly given." A constitution for Americans, said Thomas Paine, was "not a thing in name only; but in fact. . . . It is the body of elements, to which you can refer, and quote article by article; and which contains . . . every thing that relates to the complete organization of a civil government, and the principles on which it shall act, and by which it shall be bound." A constitution was thus a "thing *antecedent* to a government, and a government is only the creature of a constitution." It was truly, said Wilson, the act of the people, and "in their hands it is clay in the hands of the potter: they have the right to mould, to preserve, to improve, to refine, and to furnish it as they please." Only by conceiving of a constitution as a written delimitation of the grant of power made by the people to the government was "the important distinction so well understood in America, between a Constitution established by the people and unalterable by the government, and a law established by the government and alterable by the government" rendered truly comprehensible.[11]

In America a constitution had become, as Madison pointed out, a charter of power granted by liberty rather than, as in Europe, a charter of liberty granted by power. Magna Carta and the English Bill of Rights were not constitutions at all. They "did not," said Paine, "create and give powers to Government in the manner a constitution does." They were really only "restrictions on assumed power," bargains "which the parts of the government made with each other to divide powers, profits and privileges." "The far famed social compact between the people and their rulers," declared David Ramsay, "did not apply to the United States." "To suppose that any government can be a party in a compact with the whole people," said Paine, "is to suppose it to have existence before it can have a right to exist." In America, said Ramsay, "the sovereignty was in the people," who "deputed certain individuals as their agents to serve them in public stations agreeably to constitutions, which they prescribed for their conduct." Government, concluded Paine, "has of itself no rights; they are altogether duties."[12]

Yet if the ancient notion of a contract was to be preserved in American thinking, then it must be a Lockean contract, one formed by the individuals of the society with each other, instead of a mutual arrangement between rulers and ruled. In most countries, declared Charles Backus in 1788, the people "have obtained a partial security of their liberties, by extorted concessions from their nobles or kings. But in America, the *People* have had an opportunity of forming a compact *betwixt themselves;* from which alone, their rulers derive all their authority to govern." This image of a social contract formed by isolated and hostile individuals was now the only contractual metaphor that comprehended American social reality. Since an American constitution could no longer be regarded as a contract between rulers and people, representing distinct and unified interests, considerations like protection and allegiance lost their relevance. "Writers on government have been anxious on the part of the people," observed Nathaniel Chipman in 1793, "to discover a consideration given for the right of protection. . . . While government was supposed to depend on a compact, not between the individuals of a people, but between the people and the rulers, this was a point of great consequence." But not any longer in America, where government was based on a compact only among the people. Obedience to the government in America followed from no such traditional consideration. The flow of authority itself was reversed, and *"consent,"* which had not been the basis of magisterial authority in the past, now became "the sole obligatory principle of human government and human laws." Because of the pervasiveness of representational consent through all parts of the government, "the judgments of our courts, and the commissions constitutionally given by our governor," said John Jay, "are as valid and as binding on all our persons whom they concern, as the laws passed by our legislature." The once important distinction between magisterial authority and representative legislative authority was now obliterated. "All constitutional acts of power, whether in the executive or in the judicial department, have as much legal validity and obligation as if they proceeded from the legislature." No more revolutionary change in the history of politics could have been made: the rulers had become the ruled and the ruled the rulers.[13]

The Parceling of Power

The American governments, wrote Samuel Williams in his *Natural and Civil History of Vermont* of 1794, "do not admit of sovereignty, nobility, or any kind of hereditary powers; but only of powers granted by the people, ascertained by written constitutions, and exercised by representation for a given time." Hence such governments "do not admit of monarchy, or aristocracy; nor do they admit of what was called democracy by the ancients." The old classification of politics by the number and character of the rulers no longer made sense of American practice where "all is transacted by representation" expressed in different ways. The government in the several states thus "varies in its form; committing more or less power to a governor, senate, or house of representatives, as the circumstances of any particular state may require. As each of these branches derive their whole power from the people, are accountable to them for the use and exercise they make of it, and may be displaced by the election of others," the liberty and security of the people, as Americans had thought in 1776, no longer came from their participation in one part of the government, as the democracy balanced against the monarchy and aristocracy, "but from the responsibility, and dependence of each part of the government, upon the people."[14]

In slightly more than two decades of polemics the Americans had destroyed the age-old conception of mixed government and had found new explanations for their polities created in 1776, explanations that rested on their expansion of the principle of representation. America had not discovered the idea of representation, said Madison, but it could "claim the merit of making the discovery the basis of unmixed and extensive republics." And their republics were now peculiarly unmixed, despite the presence of senates and governors. They could in fact intelligibly be considered to be democracies, since, as James Wilson said, "in a democracy" the supreme power "is inherent in the people, and is either exercised by themselves or their representatives." Perhaps no one earlier or better described the "new and rich discoveries in jurisprudence" Americans had made than did Wilson. The British constitution, he said, had attempted to combine and to balance the three different forms of government, but it had obviously failed. And it was left to the Americans to realize that it was "not necessary to intermix the different species of government" in order to attain perfection in politics. "We have discovered, that one of them — the best and purest — that, in which the supreme power remains with the people at large, is capable of being formed, arranged, proportioned, and organized in such a manner, as to exclude the inconveniences, and to secure the advantages of all three." The federal Constitution, said Wilson, was therefore "purely democratical," even though in its outward form it resembled the conventional mixed government: "all authority of every kind *is derived by* REPRESENTATION *from the* PEOPLE *and the* DEMOCRATIC *principle is carried into every part of the government.*" The new government was in fact, incongruous as it sounded, a mixed or balanced democracy.[15]

Americans had retained the forms of the Aristotelian schemes* of government but had eliminated the substance, thus divesting the various parts of the government of their social constituents. Political power was thus disembodied and became essentially homogeneous. The division of this political power now became (in Jefferson's words) "the first principle of a good government," the "distribution of its powers into executive, judiciary, and legislative, and a sub-division of the latter into two or three branches." Separation of powers, whether describing executive, legislative, and judicial separation or the bicameral division of the legislature (the once distinct concepts now thoroughly blended), was simply a partitioning of political power, the creation of a plurality of discrete governmental elements, all detached from yet responsible to and controlled by the people, checking and balancing each other, preventing any one power from asserting itself too far. The libertarian doctrine of separation of powers was expanded and exalted by the Americans to the foremost position in their constitu-

---

Aristotelian schemes: Wood is referring to the notion that separate political institutions should draw their power from separate social orders, such as aristocrats or plebians.

tionalism, premised on the belief, in John Dickinson's words, that "government must never be lodged in a single body." Enlightenment and experience had pointed out "the propriety of government being committed to such a number of great departments"—three or four, suggested Dickinson—"as can be introduced without confusion, distinct in office, and yet connected in operation." Such a "repartition" of power was designed to provide for the safety and ease of the people, since "there will be more obstructions interposed" against errors and frauds in the government. "The departments so constituted," concluded Dickinson, "may therefore be said to be balanced." But it was not a balance of "any intrinsic or constitutional properties," of any social elements, but rather only a balance of governmental functionaries without social connections, all monitored by the people who remained outside, a balanced government that worked, "although," said Wilson, "the materials, of which it is constructed, be not an assemblage of different and dissimilar kinds."[16]

Abuse of governmental power, especially from the legislature, was now best prevented, as Madison put it in *The Federalist,* Number 51, one of the most significant expressions of the new political thinking, "by so contriving the interior structure of the government as that its several constituent parts may, by their mutual relations, be the means of keeping each other in their proper places." Perhaps the most rigorous separation of powers could be attained, suggested Madison in a revelation of the assumptions behind the new conception of government, by having all the departments of government drawn directly from the same fountain of authority, the people, "through channels having no communication whatever with one another." However, since such a plan was probably impractical, some deviations from "the principle" were necessary. Yet every effort, emphasized Madison, should be made to keep the separate departments independent, or else they could not effectively check and balance each other. The legislature must be divided and the executive fortified with a veto in order to distribute power and guard against encroachments. Moreover, continued Madison with mounting enthusiasm, the new federal government—with its new kind of "mixed character"—possessed an immense advantage over the conventional single republics which were limited in the amount of separating and dividing of powers they could sustain. "In the compound republic of America," said Madison, "the power surrendered by the people is first divided between two distinct governments, and then the portion allotted to each subdivided among distinct and separate departments." Furthermore, the partitioning of power in America would be intensified by "the extent of country and number of people comprehended under the same government," so that "the society itself will be broken into so many parts, interests and classes of citizens, that the rights of individuals, or of the minority, will be in little danger from interested combinations of the majority."[17]

It was an imposing conception—a kinetic theory of politics—such a crumbling of political and social interests, such an atomization of authority, such a parceling of power, not only in the governmental institutions but in the extended sphere of the society itself, creating such a multiplicity and a scattering of designs and passions, so many checks, that no combination of parts could hold, no group of evil interests could long cohere. Yet out of the clashing and checking of this diversity Madison believed the public good, the true perfection of the whole, would somehow arise. The impulses and passions would so counteract each other, so neutralize their potencies, as America's contending religious sects had done, that reason adhering in the natural aristocracy would be able to assert itself and dominate.

The End of Classical Politics

The Americans had reversed in a revolutionary way the traditional conception of politics: the stability of government no longer relied, as it had for centuries, upon its embodiment of the basic social forces of the state. Indeed, it now depended upon the prevention of the various social interests from incorporating themselves too firmly in the government. Institutional or governmental politics was thus abstracted in a curious way from its former associations with the society. But at the same time a more modern and more realistic sense of political behavior in the society itself, among the people, could now be appreciated. This revolution marked an end of the classical conception of politics and the beginning of what might be called a romantic view of politics. The eighteenth century had sought to understand politics, as it had all of life, by capturing in an integrated, ordered, changeless ideal the totality and complexity of the world—an ideal that the concept of the mixed constitution and the proportioned social hierarchy on which it rested perfectly expressed. In such an ideal there could be only potential energy, no kinetic energy, only a static equilibrium among synthetic orders, and no motion among the particular, miscellaneous parts that made up the society. By destroying this ideal Americans placed a new emphasis on the piecemeal and the concrete in politics at the expense of order and completeness. The Constitution represented both the climax and the finale of the American Enlightenment, both the fulfillment and the end of the belief that the endless variety and perplexity of society could be reduced to a simple and harmonious system. By attempting to formulate a theory of politics that would represent reality as it was, the Americans of 1787 shattered the classical Whig world of 1776.

Americans had begun the Revolution assuming that the people were a homogeneous entity in society set against the rulers. But such an assumption belied American experience, and it took only a few years of independence to convince the best American minds that distinctions in the society were "various and unavoidable," so much so that they could not be embodied in the government.[18] Once the people were thought to be composed of various interests in opposition to one another, all sense of a graduated organic chain in the social hierarchy became irrelevant, symbolized by the increasing emphasis on the image of a social contract. The people were not an order organically tied together by their unity of interest but rather an agglomeration of hostile individuals coming together for their mutual benefit to construct a society. The Americans transformed the people in the same way that Englishmen a century earlier had transformed the rulers: they broke the connectedness of interest among them and put them at war with one another, just as seventeenth-century Englishmen had separated the interests of rulers and people and put them in opposition to each other.

As Joel Barlow noted in 1792, the word *"people"* in America had taken on a different meaning from what it had in Europe. In America it meant the whole community and comprehended every human creature in the society; in Europe, however, it meant "something else more difficult to define." "Society," said Enos Hitchcock in 1788, "is composed of individuals—they are parts of the whole." And such individuals in America were the entire society: there could be nothing else—no orders, no lords, no monarch, no magistrates in the traditional sense. "Without the distinctions of titles, families, or nobility," wrote Samuel Williams, "they acknowledged and reverenced only those distinctions which nature had made, in a diversity of talents, abilities, and virtues. There were no family interests, connexions, or estates, large enough to oppress them. There was no excessive wealth in the hands of a few, sufficient to corrupt them." The Americans were thus both equal and unequal at the same time.

> They all feel that nature has made them equal in respect to their rights; or rather that nature has given to them a common and an equal right to liberty, to property, and to safety; to justice, government, laws, religion, and freedom. They all see that nature has made them very unequal in respect to their original powers, capacities, and talents. They become united in claiming and in preserving the equality, which nature has assigned to them; and in availing

themselves of the benefits, which are designed, and may be derived from the inequality, which nature has also established.[19]

Politics in such a society could no longer be simply described as a contest between rulers and people, between institutionalized orders of the society. The political struggles would in fact be among the people themselves, among all the various groups and individuals seeking to create inequality out of their equality by gaining control of a government divested of its former identity with the society. It was this disembodiment of government from society that ultimately made possible the conception of modern politics and the eventual justification of competing parties among the people. Those who criticized such divisive jealousy and opposition among the people, said William Hornby of South Carolina in 1784, did not understand "the great change in politics, which the revolution must have necessarily produced. . . . In *these* days we are equal citizens of a DEMOCRATIC REPUBLIC, in which *jealousy* and *opposition* must naturally exist, while there exists a difference in the minds, interests, and sentiments of mankind." While few were as yet willing to justify factionalism so blatantly, many now realized with Madison that "the regulation of these various and interfering interests forms the principal task of modern legislation, and involves the spirit of party and faction in the necessary and ordinary operations of the government." Legislation in such a society could not be the transcending of the different interests but the reconciling of them. Despite Madison's lingering hope, the public good could not be an entity distinct from its parts; it was rather "the general combined interest of all the state put together, as it were, upon an average."[20]

Under the pressure of this transformation of political thought old words and concepts shifted in emphasis and took on new meanings. Tyranny was now seen as the abuse of power by any branch of the government, even, and for some especially, by the traditional representatives of the people. "The accumulation of all powers," said Madison, "legislative, executive, and judiciary, in the same hands, whether of one, a few, or many, and whether hereditary, self-appointed, or elective, may justly be pronounced the very definition of tyranny." The separation of this governmental power, rather than simply the participation of the people in a part of the government, became the best defense of liberty. Therefore liberty, as the old Whigs had predominantly used the term — public or political liberty, the right of the people to share in the government — lost its significance for a system in which the people participated throughout.[21]

The liberty that was now emphasized was personal or private, the protection of individual rights against all governmental encroachments, particularly by the legislature, the body which the Whigs had traditionally cherished as the people's exclusive repository of their public liberty and the surest weapon to defend their private liberties. Such liberties, like that of freedom of the press, said both Madison and Paine, were now in less danger from "any direct attacks of Power" than they were from "the silent awe of a predominant party" or "from a fear of popular resentment." The assumptions behind such charges were radically new and different from those of the Whigs of 1776: men now began to consider "the interests of society and the rights of individuals as distinct," and to regard public and private liberty as antagonistic rather than complementary. In such circumstances the aim of government, in James Iredell's words, became necessarily twofold: to provide "for the security of every individual, as well as a fluctuating majority of the people." Government was no longer designed merely to promote the collective happiness of the people, but also, as the Tories had urged in the early seventies, "to protect citizens in their personal liberty and their property" even against the public will. Indeed, Madison could now say emphatically, "Justice is the end of government. It is the end of civil society." Unless individuals and minorities were protected against the power of majorities no government could be truly free.[22]

Because of this growing sense of discrepancy between the rights of the society and the rights of individuals and because the new federal government was designed to prevent the emergence of any "common passion" or sense of oneness among large numbers of persons "on any other principles than those of justice and the general good," comprehensible only by a natural elite, the older emphasis on public virtue existing throughout the society lost some of its thrust; and men could now argue that "*virtue,* patriotism, or love of country, never was nor never will be till men's natures are changed, a fixed, permanent principle and support of government." The problem was, as Charles Thompson lamented in 1786, that most Americans had no other "Object" than their own "individual happiness." While Thompson still hoped that the people would eventually become "sufficiently impressed with a sense of what they owe to their national character," others began recasting their thinking. As early as 1782 Jefferson told Monroe that it was ridiculous to suppose that a man should surrender himself to the state. "This would be slavery, and not that liberty which the bill of rights has made inviolable, and for the preservation of which our government has been changed." Freedom, said Jefferson, would be destroyed by "the establishment of the opinion that the state has a *perpetual* right to the services of all it's members." The aim of instilling a spartan creed in America thus began to seem more and more nonsensical. By 1785 Noah Webster was directly challenging Montesquieu's opinion that public virtue was a necessary foundation for democratic republics. Such virtue or patriotism, said Webster, could never predominate. Local attachments would always exist, self-interest was all there ever was. But under a democracy, argued Webster, a self-interested man must court the people, thus tending to make self-love coincide with the people's interest.[23]

William Vans Murray devoted an entire chapter of his *Political Sketches*, published in 1787, to a denial of the conventional view that republicanism was dependent upon virtue. The compulsion for such arguments was obvious. America, as Murray admitted, was "in a state of refinement and opulence," and was increasingly being permeated by "luxurious habits"— characteristics which time-honored writers on politics had declared incompatible with republican virtue and simplicity, and thus foreboding signs of an inevitable declension of the state. Yet the political scientists who spouted these maxims of republicanism had never known America. "The truth is," said Murray, "Montesquieu had never study'd a free Democracy." All the notions of these "refining speculists" had come from impressions of the ancient republics which possessed only "undefined constitutions, . . . constructed in days of ignorance." The republics of antiquity had failed because they had "attempted to force the human character into distorted shapes." The American republics, on the other hand, said Murray, were built upon the realities of human nature. They were free and responsive to the people, framed so as to give "fair play" to the actions of human nature, however unvirtuous. They had been created rationally and purposefully—for the first time in history—without attempting to pervert, suppress, or ignore the evil propensities of all men. Public virtue—the "enthusiasm," as Murray called it, of a rude and simple society, the public proscription of private pursuits for luxury—had at last "found a happy substitution in the energy of true freedom, and in a just sense of civil liberty." The American governments possessed "the freedom of Democracy, without its anarchy."[24]

Although they were "so extremely popular," wrote John Stevens, "yet the checks which have been invented (particularly in some of them) have rendered these governments capable of a degree of stability and consistency beyond what could have been expected, and which will be viewed with surprise by foreigners." Undoubtedly virtue in the people had been an essential substitute for the lack of good laws and the indispensable remedy for the traditional defects of most democratic governments. But in America where the inconveniences of the democratic form of government had been eliminated without destroying the substantial benefits of democracy—where there was introduced, said James Wilson, "into the very form of government, such particular checks and controls, as to make it advanta-

geous even for bad men to act for the public good"—the need for a society of simple, equal, virtuous people no longer seemed so critical. America
alone, wrote Murray, had united liberty with luxury and had proved "the
consistency of the social nature with the political happiness of man."[25]

Such depreciations of public virtue were still sporadic and premature,
yet they represented the beginnings of a fundamental shift in thought. In
place of individual self-sacrifice for the good of the state as the bond holding the republican fabric together, the Americans began putting an increasing emphasis on what they called "public opinion" as the basis of all
governments. Montesquieu in his *Spirit of the Laws,* wrote Madison in 1792,
had only opened up the science of politics. Governments could not be divided simply into despotisms, monarchies, and republics sustained by their
"operative principles" of fear, honor, and virtue. Governments, suggested
Madison, were better divided into those which derived their energy from
military force, those which operated by corrupt influence, and those
which relied on the will and interest of the society. While nearly all governments, including the British monarchy, rested to some extent on public
opinion, only in America had public consent as the basis of government attained its greatest perfection. No government, Americans told themselves
over and over, had ever before so completely set its roots in the sentiments
and aims of its citizens. All the power of America's governments, said
Samuel Williams, was "derived from the public opinion." America would
remain free not because of any quality in its citizens of spartan self-
sacrifice to some nebulous public good, but in the last analysis because of
the concern each individual would have in his own self-interest and personal freedom. The really great danger to liberty in the extended republic
of America, warned Madison in 1791, was that each individual may become insignificant in his own eyes—hitherto the very foundation of republican government.[26]

Such a total grounding of government in self-interest and consent had
made old-fashioned popular revolutions obsolete. Establishments whose
foundations rest on the society itself, said Wilson, cannot be overturned by
any alteration of the government which the society can make. The decay
and eventual death of the republican body politic now seemed less inevitable. The prevailing opinion of political writers, noted Nathaniel Chipman, had been "that man is fatally incapable of forming any system which
shall endure without degeneration," an opinion that appeared "to be
countenanced by the experience of ages." Yet America had lighted the way
to a reversal of this opinion, placing, as David Ramsay put it, "the science
of politics on a footing with the other sciences, by opening it to improvements from experience, and the discoveries of future ages." Governments

had never been able to adjust continually to the operations of human nature. It was "impossible," said Chipman, "to form any human institution, which should accommodate itself to every situation in progress." All previous peoples had been compelled to suffer with the same forms of government—probably unplanned and unsuitable in the first place—despite extensive changes in the nature of their societies. "The confining of a people, who have arrived at a highly improved state of society, to the forms and principles of a government, which originated in a simple, if not barbarous state of men and manners," was, said Chipman, like Chinese footbinding, a "perversion of nature," causing an incongruity between the form of government and the character of the society that usually ended in a violent eruption, in a forceful effort to bring the government into accord with the new social temperament of the people.[27]

However, the American republics possessed what Thomas Pownall called "a *healing principle*" built into their constitutions. Each contained "within itself," said Samuel Williams, "the means of its own *improvement*." The American governments never pretended, said Chipman, to perfection or to the exclusion of future improvements. "The idea of incorporating, in the constitution itself, a plan of reformation," enabling the people periodically and peacefully to return to first principles, as Machiavelli had urged, the Americans realized, was a totally new contribution to politics. The early state constitutions, David Ramsay admitted, possessed many defects. "But in one thing they were all perfect. They left the people in the power of altering and amending them, whenever they pleased." And the Americans had demonstrated to the world how a people could fundamentally and yet peaceably alter their forms of government. "This revolution principle—that, the sovereign power residing in the people, they may change their constitution and government whenever they please—is," said James Wilson, "not a principle of discord, rancour, or war: it is a principle of melioration, contentment, and peace." Americans had in fact institutionalized and legitimized revolution. Thereafter, they believed, new knowledge about the nature of government could be converted into concrete form without resorting to violence. Let no one, concluded Chipman, now rashly predict "that this beautiful system is, with the crazy empires of antiquity, destined to a speedy dissolution; or that it must in time, thro' the degeneracy of the people, and a corruption of its principles, of necessity give place to a system of remediless tyranny and oppression." By actually implementing the old and trite conception of the sovereignty of the people, by infusing political and even legal life into the people, Americans had created, said Wilson, "the great panacea of human politics."[28] The illimitable progress of mankind promised by the Enlightenment could at last be made coincident with the history of a single nation. For the Americans at least, and for others if they followed, the endless cycles of history could finally be broken.

The Americans of the Revolutionary generation believed that they had made a momentous contribution to the history of politics. They had for the first time demonstrated to the world how a people could diagnose the ills of its society and work out a peaceable process of cure. They had, and what is more significant they knew they had, broken through the conceptions of political theory that had imprisoned men's minds for centuries and brilliantly reconstructed the framework for a new republican polity, a reconstruction that radically changed the future discussion of politics. The Federalists had discovered, they thought, a constitutional antidote "wholly popular" and "strictly republican" for the ancient diseases of a republican polity—an antidote that did not destroy the republican vices, but rather accepted, indeed endorsed and relied upon them. The Federalist image of a public good undefinable by factious majorities in small states but somehow capable of formulation by the best men of a large society may have been a chimera. So too perhaps was the Federalist hope for the filtration of the natural social leaders through a federal sieve into political leadership. These were partisan and aristocratic purposes that belied the Federalists' democratic language. Yet the Federalists' intellectual achievement really transcended their particular political and social intentions and became more important and more influential than they themselves anticipated. Because their ideas were so popularly based and embodied what Americans had been groping towards from the beginning of their history, the Federalists' creation could be, and eventually was, easily adopted and expanded by others with quite different interests and aims at stake, indeed, contributing in time to the destruction of the very social world they had sought to maintain. The invention of a government that was, in James Sullivan's words, "perhaps without example in the world" could not long remain a strictly Federalist achievement. "As this kind of government," wrote Samuel Williams, "is not the same as that, which has been called monarchy, aristocracy, or democracy; as it had a conspicuous origin in America, and has not been suffered to prevail in any other part of the globe, it would be no more than just and proper, to distinguish it by its proper name, and call it, *The American System of Government.*"[29]

So piecemeal was the Americans' formulation of this system, so diverse and scattered in authorship, and so much a simple response to the pressures of democratic politics was their creation, that the originality and the theoretical consistency and completeness of their constitutional thinking have been obscured. It was a political theory that was diffusive and open-ended; it was not delineated in a single book; it was peculiarly the product of a democratic society, without a precise beginning or an ending. It was not political theory in the grand manner, but it was political theory worthy of a prominent place in the history of Western thought.

Notes

1. Madison to Jefferson, Oct. 24, 1787, Boyd, ed., *Jefferson Papers*, XII, 272; Madison (1834), quoted in Brant, *Madison*, III, 154–55; Benjamin Franklin to Du Pont de Nemours, June 9, 1788, Smyth, ed., *Writings of Franklin*, IX, 659; Wilson, in McMaster and Stone, eds., *Pennsylvania and the Federal Constitution*, 224; James Sullivan, *Observations upon the Government of the United States of America* (Boston, 1791), v.

2. Aaron Hall, *An Oration . . . to Celebrate the Ratification of the Federal Constitution by the State of New-Hampshire* (Keene, N.H., 1788), 6, 7; Paine, *Rights of Man*, in Foner, ed., *Writings of Paine*, I, 354; James Wilson, "Lectures on Law," Wilson, ed., *Works of Wilson*, II, 40; Ramsay, *American Revolution*, I, 356.

3. [Stevens], *Observations on Government*, 51; Nathaniel Chipman, *Sketches of the Principles of Government* (Rutland, Vt., 1793), 239, 277; [Murray], *Political Sketches*, 1. With the adoption of the new federal Constitution pressure was placed on the states to bring their constitutions, as one writer put it, into "closer harmony" with that of the national government. By 1790 Pennsylvania, South Carolina, and Georgia had done so; New Hampshire, Delaware, and Vermont followed in the early nineties. Hartford *Conn. Courant*, Oct. 8, 1787; Nevins, *American States*, 196–205. See also Elizabeth K. Bauer, *Commentaries on the Constitution, 1790–1860* (N.Y., 1952).

4. [Murray], *Political Sketches*, 5; [Stevens], *Observations on Government*, 50; Chipman, *Principles of Government*, 102; *The Federalist*, No. 10, No. 14; Hamilton, Notes for a Speech of July 12, 1788, in the N.Y. Ratifying Convention, Syrett and Cooke, eds., *Hamilton Papers*, V, 150; Paine, *Rights of Man*, Foner, ed., *Writings of Paine*, I, 370–71. On the confusion of terms, see Robert W. Shoemaker, "'Democracy' and 'Republic' as Understood in Late Eighteenth-Century America," *American Speech*, 41 (1966), 83–95.

5. *The Federalist*, No. 10; Williams, *History of Vermont*, 342; Pinckney (S.C.) and Randolph (Va.), in Elliot, ed., *Debates*, IV, 331, III, 199; Samuel Langdon, *The Republic of the Israelites an Example to the American States . . .* (Exeter, N.H., 1788), 7; Wilson, in McMaster and Stone, eds., *Pennsylvania and the Federal Constitution*, 222–23.

6. Williams, *History of Vermont*, 343; *The Federalist*, No. 14; Wilson, "Lectures on Law," Wilson, ed., *Works of Wilson*, I, 430, II, 57; *The Federalist*, No. 63.

7. Chipman, *Principles of Government*, 150; [Murray], *Political Sketches*, 52–53; [Stevens], *Observations on Government*, 51; Wilson, "Lectures on Law," Wilson, ed., *Works of Wilson*, I, 445. By 1823 Jefferson, who in 1776 in his desire to establish an aristocratic senate free from popular dictation had even been willing to have it elected for life, was suggesting to European constitution-makers that in order "to avoid all temptation to superior pretensions of the one over the other House, and the possibility of either erecting itself into a privileged order, might it not be better to choose at the same time and in the same mode, a body sufficiently numerous to

be divided by lot into two separate Houses, acting as independently as the two Houses in England, or in our governments, and to shuffle their names together and re-distribute them by lot, once a week for a fortnight?" Jefferson to A. Coray, Oct. 23, 1823, Andrew A. Lipscomb and Albert E. Bergh, eds., *The Writings of Thomas Jefferson* (Washington, 1905), XV, 485–86.

8. Wilson, "Lectures on Law," Wilson, ed., *Works of Wilson*, I, 398–99.

9. *The Federalist*, No. 71, No. 63, No. 28.

10. Sullivan, *Observations upon the Government*, 22, 23; Wilson, "Lectures on Law," Wilson, ed., *Works of Wilson*, I, 439–40; [Stevens], *Observations on Government*, 50.

11. Iredell (N.C.), in Elliot, ed., *Debates*, IV, 148; Paine, *Rights of Man*, Foner, ed., *Writings of Paine*, I, 278; Wilson, "Lectures on Law," Wilson, ed., *Works of Wilson*, I, 417–18; *The Federalist*, No. 53.

12. [Madison], Phila. *National Gazette*, Jan. 19, 1792, Hunt, ed., *Writings of Madison*, VI, 83–85; Paine, *Rights of Man*, Foner, ed., *Writings of Paine*, I, 382–88, 379; Ramsay, *American Revolution*, I, 355–56.

13. Backus, *Sermon Preached at Long Meadow*, 8; Chipman, *Principles of Government*, 110–11; Wilson, "Lectures on Law," Wilson, ed., *Works of Wilson*, I, 221; *The Federalist*, No. 64. See Andrew C. McLaughlin, "Social Compact and Constitutional Construction," *Amer. Hist. Rev.*, 5, (1899–1900), 467–90.

14. Williams, *History of Vermont*, 342, 343.

15. *The Federalist*, No. 14; Wilson, in McMaster and Stone, eds., *Pennsylvania and the Federal Constitution*, 230, 231, 344; Wilson, "Lectures on Law," Wilson, ed., *Works of Wilson*, I, 416–17.

16. Jefferson to John Adams, Sept. 28, 1787, Boyd, ed., *Jefferson Papers*, XII, 189; [Dickinson], *Letters of Fabius*, Ford, ed., *Pamphlets*, 182–83; Wilson, "Lectures on Law," Wilson, ed., *Works of Wilson*, I, 435.

17. *The Federalist*, No. 51.

18. Madison to Jefferson, Oct. 24, 1787, Boyd, ed., *Jefferson Papers*, XII, 277.

19. Joel Barlow, *Advice to the Privileged Orders in the Several States of Europe Resulting from the Necessity and Propriety of a General Revolution in the Principles of Government* (Ithaca, N.Y., 1956, first published London, 1792), 17; Hitchcock, *Oration, Delivered July 4, 1788*, 18; Williams, *History of Vermont*, 344, 330.

20. Charleston *Gazette of the St. of S.-C.*, July 29, 1784; *The Federalist*, No. 10; Charleston *Gazette Extra. of the St. of S.-C.*, July 17, 1784.

21. *The Federalist*, No. 47, No. 48.

22. Madison's Observations on Jefferson's Draft of a Constitution for Virginia (1788), Boyd, ed., *Jefferson Papers*, VI, 316; Paine, *Letter to Raynal*, in Foner, ed., *Writings of Paine*, II, 250, *Rudiments of Law and Government*, v; James Iredell, "To the Public" (1786), McRee, *Life of Iredell*, II, 146; *Providence Gazette*, Nov. 7, 1789; *The Federalist*, No. 51. For a new definition of liberty similar to that being formed by the Americans see De Lolme, *Constitution of England* (London, 1788), 244–46: Liberty was not, as men used to think, the establishing of a governmental order or the participating in legislation through voting for representatives; for "these are functions, are acts of Government, but not constituent parts of Liberty." "To concur by one's suffrage in enacting laws, is to enjoy a share, whatever it may be, of Power," while liberty, "so far as it is possible for it to exist in a Society of Beings whose interests are almost perpetually opposed to each other, consists in this, that, *every Man, while he respects the persons of others, and allows them quietly to enjoy the produce of their industry,*

be certain himself likewise to enjoy the produce of his own industry, and that his person be also secure."

23. *The Federalist,* No. 50, No. 51; *Providence Gazette,* Dec. 29, 1787; Thompson to Jefferson, Apr. 6, 1786, Boyd, ed., *Jefferson Papers,* IX, 380; Jefferson to Monroe, May 20, 1782, ibid., VI, 185–86; Webster, *Sketches of American Policy,* 25. For Hamilton's disavowal of "the necessity of disinterestedness in republics" and his ridiculing of the seeking "for models in the simple ages of Greece and Rome" see "The Continentalist No. VI," July 4, 1782, Syrett and Cooke, eds., *Hamilton Papers,* III, 103.

24. [Murray], *Political Sketches,* Chap. II, "Virtue," 24, 25, 28–30, 47, 43, 38, 10. On Murray and the circumstances of the writing of his pamphlet see Alexander DeConde, "William Vans Murray's *Political Sketches:* A Defense of the American Experiment," *Miss. Valley Hist. Rev.,* 41 (1954–55), 623–40.

25. [Stevens], *Observations on Government,* 51; Wilson, "Lectures on Law," Wilson, ed., *Works of Wilson,* I, 393; [Murray], *Political Sketches,* 47–48. See also [Jackson], *Thoughts upon the Political Situation,* 22–24; Taylor, *Inquiry into the Principles,* 386, 390, 461–62.

26. [Madison], Phila. *National Gazette,* Feb. 20, Jan. 19, 30, 1792, Dec. 19, 1791, Hunt, ed., *Writings of Madison,* VI, 93–94, 85, 87, 70; Williams, *History of Vermont,* 206–07, 344–45; Wilson, "Lectures on Law," Wilson, ed., *Works of Wilson,* II, 125.

27. Wilson, "Lectures on Law," Wilson, ed., *Works of Wilson,* I, 384; Chipman, *Principles of Government,* 282, 286, 288–89; Ramsay, *American Revolution,* I, 357.

28. Pownall, *Memorial to America,* 53; Williams, *History of Vermont,* 345; Chipman, *Principles of Government,* 289–90, 291–92; Ramsay, *American Revolution,* I, 357; Wilson, "Lectures on Law," Wilson, ed., *Works of Wilson,* I, 21, 420; Jefferson to David Humphreys, Mar. 18, 1789, Boyd, ed., *Jefferson Papers,* XIV, 678; Wilson, in McMaster and Stone, eds., *Pennsylvania and the Federal Constitution,* 230.

29. Sullivan, *Observations upon the Government,* 38; Williams, *History of Vermont,* 346.

Jan Lewis

"Of Every Age Sex & Condition": The Representation of Women in the Constitution

The language of the Declaration of Independence is unequivocal: "All men are created equal and . . . are endowed by their Creator with certain unalienable rights . . . and among these are life, liberty, and the pursuit of happiness." The Constitution's language is more hedged: "We the People . . . ordain and establish this Constitution" in order to "secure the Blessings of Liberty to ourselves and our Posterity." There is nothing at all in the Constitution about equality. Clearly, the Constitution was proposing to establish a "supreme law of the land" that would govern every single person within the Republic's boundaries. But whom did "the People" comprise? What of persons and groups within the Republic who did not belong to "the People"? These are not simply historians' questions. The United States Supreme Court considered them in relation to Cherokee Indians in 1831 *(Cherokee Nation v. Georgia)* and in regard to all black persons, enslaved or free, in 1857 *(Dred Scott v. Sandford)*. In both cases the Court turned to history to justify its position that the persons in question "belonged" to the United States, but only in the sense of being subjects, not in the sense of being members of "the People."

Jan Lewis, who teaches at Rutgers University, wrote the following selection as a study toward a book on women, slaves, and the creation of a liberal republic. It is commonplace to see gender forming as great an obstacle to citizenship in the early Republic as race. Lewis suggests that reality was more blurred, in regard to both categories, whatever the Supreme Court would later say. Lewis raises problems both of method and of substance. Methodologically, she turns the Constitution's complete avoidance of questions of gender from a given into a problem. Substantively, she addresses the problem of whether white women and nonwhite people of either sex in fact form a single category of exclusion. She also raises the problem of whether "citizenship" involved more than such strictly political rights as voting and holding public office. Addressing the latter question involves the problem of what kind of society the Framers and the ratifiers wanted the Constitution to protect. Turning from historians' usual concern with James Madison, Lewis pays particular attention to the Framer James Wilson, a Scottish-trained political theorist and later a justice of the Supreme Court.

Questions for a Closer Reading

1. Women are not "mentioned" in the Constitution, but were they included in some significant way among "the People"?

2. What reasoning did James Wilson follow when he included the category "sex" in his proposals for apportioning representation in the House of Representatives?

3. In what sense did Wilson think women could be citizens if they could not vote or hold public office?

4. What is the difference between Wilson's "Scottish Enlightenment sociology" and his "Lockean politics" in regard to the issue of women's place in society?

5. Did the founding generation's exclusion of women from political rights and its exclusion of black people spring from fundamentally different causes?

"Of Every Age Sex & Condition": The Representation of Women in the Constitution

It is commonly believed that women are nowhere mentioned in the American Constitution. Although the absence of women from the Constitution has seemed quite clear, scholars have not known what to make of this silence. Some argue that the authors of the Constitution intentionally framed it in a gender-neutral language so that women might be encompassed by its provisions, perhaps at some future date if not just then. It is no accident, such scholars suggest, that the Constitution repeatedly uses such words as "persons," "inhabitants," and "citizens" instead of "men."[1] Other scholars believe that the omission of women, if not intentional, reflected the patriarchal assumptions of the Founders and their belief that women had no role to play in government.[2] These debates go to the heart of a larger question, which is the relationship of women to the liberal state that the Constitution created. Is there a place for women within liberalism? Or have they always stood outside it, excluded from its inception?

These questions would be easier to answer had the authors of the Constitution been more explicit about the place they envisaged for women in the polity. As Richard B. Morris once remarked, "it would have been very helpful" if the Framers "had given us a hint" about why they were so vague in their discussion of gender.[3] But in fact, the Framers have left us a hint, in an amendment that James Wilson suggested to the resolutions then being debated in the Philadelphia Convention in the summer of 1787. Curiously, these words have attracted little attention from scholars of the Constitution and, so far as I can tell, none at all from historians of women.[4] Although these words require careful interpretation, once they are placed in the context of contemporary thinking about representation

Jan Lewis, "'Of Every Age Sex & Condition': The Representation of Women in the Constitution," *Journal of the Early Republic* 15 (1995): 359–87.

and about women, it becomes evident that the Constitution does include women, although the role it set out for them was different than the one designed for most men.

It was Monday, June 11, and the delegates who had convened in Philadelphia to revise the Articles of Confederation were now into their second week of secret meetings. The issue before the convention was who should vote for each branch of the proposed federal legislature. According to James Madison's notes, Roger Sherman of Connecticut had begun the day's session by proposing that "the proportion of suffrage" in the lower house of the national legislature, which would eventually be known as the House of Representatives, "should be according to the respective numbers of free inhabitants." Two South Carolinians, John Rutledge and Pierce Butler, immediately proposed that representation in the lower house should be based not upon the population of free persons, but upon each state's contribution to the national government. As Butler put it, "money was power." It was in this context, a debate about whether representation should be based upon population or wealth, which would include slaves, that Pennsylvania's James Wilson suggested language that would make clear that representation in the lower house would be "in proportion to the whole number of white & other free Citizens & inhabitants of every age sex & condition including those bound to servitude for a term of years and three fifths of all other persons not comprehended in the foregoing description, except Indians not paying taxes, in each state."[5] This wording was voted upon, approved, and incorporated into the resolutions that the group would continue to debate and refine throughout the summer.[6] Wilson's wording, only slightly modified, but with the words of interest to us here—"of every age, sex, and condition"—was included in the resolutions referred to the Committee of Style (chaired by William Samuel Johnson, of Connecticut, and including Alexander Hamilton, Rufus King, James Madison, and Gouverneur Morris)[7] on September 10.[8]

The Committee of Style, reporting back on September 12, compressed Wilson's language into the words that actually appear in the Constitution. The relevant clause—now the third paragraph in Article I, Section 2—specified that both representatives and direct taxes were to be "apportioned among the several states . . . according to their respective numbers, which shall be determined by adding to the whole number of free persons, including those bound to servitude for a term of years, and excluding Indians not taxed, three-fifths of all other persons."[9] This change in the wording seems to have been purely stylistic, rather than a change in meaning. The delegates voted many times over the course of the summer to change particular wordings, even on August 20 to remove the words "white & other" in the same clause as "superfluous."[10] Later, on September 13, they would replace the word "servitude" for "service," "the former being thought to express the condition of slaves, & the latter the obligations of free persons."[11] Presumably, then, when the Committee of Style dropped the words "of every age, sex, and condition," neither they nor the delegates who accepted the revision thought that the meaning of the clause had been changed.

In fact, if we follow the debate on this clause, we can see that throughout the deliberations the delegates assumed that women, as well as children, were to be included whenever the question came up of who should be counted for purposes of apportionment.[12] Wilson's original wording was part of the resolutions that the Convention was considering on June 19, and, as we have seen, most of this wording was still in the resolutions referred to the Committee of Style on September 10. But over the summer, when the delegates debated the issue of apportionment, they rendered Wilson's words in a kind of shorthand. For example, on July 5 the committee assigned the task of forging a compromise on the issue of representation reported out the following language (and here, of course, we are following the transformation in James Wilson's original wording, and not the thorny question the Convention was attempting to address): "that in the 1st branch of the Legislature each of the States . . . shall be allowed 1 member for every 40,000 inhabitants of the description reported" earlier, on June 19. On July 13, after further debate about the basis for representation, the language was modified again, to "number of inhabitants; according to the provisions hereafter mentioned," hence leaving aside for the moment the question of how to count slaves.[13]

All subsequent discussion about the question of apportioning representatives would focus on this explosive issue. The term "inhabitants"—later changed to "free persons"—now included women and children. Thus we can see what the Committee of Style probably had in mind when it dropped Wilson's original wording about age and sex. Women, then, certainly were considered by the Constitutional Convention, and although Wilson's reference to "sex" was ultimately excised, it seems clear that the Framers intended that women be included among those who were to be represented by the new government. The Constitution included women.

Because no one objected to Wilson's insertion of the word "sex," and because women seem so readily to have been comprehended by the other delegates in the terms "inhabitants" and "person," we might be tempted to think that Wilson was simply inserting words that reflected the common practice of the day. Even though no one raised an objection to Wilson's terminology, it seems to have represented a genuine innovation, and because so few have noticed since, the genuine radicalism of the Constitution's doctrine of representation has been obscured. Although, as J. R.

Pole and others have shown, in the revolutionary period democrats were beginning to insist that persons, not property, were the proper basis for representation, not until the Federal Constitution had any government based representation upon inhabitants rather than taxpayers or adult men. When Massachusetts and Pennsylvania, for example, revised their constitutions, they defined "population" as "rateable polls" or "taxable inhabitants," rather than the total number of inhabitants, whether eligible to vote or not. In fact, none of the new state constitutions enacted at the time of the Revolution numbered women and children as among those who were to be represented.[14] Similarly, the Northwest Ordinance of 1787 specified that representation was to be based upon the number of "free male inhabitants, of full age."[15]

To include female inhabitants when apportioning representatives, then, was a significant extension of democratic trends that were reshaping representation in the states. Wilson took this logic further than others had taken it until now and, in fact, further than those who would frame state constitutions in the near future would be willing to go. Kentucky's constitution of 1792 based representation on "an enumeration of free male inhabitants above twenty-one years of age," and Tennessee's, framed four years later, on "an enumeration of the taxable inhabitants."[16] But because Wilson's additional language about sex was uncontested, it is not immediately clear what he and the other delegates intended by their innovation.

When we examine Wilson's wording in the context of the convention's debate about the issue of representation, however, we may begin to understand what he and the other authors of the Constitution had in mind. The question of counting women when apportioning representatives was bound up in a matter the Framers found much more compelling, the issue of how to count slaves. While there was no discussion about including women when apportioning representatives, the Framers vigorously debated whether and how to count slaves; these discussions are quite revealing about what the delegates thought about the question of representation in general and who should be represented in particular. The slavery issue and one other, balancing the competing claims of the small and large states, were the most difficult ones the Convention faced; each threatened to send the delegates home without a plan for a national government. And both of these thorny issues touched upon the overarching question of representation. Any debate about counting slaves or small versus large states soon brought the delegates into discussions not only about very practical considerations, such as which of their states might benefit, but also theoretical views on the nature of representation in a republic. These more abstract discussions yield some clues as to what the delegates had in mind when they simplified James Wilson's original language. In fact, if we follow

Wilson himself through the debates in the Convention, his original intention in adding the language about sex becomes much more clear.

Even before he suggested the wording about "age, sex, and condition," Wilson had developed before the delegates his own theory of representation. Early in the proceedings, on June 9, Wilson "entered elaborately" into a defense of proportional representation. Representation should be based upon population; "as all authority was derived from the people, equal numbers of people ought to have an equal no. of representatives, and different numbers of people different numbers of representatives."[17] It was only two days later that he introduced his amendment to add the additional words, including the terms "of every age sex and condition," as well as the three-fifths clause. In this context, then, it seems evident that Wilson intended women to be included among the people, from whom "all authority was derived." In Wilson's mind, at least, women were included in the "We the People" who authorized the Constitution.

At this particular moment in the deliberations, Wilson was engaged in a debate about whether representation in the lower house should be based upon wealth or population. Hence, Massachusetts' Elbridge Gerry immediately objected to Wilson's amendment, addressing the three-fifths clause and asking, "Why then shd. the blacks, who were property in the South, be the rule of representation more than the Cattle & horses of the North."[18] Gerry did not, however, contest Wilson's suggestion that women should be included among the people who were to be represented.

Nor did any of the other delegates who would argue about the proper basis for representation. Pierce Butler of South Carolina would continue to argue that "property was the only just measure of representation. This was the great object of Governt: the great cause of war, the great means of carrying it on."[19] Although conservative nationalists such as New York's Gouverneur Morris agreed that "property was the main object of Society," he was troubled by the South Carolinians' desire to include slaves as part of the population.[20] He thought that the Three-Fifths Compromise was "an incoherence. If Negroes were to be viewed as inhabitants . . . they ought to be added in their entire number, and not in the proportion of 3/5." If instead, slaves were being counted as a measure of wealth, then the delegates should acknowledge that representation was being based upon population and property both.[21]

Wilson recognized the contradiction that Morris pointed out. He could not "see on what principle the admission of blacks" for purposes of representation "could be explained. Are they admitted as Citizens? Then why are they not admitted on an equality with White Citizens? Are they admitted as property? Then why is not other property admitted into the computation?"[22] Earlier New Jersey's William Paterson had made the same point even more explicitly. He "could regard negroes as in no light but as property. They are no free agents, have no personal liberty, no faculty of acquiring property, but on the contrary are themselves property, & like other property entirely at the will of the Master." After neatly distinguishing between slavery and freedom, Paterson went on to lay out his theory of representation. "What is the true principle of Representation?" he asked. "It is an expedient by which an assembly of certain individls. chosen by the people is substituted in place of the inconvenient meeting of the people themselves. If such a meeting of the people was actually to take place, would the slaves vote? they would not. Why then shd. they be represented?"[23] Although women could vote only in New Jersey, and children were not admitted to the polls anywhere,[24] Paterson made no objection to including them in the basis for representation. In some clear, if unspecified way, women were members of political society in ways that slaves simply were not.

While Wilson recognized the inconsistency of counting slaves, he was willing to compromise on this issue for the sake of the federal union. He would never concede, however, that "property was the sole or the primary object of Governt. & Society." To the contrary, "the cultivation & improvement of the human mind was the most noble object. With respect to this object, as well as to other *personal* rights, numbers were surely the natural & precise measure of Representation."[25] Now we can see what Wilson had in mind when he added the words "age sex & condition" to the resolutions the delegates were debating. If the purpose of government and society was not property, but the improvement of the human mind and the protection of other personal rights, then surely women must be included.

Although Wilson's intent seems clear enough, the delegates never commented upon Wilson's wording or the place of women in the government that they were creating. We may infer from their silence, however, a general acceptance of Wilson's reasoning, if not an understanding of its practical application. These delegates were alert to — and spent a long summer debating — the subtlest shifts of meaning; surely, then, someone would have noted and objected to Wilson's formulation had it seemed problematic for the purposes at hand. The implications of Wilson's wording on slavery, in contrast, were very much contested, and there the delegates could achieve no common understanding. The Three-Fifths Compromise, as Wilson suggested, was a compromise both on the place of slavery in the new nation and on the proper basis for representation; in a document that everywhere else insisted that persons, not property, were to be represented, the compromise inserted the principle of the representation of wealth. James Madison would later attempt to wrest a logic out of this "incoherence" by arguing in *The Federalist* Number 54 that the Constitution intentionally recognized slaves' "mixt character of persons and property." "This is in fact their true character," Madison asserted. And "if the laws were to restore the rights which have been taken away, the negroes could no longer be refused an equal share of representation with the other inhabitants."[26] By necessary implication, women, who were counted fully, were to be represented fully as well.

In none of these discussions was it argued that slaves, free blacks, women, or children should vote, although in some states free blacks and in one women were exercising the franchise.[27] Instead democrats such as Wilson and Madison believed that all free inhabitants were part of the "imagined community" that they called the United States.[28] They drew a distinction between being a member of the nation or community, which they called civil society, and voting. Every state in the new nation restricted the suffrage on the basis of not only age, sex, race, and freedom, but also wealth as well.[29] Not even all adult white men could vote. According to the tenets of republicanism, participation in the republic, and not simply voting, should have been restricted only to those who held enough property to secure a stake in the community and maintain their independence. Nascent liberals such as Wilson and Madison thought of the nation in much more expansive terms. Every free person who inhabited it was, in fact, a citizen, deserving of its protection and entitled to representation in the halls of government. In this context, women, who explicitly were to be represented but who just as explicitly were not permitted to represent themselves, became the touchstone of the modern, liberal state. By construing women as interested citizens incapable of representing themselves, liberalism provided a justification for the state: protecting those who could not protect themselves.[30]

James Wilson set out this theory of representation in his *Lectures on Law*. Over the winters of 1790–1791 and 1791–1792, he delivered two sets of lectures at the College of Philadelphia, but he never completed the entire course, nor had he even completed revisions on the entire set of lectures at the time of his death in 1798.[31] Born in Scotland in 1742, Wilson was not quite fifty years old when he was appointed the first Professor of Law at the College of Philadelphia, yet he had already played a prominent role in the critical political events of the era. Educated at St. Andrews and the University of Edinburgh, he moved to America in 1765, settling in Philadelphia where he studied law with John Dickinson. He became active in the revolutionary movement, serving in a number of important capacities at the state and national level. His "Considerations on the Nature and Extent of the Legislative Authority of the British Parliament" (1774) was one of the models for the Declaration of Independence, and Wilson himself was one of only six men to sign both the Declaration of Independence and the

Constitution. In 1789, George Washington made him one of the original associate justices of the Supreme Court.[32]

Even in the incomplete form in which Wilson's *Lectures* were published after his death, they constitute one of the most significant—and least explored—documents in political and social thought from this period of American history. If they lack the focus of *The Federalist,* they make up for it with their sweep. And although coherent political and social theories are embedded in the writings of the great thinkers of the age—Jefferson, Madison, Hamilton, Adams—none of them set out as systematically to articulate a comprehensive theory of society and politics. In their subject matter, the *Lectures* invite comparison with John Locke's *Two Treatises of Government,* and as such, they are a key text in the history of liberal thought in America. Moreover, because Wilson was self-consciously a synthesizer,[33] which is another way of saying that he was not always original, he is an especially useful guide to the assumptions shared by a wide range of political thinkers, particularly those whose thinking ran along liberal lines. Furthermore, because the lectures attempted to discuss systematically the relationship between society and government, they illuminate connections that others left unstated.

All of the dignitaries of the new federal government turned out for Wilson's inaugural lecture as Professor of Law at the College of Philadelphia. Women also were among the audience—not an unusual occurrence for such events, and at one point Wilson addressed them directly. "Methinks I hear one of the female part of my audience exclaim—What is all this to us? We have heard so much of societies, of states, of governments, of laws, and of a law education. Is everything made for your sex? why should not we have a share? Is our sex less honest, or less virtuous, or less wise than yours?" Women were not, Wilson averred, any less honest, virtuous, or wise than men. Moreover, although he doubted "whether it would be proper" for women "to undertake the management of publick affairs," they had an important role to play in society. He told the women in his audience that "you have indeed heard much of publick government and publick law; but these things were not made for themselves: they were made for something better, and of that something better, you form the better part—I mean society—I mean particularly domestick society. . . . "[34] Wilson continued with a discussion of the relationship between government and society that recalls Thomas Paine's famous dictum that "society in every state is a blessing, but government even in its best state is a necessary evil."[35] Wilson noted that

> By some politicians, society has been considered as only the scaffolding of government; very improperly, in my judgment. In the just order of things,

government is the scaffolding of society: and if society could be built and kept entire without government, the scaffolding might be thrown down, without the least inconvenience or cause of regret.

Government is indeed highly necessary; but it is highly necessary to a fallen state. Had man continued innocent, society, without the aids of government, would have shed its benign influence even over the bowers of Paradise.[36]

Government was created to serve society, not as an end in itself. Wilson would return to this point so frequently in his lectures that it is evident that it was not simply a passing thought, intended to placate the women in his audience. Instead, it was one of the central tenets in his political canon.[37] "Government," to put it succinctly, "was instituted for the happiness of society."[38] Like John Locke, Wilson believed that government originated in a social compact. As Wilson explained it, in terms reminiscent of Locke, government was created "by a human establishment, to acquire a new security for the possession or the recovery of those rights, to which we were previously entitled by the immediate gift, or by the unerring law, of our all-wise and all-beneficent Creator."[39]

For the past several decades, however, historians have been at pains to discount the influence of Locke in revolutionary thought, placing much more emphasis upon its sources in civic humanism, British Opposition party ideas, and the Scottish Enlightenment. As a consequence, it no longer seems possible to make a statement so simple as Carl Becker's comment in 1922 that "Jefferson copied Locke."[40] Still, the influence of Locke on thinkers such as Wilson is so clear that it requires our continued attention; we must ask how he and those who thought like him integrated Lockean ideas with ones they adopted from the British Opposition and the Scottish Enlightenment. We might begin this task by examining how Wilson understood the Lockean social contract, and what his interpretation of it meant for women.

Before we proceed with this analysis, we should note that feminist political theorists such as Carole Pateman have argued that women were left out of the social contract that created the liberal state. Applying Pateman's formulation to early America, Linda K. Kerber has recently written that "men and women have been differently situated in relation to consent theory. . . . Men are imagined as entering the social contract as free agents, but most women enter the social contract already bound by marriage and by antecedent obligations to their husbands." It is undeniable that, as Kerber and others have shown, the Common Law doctrine of coverture, which held that upon marriage a woman's legal personality was merged into that of her husband, remained the basis for property and domestic relations law after the Revolution.[41] It is equally true, however, as Kerber herself has demonstrated, that while some used coverture as a model for women's political position as well, others were beginning to imagine that women could be participants in the social compact, acting independently of their husbands or other male protectors.[42] James Wilson was one of those who found a place for women in the social compact.

One of Wilson's earliest statements about the nature of political society succinctly outlined the fundamental beliefs that he would develop at greater length in his *Lectures on Law.* "All men are," Wilson asserted in 1774, recapitulating Locke and anticipating Jefferson,

> by nature, equal and free: no one has a right to any authority over another without his consent: all lawful government is founded on the consent of those who are subject to it: such consent was given with a view to ensure and to increase the happiness of the governed, above what they could enjoy in an independent and unconnected state of nature. The consequence is, that the happiness of the society is the *first* law of every government.[43]

Some of the terms—freedom, equality, the state of nature, the requirement of consent—are familiar from Locke's *Second Treatise.*[44] Other elements, however, betray Wilson's Scottish upbringing and education and his wide reading among ancient and modern authorities both; according to the editor of Wilson's published works, he cited almost two hundred different sources. Moreover, as Morton White has demonstrated, Wilson was something of a plagiarist, sometimes copying a line here or there without citing his source. Perhaps even more important, Wilson was self-consciously a synthesizer who tried to reconcile what seemed to be contradictory points of view.[45]

Wilson's accomplishment was to merge a Scottish Enlightenment sociology and a Lockean politics; accordingly the happiness of society, a concept that is undeveloped in Locke, becomes the object of government. Although Locke seems to have posited a sphere of civil society, standing between the private realm of family and work and the public domain of government, he did not describe it in any detail or fit it into his social or political theory. In fact, in some places he made it appear as if civil society and government were one and the same.[46] A century later, when civic culture itself was a much more visible feature of public life and such philosophers of the Scottish Enlightenment as Francis Hutcheson and Thomas Reid had helped shift the focus from the individual to society,[47] James Wilson could write with much more specificity about both civil society and women's role in it.

Men and women were, by nature, social beings. "We are fitted and intended for society, and . . . society is fitted and intended for us," Wilson asserted in his *Lectures on Law*.

> We have all the emotions, which are necessary in order that society may be formed and maintained: we have tenderness for the fair sex: we have affection for our children, for our parents, and for our other relations: we have attachment to our friends: we have a regard for reputation and esteem: we possess gratitude and compassion: we enjoy happiness and pleasure in others, especially when we have been instrumental in procuring it: we entertain for our country an animated and vigorous zeal: we feel delight in the agreeable conception of the improvement and happiness of mankind.

Sociability, then, was nurtured in the family, and the bonds of affection that were created there stretched ever outward, from the family, to friends, the community, the nation, and even to humankind itself.[48]

It was for this reason that Wilson would say again and again that government was "instituted for the happiness of society." Although women could play no part in the masculine realm of government without jeopardizing their femininity,[49] they certainly had an important role to play in constituting society. Indeed, marriage was the pattern for all other social relationships and for patriotism itself. Yet while that other influential Scottish émigré John Witherspoon could use this logic to assert the "absolute necessity of marriage for the state,"[50] Wilson would turn that logic around and insist that government was created for society and for domestic society in particular. Because the purpose of government was to protect and even improve "social life," although women could not participate in the running of government, they had "a most intimate connexion with the effects, of a good system of law and government."[51] Women in this sense were the very object of government, and that was precisely why they had to be represented by the new government created by the Constitution.

From our present perspective, perhaps what we confront here is the question of whether the glass of political thought is half empty or half full. It is undeniable that Wilson's philosophy of government justified the exclusion of women from the vote and from office holding, and that basing this exclusion upon women's feminine nature would ultimately make it difficult for women to enter these political spheres.[52] Yet at the same time, Wilson's liberalism made a place for women not simply in the family, but in the large and important sphere of civil society—what Jürgen Habermas has called the "bourgeois public sphere."[53] In fact, although Habermas based his theoretical discussion of society upon European nations, it bears an uncanny resemblance to Wilson's description of the ideal society that he hoped would be sustained by a republican form of government. After expatiating upon the nobility of the individual voter, Wilson reflected, however, that "I am far from insinuating that every citizen should be an enthusiast in politicks, or that the interests of himself, his family, and those who depend on him for their comfortable situation in life, should be absorbed in Quixote speculations about the management or the reformation of the state." As he would frequently note, government was not, after all, the object of society. "There is a golden mean in things and there can be no incompatibility between the discharge of one's [sic] publick and private duty. Let private industry receive the warmest encouragement; for it is the basis of publick happiness." Government, then, was both good and necessary, and so was private enterprise, but neither attracted Wilson's full attention. Instead, Wilson recommended "a little relaxation. . . . It may consist in reading a newspaper, or in conversing with a fellow citizen. May not the newspaper convey some interesting intelligence, or contain some useful essay? . . . May not the conversation take a pleasing and an improving turn?"[54] This, then, was the very stuff of life: the reading of newspapers and conversation among friends. Wilson was describing the bourgeois public sphere, and, at a time when literacy rates for women were increasing,[55] it was a realm that included women.

The public sphere or civil society,[56] as Wilson described it and Habermas more recently has explained it, is the realm of society that was created when ordinary people emerged from their homes to engage in conversation. Habermas defines it as "the sphere of private people com[ing] together as a public,"[57] and although these are not the precise words that Wilson used, they convey his understanding too of the relationship between domestic and civil society.[58] As Habermas recognized and several historians have noted more recently, women participated in the public sphere.[59] Much like Wilson, Habermas has suggested that the notion of humanity that was cherished by the rising bourgeoisie of the eighteenth century was born and nourished in the family, which served as a model for all other relationships in society. The family, he wrote, "seemed to be established voluntarily and by free individuals and to be maintained without coercion; it seemed to rest on the lasting community of love on the part of the two spouses; it seemed to permit that non-instrumental development of all faculties that marks [sic] the cultivated personality." The family, then, contributed to society precisely the ingredients that defined humanity itself: "voluntariness, community of love, and cultivation."[60]

Little wonder, then, that Wilson would insist that government was created to protect society and domestic society in particular, for it was the source of all that was most valuable in life. Moreover, when any government subverted that end, or even when it failed to protect society, then the people might abolish, alter, or amend their government "at whatever time, and in whatever manner, they shall deem expedient."[61] Here Wilson synthesized Locke and the Radical Whigs into his Scottish Common Sense philosophy. Although government may be necessary to protect society and provide for its security, it is government as well that presents the greatest threat to happiness. Here, once again, Wilson's political thought anticipated that of Habermas, who argues that the bourgeois public sphere defined itself historically in opposition to the authoritarian early modern state. Indeed, political consciousness developed as people began to insist, "in opposition to [the] absolute sovereignty" of a monarch, that the only basis for law was the human values, what Habermas calls "general and abstract laws,"[62] that they had learned within the family.

It is for this reason that thinkers such as Wilson did not worry as much about the conflicts between individuals as those between society and the state. In part, they reflected the continuing republican obsession with the threat of governmental tyranny and a difficulty in thinking about the "people" in anything other than corporate terms. In this context, a "right" was a corporate liberty, secured from the state.[63] Yet Wilson's thinking incorporated liberal influences as well, in particular Locke filtered through a Scottish lens. As a consequence, his vision of society and of the rights that might be enjoyed in it was much richer than that of republican thinkers or even Locke. The primary focus always was upon society, for it was only there that individuals could become fully human.[64]

Just as Wilson's larger political and social philosophy synthesized republican and liberal themes, so also did his views on women. Although in other instances Wilson rejected the English jurist Blackstone as an authority,[65] he cribbed Blackstone's description of the common law principle of coverture: "The most important consequence of marriage is, that the husband and the wife become, in law, only one person: the legal existence of the wife is consolidated into that of the husband."[66] Yet if the common law doctrine of coverture reflected and perpetuated the dependent social relations of feudal society and helped assure the preservation of property in the male line of descent,[67] Wilson gave that doctrine a sentimental gloss. He rhapsodized it as "sublime and refined." For Wilson, coverture was not so much a legal fiction or even a mechanism for the transmission of property. Rather, it was the ideal of marriage itself. "By that institution the felicity of Paradise was consummated; and since the unhappy expulsion from thence, to that institution, more than to any other, have mankind been indebted for the share of peace and harmony which has been distributed among them."[68] In other words, if peace and harmony were to be found anywhere, it was in marriage. Hence, the doctrine of marital unity—that two persons would function as one—became the cornerstone of society.

Like a number of democrats at the time,[69] Wilson was willing to countenance divorce for marriages that had failed. As he put it, "When . . . the impression of happiness must be obliterated from every succeeding part of the conjugal history, why should any more blackened pages be added to the volume?"[70] Wilson's principal concern was not the orderly transmission of property but the happiness of society.

Indeed by recognizing divorce as the remedy for marriages gone wrong, Wilson was protecting the institution from what he considered more dangerous interventions. Marriage was a civil contract, and like other civil contracts, it could be dissolved under certain circumstances.[71] But this was the only option available. An aggrieved party could not summon the government to her support, nor could the community routinely call a husband or wife to account.[72] Wilson made the doctrine of marital unity a bulwark to protect the family from the state. In so doing, he transformed a wholly patriarchal vision of the family, in which a father ruled as a king over the dependents in his household, into a liberal one, in which the privacy of the sentimental family must be protected from the interventions of the state. "The rights, the enjoyments, the obligations, and the infelicities of the matrimonial state" all were "removed" from the "protection or redress" of the state. Instead, the state must stand aside, adopting the stance of "a candid and benevolent neighbour," who must "presume, for she wishes, all to be well."[73] The social order, then, rested upon a sort of wish-fulfillment: families that were presumed to be happy.[74]

Yet if Wilson's social and political theory held out little hope for women who were suffering at the hands of their families, it implicitly promised them the full array of civil liberties. To be sure, the doctrine of women's civil rights would come into conflict with the older doctrine of coverture and, as Linda Kerber has suggested, when it did, the more restrictive interpretation of women's citizenship might prevail.[75] The men who created the new national and state governments after the Revolution barely discussed the question of female citizenship. Hence, even when, as in the case of James Wilson, they seemed to expand the sphere of women's civil liberties, the Framers offered very little guidance about how those rights should be defined or enforced.

Nonetheless, during the first three-quarters of the nineteenth century, the constitutional foundation for women's citizenship—that is, women's entitlement to civil, but not political rights—was made increasingly secure. Although these conclusions must be offered cautiously, as there is much research to be done on this topic, women's membership in civil society would be defined in relationship to that of free blacks. Just as the issues of race and gender had been joined in James Wilson's language on representation offered to the Constitutional Convention, so too would they be linked in subsequent discussions in the nineteenth century. In fact, the understanding of women's civil rights emerged most clearly in discussions about attempts to limit the civil rights of free blacks. These discussions suggest that women were considered as members of civil society, entitled to representation and the rights of citizens, even if they could not themselves participate in government.[76]

This understanding emerged as state courts began to define the rights of free blacks. For those states that wished to restrict them from voting, women served a useful purpose as an example of another class of adult citizens who could not vote. In 1838, for example, the North Carolina Supreme Court observed, "Surely the possession of political power is not essential to constitute a citizen. If it be, then women, minors, and persons who have not paid public taxes are not citizens."[77] Yet at the same time, women could be used to illustrate the sorts of civil rights that had to be extended to all citizens, whether they voted or not. A provision in the proposed Missouri constitution, which would have prevented free blacks and mulattoes from entering the state, kindled a heated controversy when Congress debated Missouri's admission into the Union in 1820. Opponents argued that since free blacks were neither aliens nor slaves, they surely were entitled to the privileges of citizens, including the right to move from one state to another. Once again, women served as a point of reference for those who, while not holding political rights, nevertheless enjoyed the protections of citizens.[78] And in this case, the right under discussion was fundamental to liberalism, the right of a citizen to move freely within the nation.

Women, then, came to play a critical role in the way that democratic liberalism defined itself in practice. They became the referent for citizens who were not members of political society, that is, who could not vote or hold office. In this way, they helped legitimate not so much their own inequality as that of free blacks. In fact, when New Jersey women lost the vote in 1808, so did free blacks.[79] In other words, although the category of female citizenship—as members of civil but not political society—was contested,[80] it was more stable than that of free blacks, and hence could be used in attempts to stabilize the status of free blacks.

Such efforts to stabilize the position of free blacks could not entirely succeed, however, because they rested upon the assumption that all members of society were members of that imagined community known as the nation. Although white men could accept the general principle that women were part of the nation, the notion that blacks were to be included too was considerably more problematic. Here it was not so much the specific implications of that assumption that proved difficult for whites to accept as the fundamental principle itself. The first federal naturalization act of 1790, while liberal in other regards, offered citizenship to "free white" persons only. When white Americans drew the boundaries between themselves and other nations, their first impulse was to keep dark-skinned people out.[81]

Although Wilson's social theory was not intrinsically racist—and he himself was an opponent of slavery—it was ill-equipped to deal with the increasing racism of the new nation.[82] Because Wilson's version of liberalism rested upon the family, it could easily integrate women into its social vision; indeed, they were necessary to it. The same was not true for free blacks. Political pronouncements such as, "We see those persons possess the greatest share of happiness, who have about them many objects of love and endearment," had a certain amount of resonance in a society that was beginning to pay homage to the affectionate family.[83] It was not at all clear, however, that free blacks could as easily be integrated into a political society premised upon the affectionate family and the emotions of love and endearment.

Because of their social unacceptability to whites, free blacks presented a challenge to the liberal notion of social citizenship, that is, the sort of citizenship enjoyed by women. As a number of historians have shown, increasingly public life in the North as well as the South was being segregated. In the North, some public spaces, such as restaurants and hotels, were closed to blacks entirely, while others, such as theaters, churches, and various modes of transportation offered them only segregated spaces. In many places schools, also, were segregated. In the South, all of these places and more were off limits for free blacks.[84] Indeed, much of the public sphere—that is, civil society itself—was closed to free blacks. In this context, blacks' civil rights became problematic.

Again and again in the antebellum period, as James H. Kettner has shown, courts in the North and South both would confront the dilemma presented by black citizenship. In general, northern courts would accept the doctrine of free black citizenship, although on occasion begrudgingly. Southern courts until about the second third of the century often were prepared to acknowledge free black citizenship as well, but as the slave system became more entrenched and challenges to it from outside mounted, southern jurists shifted their approach. Increasingly they looked for a new way to define free blacks—as more than slaves, but less than citizens. A South Carolina court dubbed free blacks "subjects" instead of "citizens." A Kentucky judge termed them "quasi citizens, or at least denizens." One in Georgia called them "our wards," while Mississippi offered the term "*alien strangers,*" and Louisiana suggested "strangers to our Constitution." Other states settled upon "degraded race" or "third class."[85] Understanding full well what citizenship meant, even in the absence of full political rights,

Southern courts flailed about looking for a category that was different—and less—than that occupied by women.

The worst blow to free blacks came, of course, with the *Dred Scott* decision in 1857. Ruling for the majority, Chief Justice Roger B. Taney argued that blacks, whether slave or free, could not be citizens of the United States.[86] A little over two decades and more than half a million lives later, that decision would be reversed, with the Fourteenth Amendment; two years later, free black males were given the right to vote. Then, in another two years, in 1872, Virginia Minor would sue the clerk in her home town in Missouri who refused to register her to vote. Her case made it to the Supreme Court that, in denying her the right to vote, confirmed what had become the prevailing wisdom: "There is no doubt that women may be citizens. . . . There cannot be a nation without a people. The very idea of a political community, such as a nation is, implies an association of persons for the promotion of the general welfare. Each one of the persons associated becomes a member of the nation formed by the association." Here, finally, was the explicit application of consent theory to women—but for the purpose of denying them the right to vote. The only real question, the Court insisted, was "whether all citizens are voters."[87] The answer, the Court held, was no.

Less than a century after the ratification of the Constitution, then, the vision of the public sphere that it had embodied had faded badly. While it is certainly true, as a number of historians have pointed out, that over the course of this period, the meaning of political participation changed, so also did the context in which it was exercised. As the act of voting became increasingly important—and ever more widely shared[88]—women's exclusion from that privilege of citizenship became all the more glaring. At the same time, free blacks, whose ranks were expanded ten-fold by the termination of slavery in the South at the end of the Civil War, were increasingly segregated from those places that constituted the public realm,[89] and that sphere consequently took up less and less space. James Wilson's suggestion that persons "of every age sex & condition" should be counted was never, of course, an accurate description of social practices in the new nation. But it was also more than a Constitutional mechanism for apportioning representatives in the national government. It was also a close enough rendering of the public sphere that had emerged in American society in the eighteenth century to make it the sketch from which a more inclusive social and political vision might be imagined. Departing as it did from traditional formulas for representation, James Wilson's words made a radical and hopeful statement about what the new nation might be.

That vision of a broadly inclusive society and a government that worked always on its behalf was not realized then, nor has it been since. From the outset, female citizenship had been defined in relationship not so much to white male citizenship, but to that of blacks, both slave and free. Originally, women were the paradigmatic citizens of liberalism; that is, they constituted society, enjoyed its rights, and demanded its protection. Increasingly however, women came to stand for those who were members of society but who did not enjoy full political rights and could not represent themselves. At the same time, free blacks would come to stand for those who enjoyed, nominally at least, complete political rights, but who were excluded from full membership in society. In this manner, the gap between politics and society, which had narrowed considerably in the Revolutionary period as liberal theories of government and society were brought to bear, was forced wider.[90] As gender has been used to construct the political and social practices of race, and race to construct the practices of gender, the fleeting vision of a wide public sphere open to persons of every age, sex, race, and condition has faded, leaving barely a trace.

Notes

1. See for example, Herman Belz, "Liberty and Equality for Whom? How to Think Inclusively about the Constitution and the Bill of Rights," *The History Teacher,* 25 (May 1992), 263–77; Robert A. Goldwin, *Why Blacks, Women, and Jews Are Not Mentioned in the Constitution* (Washington, DC, 1990). Men, it should be noted, are not mentioned in the Constitution either, except when the male pronoun "he" is used to refer to an officeholder, such as a senator or president.

2. See for example, Joan Hoff, *Law, Gender, and Injustice: A Legal History of U.S. Women* (New York, 1991), esp. 117–18. A number of historians have similarly argued that the exclusion of women from the political life and structures of the new nation was intrinsic, rather than incidental. See, for example, Linda K. Kerber, "A Constitutional Right to Be Treated like Ladies: Women and the Obligations of Citizenship," in *U.S. History as Women's History,* ed. Linda K. Kerber, Alice Kessler-Harris, and Kathryn Kish Sklar (Chapel Hill, 1995), 17–35; Carroll Smith-Rosenberg, "Dis-covering the Subject of the 'Great Constitutional Discussion,' 1786–1789," *Journal of American History,* 79 (Dec. 1992), 841–73; "Subject Female: Authorizing American Identity," *American Literary History,* 5 (Fall 1993), 481–511; Susan Juster, *Disorderly Women: Sexual Politics and Evangelicalism in Revolutionary New England* (Ithaca, 1994), esp. 210–11; and Rogers M. Smith, "'One United People': Second-Class Female Citizenship and the American Quest for Community," *Yale Journal of Law and the Humanities,* 1 (1989), 229–93.

3. Richard B. Morris, *The Forging of the Union, 1781–1789* (New York, 1987), 190.

4. They were, however, noticed on at least several occasions in the nineteenth century. "A Petition for Universal Suffrage" presented to Congress in January 1866 by Elizabeth Cady Stanton and several other feminists noted that "the Constitution classes us as 'free people,' and counts us as *whole* persons in the basis of representation. . . . " Records of the House of Representatives (National Archives and

Records Administration, Washington, DC); copy in Papers of Stanton and Anthony (Rutgers University). See also Senator Samuel Latham Mitchill's 1804 letter to his wife Catherine: "You must remember . . . that you are one of my constituents, and that I am in some degree responsible to you for my public conduct. In the theory of our Constitution women are calculated as political beings. They are numbered in the census of inhabitants to make up the amount of population, and the Representatives are apportioned among the people according to their numbers, reckoning the females as well as the males. Though, therefore, women do not vote, they are nevertheless represented in the national government to their full amount." "Dr Mitchill's Letters from Washington, 1801–1805," *Harper's New American Magazine* (Apr. 1879), 748.

5. *The Records of the Federal Convention of 1787,* ed. Max Farrand (1911; rep., 4 vols., New Haven, 1966), I, 201.

6. Ibid., I, 201, 227, 236; James Madison, *Notes of Debates in the Federal Convention of 1787, reported by James Madison* (New York, 1987), 149–50.

7. Ibid., II, 547, 553, 554.

8. Ibid., 571.

9. Ibid., 590.

10. Ibid., 350.

11. Ibid., 607.

12. Needless to say, the inclusion of children in the formula for representation had important implications in political thought. A discussion of this issue lies beyond the scope of this article. For a masterful analysis of the place of children in early American political thought and law, see Holly Brewer, "Constructing Consent: How Children's Status in Political Theory Shaped Public Policy in Virginia, Pennsylvania, and Massachusetts before and after the American Revolution" (Ph.D. diss., University of California, Los Angeles, 1994).

13. Farrand, ed., *Records of the Federal Convention,* I, 526, 603.

14. J. R. Pole, *Political Representation in England and the Origins of the American Republic* (1966; rep., Berkeley, 1971), 204, 274–75. See also Rosemarie Zagarri, *The Politics of Size: Representation in the United States, 1776–1850* (Ithaca, 1987), 39–42, 57–60; and, for a concise overview, Peter S. Onuf, "The Origins and Early Development of State Legislatures, in *Encyclopedia of the American Legislative System,* ed. Joel Silbey (3 vols., New York, 1994), I, 175–94. For the relevant sections in the constitutions of Massachusetts and Pennsylvania, see *The Federal and State Constitutions, Colonial Charters, and Other Organic Laws of the State, Territories, and Colonies Now or Heretofore Forming the United States of America,* ed. Francis Newton Thorpe (7 vols., Washington, DC, 1909), V, 1898, 3086–87. New York's 1777 constitution specified that in years to come, the legislature should be reapportioned on the basis of the "number of electors" in each county (V, 2629). The following states assigned each county, and in some cases town, a certain number of representatives in the lower house: Delaware (I, 562); Georgia (II, 778–79); Maryland (III, 1691); New Hampshire (IV, 2452); New Jersey (V, 2595); New York (V, 2629); North Carolina (V, 2790); South Carolina (VI, 3244–45); Virginia (VII, 3815–16). When the Georgia Constitution was rewritten in 1798, the basis for representation was changed to the "numbers of free white persons, and including three fifths of all the people of color"; that is, the basis for representation was essentially that of the Federal Constitution, except that race, rather than freedom was to be used as the principle of inclusion (II, 791).

15. "Northwest Ordinance," in *The Founders' Constitution,* ed. Philip B. Kurland and Ralph Lerner (5 vols., Chicago, 1987), I, 27. Each of the states created out of the territory, however, was to be eligible for admission to Congress once it had "sixty thousand free inhabitants" (Article V, I, 29). Representation, however, was to be based upon the number of free adult males.

16. Thorpe, ed., *Federal and State Constitutions,* III, 1265, VI, 3414.

17. Farrand, ed., *Records of the Federal Convention,* I, 179.

18. Ibid., 201.

19. Ibid., 542; see also, ibid., 562.

20. Ibid., 533.

21. Ibid., 603–04.

22. Ibid., 587.

23. Ibid., 561.

24. For the case of New Jersey, see Judith Apter Klinghoffer and Lois Elkis, "'The Petticoat Electors': Women's Suffrage in New Jersey, 1776–1807," *Journal of the Early Republic,* 12 (Summer 1992), 161–93. For children, see Holly Brewer, "Constructing Consent."

25. Farrand, ed., *Records of the Federal Convention,* I, 605.

26. *The Federalist,* ed. Jacob E. Cooke (Middletown, CT, 1961), 368.

27. Of course, the Constitution left the qualifications for suffrage up to the states. For free blacks voting in state elections, see James Oliver Horton, *Free People of Color: Inside the African American Community* (Washington, DC, 1993), 151. For women, see Klinghoffer and Elkis, "'Petticoat Electors.'"

28. Benedict Anderson, *Imagined Communities: Reflections on the Origin and Spread of Nationalism* (New York, 1991); Michael Walzer uses the term "political community" in *Spheres of Justice: A Defense of Pluralism and Equality* (New York, 1983), 28–30.

29. See the useful summary in James Wilson, *Lectures on Law,* in *The Works of James Wilson,* ed. Robert Green McCloskey (2 vols., Cambridge, MA, 1967), I, 408–11.

30. Here again, the distinction between a republican and liberal understanding of citizenship becomes more clear. For republican thinkers, liberty means the right to self-government, and because only those who are independent may participate in government, the scope of republican liberty is restricted. That is, even though republicans distinguished between personal liberty—which included an array of civil rights—and public liberty—the right of a people to govern itself, they thought of freedom fundamentally as the right to participate in government. See Gordon S. Wood, *The Creation of the American Republic, 1776–1787* (Chapel Hill, 1969), 18–28; and Alan Craig Houston, *Algernon Sydney and the Republican Heritage in England and America* (Princeton, 1991), 118. Liberals such as Wilson shifted the emphasis or, perhaps more precisely, expanded the compass to include protection of life, liberty, and happiness, for the entire society, not simply those who participated directly in government.

31. "Introduction," McCloskey, ed., *Works of Wilson,* I, 28–30.

32. There is no modern biography of Wilson. For brief treatments, see ibid., and "James Wilson (Sept. 14, 1742–Aug. 21, 1798)" *Dictionary of American Biography* (22 vols., New York, 1928–1958), XIX, 326–30.

33. Stephen A. Conrad, "Polite Foundation: Citizenship and Common Sense in James Wilson's Republican Theory," in *Supreme Court Review,* ed. Philip B. Kurland,

Gerhard Casper, and Dennis Hutchinson (Chicago, 1985), 359–88, esp. 386–87; Shannon Stimson, "'A Jury of the Country': Common Sense Philosophy and the Jurisprudence of James Wilson," in *Scotland and America in the Age of the Enlightenment,* ed. Richard B. Sher and Jeffrey R. Smitten (Princeton, 1990), 193–208.

34. Wilson, *Lectures on Law,* in McCloskey, ed., *Works of Wilson,* I, 85–86. For the presence of women in similar audiences at this time, see Jan Lewis, "Politics and the Ambivalence of the Private Sphere: Women in Early Washington, D.C.," in *A Republic for the Ages: The United States Capitol and the Political Culture of the Early Republic,* ed. Donald Kennon and Barbara Wolanin (forthcoming).

35. Thomas Paine, *Common Sense,* ed. Isaac Kramnick (London, 1976), 64. Consider also the philosophy of government embedded in Jefferson's First Inaugural Address, particularly by reading his encomium to "a wise and frugal Government, which shall restrain men from injuring one another, shall leave them otherwise free to regulate their own pursuits of industry and improvement," in the light of his injunction to his fellow citizens to "restore to social intercourse that harmony and affection without which liberty and life itself are but dreary things." Thomas Jefferson, *Writings,* ed. Merrill D. Peterson (New York, 1984), 494, 493.

36. Wilson, *Lectures on Law,* in McCloskey, ed., *Works of Wilson,* I, 86–87.

37. Near the end of his *Lectures on Law* Wilson quoted from his Introduction that "'publick law and publick government were not made for themselves;' but that 'they were made for something better;' that 'I meant society;' that 'I meant particularly domestick society.'" This was no "encomium," he insisted, but a principle "founded in sound politicks and genuine philosophy." Ibid., II, 608. For a different reading, see Smith, "'One United People,'" 245–47.

38. Wilson, *Lectures on Law,* in McCloskey, ed., *Works of Wilson,* I, 239; see similarly I, 284, 283, II, 585.

39. Ibid., II, 583.

40. Carl L. Becker, *The Declaration of Independence: A Study in the History of Ideas* (1922; 3rd ed., New York, 1970), 79. For the influence of civic humanism, see, for example, J. G. A. Pocock, *The Machiavellian Moment: Florentine Political Thought and the Atlantic Republican Tradition* (Princeton, 1975). For British Country thought, see, for example, Wood, *Creation of the American Republic.* For the Scottish Enlightenment, see, for example, Morton White, *The Philosophy of the American Revolution* (New York, 1978); Garry Wills, *Inventing America: Jefferson's Declaration of Independence* (Garden City, 1978); and Henry F. May, *The Enlightenment in America* (New York, 1976).

41. Carole Pateman, *The Sexual Contract* (Stanford, 1988); Kerber, "A Constitutional Right to Be Treated like American Ladies," 17–35 (quotation at 20). For coverture, see Norma Basch, *In the Eyes of the Law: Women, Marriage, and Property in Nineteenth-Century New York* (Ithaca, 1982); and Basch, "Equity v. Equality: Emerging Concepts of Women's Political Status in the Age of Jackson," *Journal of the Early Republic,* 3 (Fall 1983), 297–318.

42. Kerber, "The Paradox of Women's Citizenship in the Early Republic: The Case of *Martin* v. *Massachusetts,* 1805," *American Historical Review,* 97 (Apr. 1992), 349–78.

43. Wilson, "Considerations on the Nature and Extent of the Legislative Authority of the British Parliament," in McCloskey, ed., *Works of Wilson,* II, 723.

44. John Locke, *Two Treatises of Government,* ed. Peter Laslett (2 vols., Cambridge, Eng., 1960).

45. Wilson, "Bibliographical Glossary," in McCloskey, ed., *Works of Wilson,* II, 849–56; White, *Philosophy of the Revolution,* 133; Conrad, "Polite Foundation," esp. 386; Stimson, "'A Jury of the Country.'" As Jay Fliegelman has recently noted, plagiarism was almost an accepted intellectual practice in this period. See *Declaring Independence: Jefferson, Natural Language, and the Culture of Performance* (Stanford, 1993), 164–89.

46. Locke observed, "The only way whereby any one divests himself of his Natural Liberty, and *puts on the bonds of Civil Society* is by agreeing with other Men to joyn and unite into a Community for their comfortable, safe, and peaceable living one amongst another, in a secure enjoyment of their Properties.... When any number of Men have so *consented to make one Community* or Government, they are thereby presently incorporated, and make *one Body Politick.* ... " Locke, *Two Treatises of Government,* II, 124.

47. On the influence of the Scottish Enlightenment, see White, *Philosophy of the American Revolution;* Wills, *Inventing America;* Conrad, "Citizenship and Common Sense"; and David Daiches, "John Witherspoon, James Wilson and the Influence of Scottish Rhetoric on America," *Eighteenth-Century Life,* 15 (Feb. 1991), 163–80.

48. Wilson, *Lectures on Law,* in McCloskey, ed., *Works of Wilson,* I, 233; see also I, 241–42. So important was this point to Wilson that he would repeat it verbatim in his lecture on "Natural Rights," II, 587. See also Thomas Jefferson to Thomas Law, June 13, 1824, in Peterson, ed., *Writings,* 1335–39. Consider as well James Madison's *Federalist* Number 14, in Cooke, ed., *The Federalist,* 88.

49. Wilson, *Lectures on Law,* in McCloskey, ed., *Works of Wilson,* I, 85–88. As Rosemarie Zagarri has pointed out, Wilson followed the lead of Scottish thinkers in advocating social equality for women while insisting upon political inequality. See her "Morals, Manners, and the Republican Mother," *American Quarterly,* 44 (June 1992), 207. Wilson's thinking about women, like that of many of his contemporaries, was contradictory. He argued that women could not enter politics both because of their status, as unpropertied dependents, and their nature, which he called "female virtue." Wilson, *Lectures on Law,* in McCloskey, ed., *Works of Wilson,* I, 411, 86–88. Paul A. Rahe has suggested that Wilson's paean to female virtue was "inspired by Jean-Jacques Rousseau's celebration of domesticity as a bulwark against the psychologically debilitating effects of the corrosive individualism at the core of modern life," but there is little evidence that Wilson was particularly concerned by modern individualism or that he shared Rousseau's notorious misogyny. See Paul A. Rahe, *Republics Ancient and Modern: Classical Republicanism and the American Revolution* (Chapel Hill, 1992), 564–65. It may be useful to note that the tendency to assign political roles on the basis of status is characteristic of republican approaches to government, while assigning them on the basis of "nature" is more typical of liberal thought. At the same time it should be remembered that each approach to government offered means both for including and excluding. Because republicanism excluded the poor, the propertyless, and the dependent, it left open the possibility that single, propertied women might vote, which is precisely what happened in New Jersey between 1776 and 1807. See Klinghoffer and Elkis, "'Petticoat Electors.'" As republican approaches to government were replaced by liberal ones, women would be excluded on the basis of their (supposed) nature, including their special virtue. Yet if post-revolutionary liberalism restricted women from the suffrage and office-holding, it also, as will be suggested, opened up a space for them as members of civil society.

50. "Reflections on Marriage," *Pennsylvania Magazine* (Philadelphia), Sept. 1775, 408, later published as "Letters on Marriage," in *The Works of the Rev. John Witherspoon* (2d ed., 4 vols., Philadelphia, 1802), IV, 161–83. See also Jan Lewis, "The Republican Wife: Virtue and Seduction in the Early Republic," *William and Mary Quarterly*, 44 (Oct. 1987), 689, 709.

51. Wilson, *Lectures on Law*, in McCloskey, ed., *Works of Wilson*, I, 88.

52. See Rowland Berthoff, "Conventional Mentality: Free Blacks, Women, and Business Corporations as Unequal Persons, 1820–1870," *Journal of American History*, 76 (Dec. 1989), 753–808. Berthoff, however, overemphasizes the persistence of classical republican themes in mid-nineteenth-century justifications for the exclusion of women from politics.

53. Jürgen Habermas, *The Structural Transformation of the Public Sphere: An Inquiry into a Category of Bourgeois Society*, trans. Thomas Burger (Cambridge, MA, 1991).

54. Wilson, "Speech on Choosing the Members of the Senate by Electors," in McCloskey, ed., *Works of Wilson*, II, 787–88. Wilson liked these ideas so much that he repeated them in his *Lectures on Law*. Stephen A. Conrad notes that this passage "captures the essence of Wilson's polite theory of republicanism" in which "the essential opportunities for a true republicanism in America can be realized only in the fundamental sphere of the social life of the People 'out of doors.'" Conrad, "Polite Foundation," 384.

55. Kenneth A. Lockridge, *Literacy in Colonial New England: An Enquiry into the Social Context of Literacy in the Early Modern West* (New York, 1974).

56. As Stephen A. Conrad has pointed out, Wilson used the terms "civil society," "People," and "state" interchangeably. See Conrad, "James Wilson's 'Assimilation of the Common Law Mind,'" *Northwestern University Law Review*, 84 (Fall 1989), 218–19.

57. Habermas, *Structural Transformation of the Public Sphere*, 27.

58. See Wilson, *Lectures on Law*, in McCloskey, ed., *Works of Wilson*, I, 238–40. Habermas uses the term "civil society" to encompass the "realm of commodity exchange and social labor"; Wilson uses the term "private industry" instead.

59. See in particular Dena Goodman, "Public Sphere and Private Life: Toward a Synthesis of Current Historiographical Approaches to the Old Regime," *History and Theory*, 31 (1992), 1–20; Keith Michael Baker, "Defining the Public Sphere in Eighteenth-Century France: Variations on a Theme by Habermas," *Habermas and the Public Sphere*, ed. Craig Calhoun (Cambridge, MA, 1992), 198–207. Both Goodman and Baker critique Joan Landes's use of Habermas to explain women's supposed exclusion from the public sphere. See Landes, *Women and the Public Sphere in the Age of the French Revolution* (Ithaca, 1988), in particular her claim that "the exclusion of women from the bourgeois public was not incidental, but central to its incarnation. . . . " Ibid., 7. See as well Dena Goodman, *The Republic of Letters: A Cultural History of the French Enlightenment* (Ithaca, 1994), esp. 3–11. For evidence of women in the postrevolutionary American public and an explanation of why they were there, see Lewis, "Politics and the Ambivalence of the Private Sphere"; and Elizabeth Regine Varon, "'We Mean to be Counted': White Women and Politics in Antebellum Virginia" (Ph.D. diss., Yale University, 1993).

60. Habermas, *Structural Transformation of the Public Sphere*, 46–47.

61. Wilson, *Lectures on Law*, in McCloskey, ed., *Works of Wilson*, I, 77.

62. Habermas, *Structural Transformation of the Public Sphere*, 54.

63. See, in particular, Wood, *Creation of the American Republic,* Part 1.

64. See for example, Wilson, *Lectures on Law,* in McCloskey, ed., *Works of Wilson,* I, 227: "Society is the powerful magnet, which, by its unceasing though silent operation, attracts and influences our dispositions, our desires, our passions, and our enjoyments."

65. See for example, ibid., 77–79. See also Conrad, "Wilson's 'Assimilation,'" 197–215.

66. Wilson, *Lectures on Law,* in McCloskey, ed., *Works of Wilson,* II, 601.

67. Basch, *In the Eyes of the Law,* 45–54.

68. Wilson, *Lectures on Law,* in McCloskey, ed., *Works of Wilson,* II, 598.

69. Norma Basch, "From the Bonds of Empire to the Bonds of Matrimony: The Emerging Right of Divorce in the Context of Independence," in *Devising Liberty: Creating the Conditions of Freedom in the New American Republic,* ed. David T. Konig (forthcoming).

70. Wilson, *Lectures on Law,* in McCloskey, ed., *Works of Wilson,* II, 603.

71. Contrast his view to that of Blackstone who, as Norma Basch has explained, dispelled "the notion that marriage is a contract like any other; marriage once contracted is a status." Basch, *In the Eyes of the Law,* 48.

72. Community intervention had been routine in the Puritan colonies of New England. See, for example, John Demos, *A Little Commonwealth: Family Life in Plymouth Colony* (New York, 1970), 82–106; and Nancy F. Cott, "Eighteenth-Century Family and Social Life Revealed in Massachusetts Divorce Records," *Journal of Social History,* 10 (Fall 1976), 20–43. For changing standards, see Michael Grossberg, *Governing the Hearth: Law and the Family in Nineteenth-Century America* (Chapel Hill, 1985), 17–21.

73. Wilson, *Lectures on Law,* in McCloskey, ed., *Works of Wilson,* II, 603–04. Note also Morton J. Horwitz's observation that "nineteenth-century political, social, and economic thought . . . sought to establish a separate, 'natural' realm of non-coercive and non-political transactions free from the dangers of state interference and redistribution." Horwitz, *The Transformation of American Law, 1870–1960* (1977; 2d ed., New York, 1992), 11.

74. I have explored the roots in republican thought of this assumption that marriages must be free of conflict in "The Republican Wife," 689–721. If liberals would be more willing than republicans to confront the reality of conflict in the economy and society—Madison's *Federalist* Number 10 is the key text here—they continued to assume that families were intrinsically free from conflict.

75. Kerber, "The Paradox of Women's Citizenship," 349–378 (quotation at 371). As Kerber has demonstrated in her illuminating analysis of *Martin* v. *Massachusetts,* when the doctrine of coverture came into conflict with the liberal faith in an individual's ability to make her own choices, judges had no clear guide. They might, as did the Supreme Judicial Court of Massachusetts in 1805, decide that the principle of coverture took precedence, and that a woman married to a Loyalist had effectively no choice but to abandon her country and her property and accompany her husband when he left Massachusetts for England. But before they made that ruling they had to consider Attorney General James Sullivan's argument that a married woman could be "an inhabitant in every sense of the word. Who are the members of the body-politic? are not all the *citizens,* members; infants, idiots, insane, or whatever may be their *relative* situations in society?" Like James Wilson, Sullivan was a liberal, who believed that women were members of the original social compact that established government.

76. This conclusion must be advanced cautiously, as most of these statements about women's civil rights were, like Wilson's, abstract and categorical, and were advanced to explain why free blacks should or should not have certain rights, not why women should or should not enjoy them. Moreover, although the passing of Married Women's Property Acts in various states, beginning with New York in 1848, would begin to chip away at the doctrine of coverture, the legal fiction of marital unity continues even today to cast a shadow over women; consider only the reluctance of the police to intervene in so-called "domestic disputes." Nonetheless, the fundamental civil rights of liberalism—freedom of assembly, freedom of religion, freedom of speech, freedom from the oppressions of the state, and perhaps the most fundamental right of all, to own oneself—are far from trivial, and the extension of them to women, even in the abstract, is of considerable significance. For the persistence of coverture, see Kerber, "Obligations of Citizenship," 34, 355n. For the concept of self-ownership, see Locke, *Two Treatises of Government*, II, 27.

77. *State* v. *Manuel*, 4 *Devereaux & Battle*, 25–26 (NC, 1838), quoted in James H. Kettner, *The Development of American Citizenship, 1608–1870* (Chapel Hill, 1978), 317. Significantly, the case was about whether free blacks were citizens; the court concluded that they were.

78. Kettner, *Development of American Citizenship*, 312–14.

79. Klinghoffer and Elkis, "'Petticoat Electors,'" 74. Before 1820 free blacks also lost the right to vote in Connecticut and Pennsylvania, while in New York they had to meet a property requirement no longer demanded of whites. See Horton, *Free People of Color*, 151.

80. See for example, Ellen Carol DuBois, *Feminism and Suffrage: The Emergence of an Independent Women's Movement in America, 1848–1869* (Ithaca, 1978); and Berthoff, "Conventional Mentality." Although Berthoff suggests that state constitutional debates between 1820 and 1870 reveal the persistence of republican notions of the political incapacity of both women and blacks, it is possible to interpret his material in another way. In a more republican political culture, the exclusion of women and blacks from the polity would not have occasioned much debate; after all, women were barely mentioned in the constitutional debates of the revolutionary period, and it was slavery, not the status of free blacks, that attracted most attention. That there was debate at all suggests the problematic nature of female and black citizenship, leading some to argue for a fuller inclusion for both, and others to justify the status quo or even, in the case of free blacks, to argue for the rescission of those civil rights they already enjoyed. For another argument that American doctrines of female citizenship incorporated a republican assumption of female dependency, see Joan R. Gundersen, "Independence, Citizenship, and the American Revolution," *Signs*, 13 (Autumn 1987), 59–77.

81. Kettner, *Development of American Citizenship*, 236. See also Walzer, *Spheres of Justice*. In this context, the termination of the slave trade may be considered not only an attack upon slavery but as an attempt to prevent the entry of any more Africans into the nation. See James Oakes, "The Rhetoric of Reaction: Justifying a Proslavery Constitution," unpublished paper presented at Symposium of Bondage, Freedom, and the Constitution, Benjamin N. Cardozo School of Law/Yeshiva University, February 20, 1995.

82. For the growth of racism in this period, see Winthrop D. Jordan, *White over Black: American Attitudes toward the Negro, 1550–1812* (Chapel Hill, 1968), 429–569.

83. Wilson, *Lectures on Law*, in McCloskey, ed., *Works of Wilson* I, 237. See Lewis, "Republican Wife"; and Jay Fliegelman, *Prodigals and Pilgrims: The American Revolution against Patriarchal Authority, 1750–1800* (New York, 1982).

84. Ronald T. Takaki, *Iron Cages: Race and Culture in Nineteenth Century America* (New York, 1979); Leon Litwack, *North of Slavery: The Negro in the Free States, 1790–1860* (Chicago, 1961); Ira Berlin, *Slaves without Masters: The Free Negro in the Antebellum South* (New York, 1974), 321–27.

85. This paragraph is drawn from Kettner, *Development of American Citizenship*, 287–324 (quotations at 319–20).

86. Don E. Fehrenbacher, *The Dred Scott Case: Its Significance in American Law and Politics* (New York, 1978), 335–64. After asserting that at the time the nation was created, blacks "had no rights which the white man was bound to respect," Taney went on to list some of those rights that the recognition of black citizenship would necessarily confer. It is a veritable catalogue of the civil rights upon which participation in the public sphere depends: ". . . the right to enter every other State whenever they pleased . . . to go where they pleased at every hour of the day or night without molestation . . . the full liberty of speech in public and in private upon all subjects upon which . . . citizens might speak; to hold public meetings upon political affairs. . . . " Ibid., 347, 355.

87. *Minor* v. *Happersett*, 88 US 165–66, 170 (1875). For an analysis of this case, see Norma Basch, "Reconstructing Female Citizenship: *Minor* v. *Happersett*," in *The Constitution, Law, and American Life: Critical Aspects of the Nineteenth-Century Experience*, ed. Donald G. Nieman (Athens, 1992), 52–66.

88. Michael E. McGerr, *The Decline of Popular Politics: The American North, 1865–1928* (New York, 1986), 5, 40–41; Morton Keller, *Affairs of State: Public Life in Late Nineteenth Century America* (Cambridge, MA 1977), chap. 7.

89. A number of students of Habermas have questioned whether the bourgeois public sphere that he posited could ever have or did include persons other than bourgeois white males. Michael Warner, for example, has argued that the limitations of literacy, which made it disproportionately a privilege of propertied white males, effectively excluded women, racial minorities, and poor white men from the public sphere created by print in the eighteenth century. See Warner, *The Letters of the Republic: Publication and the Public Sphere in Eighteenth-Century America* (Cambridge, MA 1990), 15–16, 48–49. More recently he has argued that the exclusion from the public sphere of those who were not white males was not simply contingent, for the way in which the public sphere represented the individual presumed a white male body. See "The Mass Public and the Mass Subject," in Calhoun, ed., *Habermas and the Public Sphere*, 382–83. The presence of women in the public sphere, however, renders Warner's formulation somewhat problematic. See note 59 supra.

90. For a different approach to this problem—the growing gap between society and politics—see Wood, *Creation of the American Republic*, 562.

Jack N. Rakove

The Perils of Originalism

From *Original Meanings: Politics and Ideas
in the Making of the Constitution*

One powerful position among present-day legal thinkers
holds that in constitutionally significant cases the Supreme
Court ought to be guided by the "original intent" of the document's creators. Ascertaining original intent is a historical
question, but not necessarily a historian's one. A number of
important legal thinkers have offered "originalism" as a general strategy that jurists ought to employ when they decide
constitutional cases, and the Supreme Court frequently does
turn to *The Federalist* for evidence about what the Framers
and the ratifiers intended. The final selection, by Jack N.
Rakove, Coe Professor of History at Stanford University,
raises the problem of where to look to find the Constitution's original meaning. Do we find it among the delegates
to the Philadelphia Convention? If so, what relative weight
should we give to, say, James Madison, who masterminded
the Convention's agenda and whose ideas underpinned the
final result, and to Edmund Randolph, who presented Madison's ideas to the Convention but opposed the final document? Or do we find the Constitution's original meaning
among "the People," who ratified it, rather than among the
handful of men who wrote it? Is it possible to know the mind
of a whole nation, even at a moment of crisis? What reason
might there be that a single generation's understanding and
meaning ought to be binding upon that generation's de-
scendants, however much conditions change? Rakove won
the Pulitzer Prize for *Original Meanings: Politics and Ideas in*

the Making of the Constitution (1996), of which "The Perils of Originalism" is the first chapter.

Questions for a Closer Reading

1. In the light of Rakove's argument, who were the real "founders" of the American Republic?

2. How are the notions of meaning, intention, and understanding *different* tools for understanding why the Framers established the Republic?

3. Can a historian's answer to the problem of constitutional originalism really address the needs and concerns of the judge who posed it?

4. In what ways is it appropriate to use *The Federalist* for enlightenment on the question of the Constitution's meaning?

5. What problems do historians face if they turn to the Constitution's intellectual context to address the question of its original meaning?

The Perils of Originalism

"The infant periods of most nations are buried in silence, or veiled in fable," James Madison observed in July 1819; "and perhaps the world may have lost but little which it need regret." This was no casual observation. Years earlier, Madison had mounted a serious historical project of his own, studying the "History of the most distinguished Confederacies, particularly those of antiquity," as part of his preparations for the great Federal Convention of 1787. It was "the curiosity I had felt during my researches," he recalled near the close of his life, "and the deficiency I found in the

Jack N. Rakove, "The Perils of Originalism," in *Original Meanings: Politics and Ideas in the Making of the Constitution* (New York: Knopf, 1996), 3–22.

means of satisfying it more especially in what related to the process, the principles—the reasons, & the anticipations which prevailed in the formation"
of these confederations, that convinced Madison to "preserve as far as I
could an exact account of what might pass in the Convention" at Philadelphia. If the Convention fulfilled "its trust," his notes would enable future generations to recover "the objects, the opinions & the reasonings" from which
the "new System of Govt." had taken its form. "Nor was I unaware of the value
of such a contribution to the fund of materials for the History of a Constitution on which would be staked the happiness of a young people great even
in its infancy, and possibly the cause of Liberty through[ou]t the world."[1]

Madison recorded these thoughts in the preface he wrote to accompany
the posthumous publication of his notes of debates at Philadelphia. "A
sketch never finished or applied," he called it—and in truth, this preface
offered only a brief overview of the events leading to the calling of the
Federal Convention. But its rough quality did not trouble Madison. For
sound history, he believed, could never be written by the participants in
great events, however momentous their deeds or intimate their knowledge. "It has been the misfortune of history," he wrote in 1823,

> that a personal knowledge and an impartial judgment of things rarely meet
> in the historian. The best history of our Country, therefore, must be the fruit
> of contributions bequeathed by contemporary actors and witnesses to suc-
> cessors who will make an unbiassed use of them. And if the abundance and
> authenticity of the materials which still exist in the private as well as public
> repositories among us should descend to hands capable of doing justice to
> them, the American History may be expected to contain more truth, and
> lessons certainly not less valuable, than those of any Country or age.[2]

So Madison urged friends and correspondents to preserve their vital papers, and he took great care to gather and safeguard his own: letters, memoranda, and, most prized of all, the notes of debates which he regarded as
his great testamentary legacy to the American republic. Yet during the half
century between the adoption of the Constitution and his death in 1836,
Madison never thought to draft the first-person account of that momentous
event that historians—with all their mistrust of memoirs—would dearly
love to have.

Even so, a historian reading Madison's "Sketch" and his carefully preserved papers immediately recognizes a kindred spirit at work—so much
so, in fact, that Madison may well be regarded as a patron saint of American history. Without his notes of debates, it would be nearly impossible to
frame more than a bare-bones account of how the Constitution took
shape. They alone make it possible to follow the *flow* of debate within the

Convention, to detect the imprint of individual personalities and rhetorical styles, and, most important, to identify the shifting concerns that prevailed at different points during the deliberations.

Like so many of his colleagues and "cotemporaries," Madison was acutely and rightly aware that posterity would find his generation's experiments in self-government intensely interesting. In exchange for his own sensitivity to their needs, Madison asked only that those who later used his records should seek to write the "unbiassed" history the subject deserved. In one sense, his request sets an admirable standard to which all historians should naturally aspire: What self-respecting scholar sets out to write an avowedly "biased" history? Yet objectivity is, of course, an elusive ideal, and Madison's hopes express a faith in the possibilities of obtaining objective knowledge of the past that many modern scholars would find touchingly naive. For two sets of reasons—one tied to the character of the Constitution itself, the other involving more general issues of historical knowledge—the task of "doing justice" to "The Founding" of the American republic is more demanding than Madison ever suspected.

Precisely because the Constitution has always played a central role in American politics, law, and political culture, as both a continuing source of dispute and a legitimating symbol of national values, the interpretation of its historical origins and meaning has rarely if ever been divorced from an awareness of contemporary ramifications. When the early-twentieth-century Progressive historians portrayed the framers as a propertied elite intent on preserving the powers of their own class, they were mindful of the uses of public power in an industrializing America.[3] Or again, the emphasis that political scientists such as James MacGregor Burns and Robert Dahl place on the anti-democratic tendencies of the Constitution is derived from a frustration with the seeming inability of the political system to fashion effective governing coalitions.[4] No less political is the celebratory attitude toward the higher wisdom of the founders that marks the work of recent conservative political theorists who prefer the framers' ideas of natural rights and federalism to the result-oriented reasoning of contemporary legal theory and its accompanying willingness to expand the authority of federal courts at the expense of the democratic autonomy of communities and states.[5] Because any portrait of the Founding and the Founders—whether cynical or heroic—affects how we imagine these great symbols of American political life, even the most objective scholar may find it difficult to avoid an appearance of bias, however slight or inadvertent.

Madison himself was not immune to this danger. In his own way, he sought to enhance the heroic aura that already surrounded the Convention. For if the origins of the Constitution would never be lost in the dim reaches of legend and fable, opportunity still remained to portray its adoption and its framers in mythic terms. While recognizing that the "character" of the Constitution "must be tested by the experience of the future," Madison used the final paragraph of his "Sketch" to

> express my profound and solemn conviction, derived from my intimate opportunity of observing and appreciating the views of the Convention, collectively and individually, that there never was an assembly of men, charged with a great and arduous trust, who were more pure in their motives, or more exclusively or anxiously devoted to the object committed to them, than were the members of the Federal Convention of 1787. . . . [6]

An "unbiassed" view of the framers, in other words, was one that would discover their political integrity and benevolence — and one that would provide an exemplary lesson in the possibilities of republican politics to a generation that the aging statesman of the 1830s feared was learning to prefer confrontation to accommodation.

A history written in that way would necessarily tell the story of the framing of the Constitution not only from the vantage point of the framers but even, perhaps, as they would most have wanted it to be told. Understanding events as participants themselves did has always been one of the great goals and challenges of historical writing. Yet in recent years historians have become ever more insistent on the limitations of any form of storytelling — that is, of the narrative conventions traditionally used in reconstructing the epochal events of the past. Historians may think they are writing objective accounts of definable phenomena. But in practice (it is argued) there can be no single story of any event — least of all, so complex an event as the adoption of the Constitution. Moreover, the composition of any narrative history requires decisions as to perspective and dramatic structure that differ little from the imaginative contrivances of the novelist.

Even if a historian confident in his empiricism can dismiss such radical doubts as the mischievous intrusion of overly refined literary theories, the problem of perspective remains crucial for another reason. Both the framing of the Constitution in 1787 and its ratification by the states involved processes of collective decision-making whose outcomes necessarily reflected a bewildering array of intentions and expectations, hopes and fears, genuine compromises and agreements to disagree. The discussions of both stages of this process consisted largely of highly problematic predictions of the consequences of particular decisions. In this context, it is not immediately apparent how the historian goes about divining the true intentions or understandings of the roughly two thousand actors who served in the various conventions that framed and ratified the Constitution, much less the larger electorate that they claimed to represent. Economists and political scientists have developed highly sophisticated models to analyze collective voting on complex issues, but the evidence on which historians of eighteenth-century America rely cannot readily be compared with the databases of contemporary social science.

For all these reasons, then, the ideal of "unbiassed" history remains an elusive goal, while the notion that the Constitution had some fixed and well-known meaning at the moment of its adoption dissolves into a mirage. Yet in the end, what is most remarkable about our knowledge of the adoption of the Constitution is not how little we understand but how much. Historians familiar with the extant records may well feel that Associate Justice Robert Jackson rather overstated the point when he complained that the ideas of the framers had to be "divined from materials almost as enigmatic as the dreams Joseph was called upon to interpret for Pharaoh."[7] However indeterminate some of our findings may be, however much more evidence we could always use, the origins of the Constitution are not "buried in silence or veiled in fable." Not only do Madison's notes and other sources allow us to track the daily progress of the deliberations at Philadelphia, but the records of the ensuing ratification debates reveal the range of meanings that the American political nation first attached to the proposed Constitution. Nor are the relevant sources confined to what was said and written during the intense debates of the late 1780s. The larger intellectual world within which the Constitution is often located—the Enlightened world of Locke and Montesquieu, Hume and Blackstone,* plain whigs and real whigs, common lawyers and Continental jurists—has been the subject of extensive analysis. Nor is the prior political history of the Revolution a neglected episode in the study of the American past.

Questions of bias, perspective, and the intelligibility of collective action will remain vexatious, of course. But so they do in almost any kind of historical writing. Rather than fret about these problems in the abstract or bemoan the limits of the evidence, it makes more sense to ask how well particular types of sources can be brought to bear on the range of questions that arise when we ask what the Constitution originally meant, or what its framers originally intended, or what its ratifiers (and the electorate beyond them) originally understood they were being asked to endorse or reject.

Meaning, intention, understanding—these are the three terms that the historians, political theorists, and legal scholars who engage in originalist analy-

---

Locke and Montesquieu, Hume and Blackstone: Rakove is using these four European political and legal thinkers as instances of writers whom sophisticated Americans with an interest in politics and law were likely to have read.

ses of the Constitution commonly use to title their research. The terms are often used loosely and synonymously, at some cost to the clarity that this interpretive method ostensibly seeks. But they are not fully interchangeable — or at least they need not be — and distinguishing them more carefully exposes some of the conceptual traps that ensnare the unwary.

The Constitution is the text whose meaning interpretation seeks to recover, and the term "original meaning" can accordingly be applied to the literal wording — the language — of its many provisions. For example, what does Article I mean when it talks of "commerce" (a word famously glossed in the most controversial twentieth-century exegesis of the Constitution, a cometary work which once blazed across the academic sky and has long since vanished beneath its horizon)?[8] What does Article II mean when it vests something called "the executive power" in the president (the question that underlay the most important disputes of the 1790s)? Or again, what is the "establishment of religion" that the First Amendment prohibits Congress from making any laws respecting?

Meaning must be derived from usage, however, and it is at this point that the alternative formulations of original intention and understanding become pertinent. *Intention* connotes purpose and forethought, and it is accordingly best applied to those actors whose decisions produced the constitutional language whose meaning is at issue: the framers at the Federal Convention or the members of the First Federal Congress (or subsequent congresses) who drafted later amendments. Theirs were the choices of wording that produced the literal text, adding the phrase "This Constitution" at the beginning of the supremacy clause, for example, or substituting "declare" for "make" in the war-power clause. Knowing why they preferred one term to another is surely relevant to recovering the original meaning of the Constitution. Original intention is thus best applied to the purposes and decisions of its authors, the framers.

Understanding, by contrast, may be used more broadly to cover the impressions and interpretations of the Constitution formed by its original readers — the citizens, polemicists, and convention delegates who participated in one way or another in ratification. Unlike the framers, they had no authorial control over the content of the Constitution, and the only intentions they were ultimately allowed to exercise were to confirm or reject it in its entirety, sometimes hoping, but not assuredly knowing, that subsequent amendments might allay their worst fears. But this public debate was nevertheless very much concerned with how the manifold provisions of the Constitution were commonly or popularly understood — though here, of course, the range of understandings that emerged often produced rather less than a consensus.

Perhaps these distinctions seem labored or overly precise. But the value of thinking rigorously about the separate elements of originalism is compounded by the different purposes that this theory may serve. If its purpose is merely to gain a general sense of what a term meant, or why a given provision was adopted, *without treating its original meaning as dispositive,* then it is permissible to slide promiscuously among these sources and even to regard early interpretations adopted after the Constitution took effect as reasonably authoritative because of their propinquity to the deliberations of 1787–88. The greater the remove in time from the moment of founding, the greater the inclination to collapse the distinct phases of framing, ratifying, and implementing the Constitution into one composite process of original interpretation.

But this latitudinarian attitude becomes less defensible if originalism seeks to provide something more than an informed point of departure for a contemporary decision. For the argument that the original meaning, once recovered, should be binding presents not only a strategy of interpretation but a rule of law. It insists that original meaning should prevail— regardless of intervening revisions, deviations, and the judicial doctrine of *stare decisis**—because the authority of the Constitution as supreme law rests on its ratification by the special, popularly elected conventions of 1787–88. The Constitution derives its supremacy, in other words, from a direct expression of popular sovereignty, superior in authority to all subsequent legal acts resting only on the weaker foundations of representation. If this becomes the premise of interpretation, it follows that the understanding of the ratifiers is the preeminent and arguably sole source for reconstructing original meaning. The prior editorial decisions and revisions of the Convention recede to the status of mere proposals, while actions taken by any branch of government *after* the Constitution took effect themselves become mere interpretations. Both may still offer corroboratory evidence of how the Constitution was understood, for its framers and early implementers shared a common political vocabulary with its ratifiers. But that elision should not erase the real distinction and premise upon which a strong theory of originalism logically depends.

Whether one pursues the loose or strict versions of this method of interpretation, it should be evident that all appeals to the original meaning, intention, and understanding of the Constitution are inherently historical in nature. This does not mean, however, that these are the kinds of questions historians would ordinarily ask. A historical account of a particular clause would certainly want to address why it became part of the Constitution and

---

*stare decisis: The principle employed by judges that a rule or precedent established in a previous analogous case should be allowed to stand.

how its later interpretation evolved in response to events and the concerns of political leaders, jurists, particular interests, or the public at large. It would also have room to reflect on the ironic twists and turns that have often carried interpretation away from the apparent intentions and understandings of 1787–88. But historians have little stake in ascertaining the original meaning of a clause for its own sake, or in attempting to freeze or distill its true, unadulterated meaning at some pristine moment of constitutional understanding. They can rest content with—even revel in—the ambiguities of the evidentiary record, recognizing that behind the textual brevity of any clause there once lay a spectrum of complex views and different shadings of opinion. "It may be a necessary fiction for lawyers and jurists to believe in a 'correct' or 'true' interpretation of the Constitution, in order to carry on their business," Gordon Wood has observed, "but we historians have different obligations and aims." The foremost of these tasks is to explain why "contrasting meanings" were attached to the Constitution from its inception.[9] And, if anything, this is a task that recent controversies over the feasibility of a "jurisprudence of original intention" have inspired historians to pursue with relish.[10]

To borrow a dictum from John Marshall, the great chief justice (and constitutional ratifier), historians can never forget that it is a debate they are interpreting. They have a further obligation not easily reconciled with the strong form of originalism. With its pressing ambition to find determinate meanings at a fixed moment, the strict theory of originalism cannot capture everything that was dynamic and creative, and thus uncertain and problematic, in the constitutional experiments of the Revolutionary era—which is why, after all, the debates of this era were so lively and remain so engaging. Where we look for precise answers, the framers and ratifiers were still struggling with complex and novel questions whose perplexities did not disappear in 1788.

Yet historians have other duties that complicate their relation to the recurring question of the role that originalism can play in constitutional controversy and adjudication. As critics, consultants, or citizens, they are called upon (or volunteer) to assess the historical claims that judges make while resolving a judicial case in controversy or which partisan advocates express while contesting political issues with constitutional implications. Like other experts, historians guard their professional terrain jealously, and they may rise in righteous anger when opinions they believe to be dubious and false are advanced with dogmatic certitude. But also like other experts, they possess valuable information which they can be enticed to yield up, and which may well suggest that one account of the original meaning of the Constitution appears more persuasive or better founded than another. It is one thing to say that few interpretations of the more ambiguous and disputable clauses of the Constitution can be established conclusively, another to treat all interpretations as equally plausible or representative of the prevailing ideas of the time. Historians who pursue or merely observe the ongoing quest for the Holy Grail of original meaning thus occupy an awkward position vis-à-vis other knights-errant. Their research can lay an evidentiary basis for originalist interpretation, but it can also undermine critical assumptions on which invocations of original meaning depend, and expose the flawed conclusions they reach. And as Leonard Levy, the dean of American constitutional historians, has argued, the Supreme Court's use of originalist evidence is best described as a mix of "law office history" and justificatory rhetoric which offers little reason to think that this method of interpretation can provide the faithful and accurate application of the original constitutional understandings its advocates promise. William E. Nelson reaches a similar conclusion in his study of the adoption and early interpretation of the Fourteenth Amendment.[11]

It is not the province of the historian to decide questions of law. But by thinking about the original meanings, intentions, and understandings of 1787–91 as a problem of historical knowledge, it may be possible to give this recurring motif of constitutional interpretation a rigor it often lacks.

From the moment of its publication in a special issue of the *Pennsylvania Packet* on September 19, 1787, Americans have endowed the Constitution with two complementary sets of meanings. Taken as a whole—which is how the ratifiers had to take it—the Constitution symbolizes the "more perfect union" its framers proposed to put in place of the "imbecile" Articles of Confederation. In practice, the sole choice the Federal Convention and its Federalist supporters succeeded in forcing upon the nation at large was binary: The Constitution could be either accepted or rejected, but it could be altered only after it had been ratified. Thus ratification ultimately depended on the gross comparison of the Confederation and the Constitution. Structuring the decision in this way gave the Federalists the crucial political advantage of being able to equate support for the Constitution with support for the Union. There was nothing ambiguous about the nature of this choice at the time it was made, but it certainly became so later, as southern states'-rights theorists argued that the states that had been the parties to the original compact retained a sovereign right to reverse their decision.[12]

The Constitution has thus always represented something more than the sum of its parts. But since 1789, most disputes about its meaning have necessarily centered on its individual clauses. No single clause or provision can be interpreted without considering its relation to the document as a whole. Yet in practice, the enterprise of interpretation often requires an intense analysis of key words and brief phrases that the Constitution itself does not define. No explanatory footnotes or midrashic columns encumber the text, defining what such key terms as "necessary and proper" or "the executive power" or an "establishment of religion" were meant or understood to signify.

These two conceptions of the meaning of the Constitution are complementary, not contradictory. But they do lead historians to ask different kinds of questions about its adoption. The task of explaining *why* the Constitution was adopted does not involve paying close attention to its actual drafting or the origin and evolution of particular clauses. The central issue instead is to identify the political and social alignments that favored or opposed the creation of a stronger national government. Thus long after Charles Beard offered his *Economic Interpretation of the Constitution* in 1913, many historians still view the adoption of the Constitution largely in the context of a political struggle between identifiable constituencies and interests. Though the terms used to describe these different coalitions have changed over time, the thrust of inquiry has shifted less than one might suppose. Even in Gordon Wood's monumental study, *The Creation of the American Republic,* the substance of the Constitution matters less than the way in which the struggle over its ratification catalyzed a larger gulf between democratic and aristocratic elements in American society.[13] Within this context, it is enough to identify the most conspicuous differences between the Articles of Confederation and the Constitution; the basic story will not be altered if many of the particularities of the Constitution are ignored. Indeed, some of the concerns that most troubled the framers at Philadelphia—such as the extended impasse between small and large states—may prove only marginally relevant.

By contrast, the task of recovering the original meaning of the Constitution in all its detail raises a series of complex questions. Where do we turn when the meaning of the text—or more accurately, the meaning of a particular passage embedded in a larger text—is open to dispute?

An avowedly historical approach to the problem of original meaning involves something more than aggregating all relevant references to a particular provision of the Constitution or an aspect of constitutional thinking. It requires us to assess the probative value of any piece of evidence as well as to think systematically about the different types of evidence with which we work. In practice, there are four sets of sources that can be brought to bear to solve problems or puzzles about the original meaning of the Constitution. Two of these sets of sources can be described as *textual* in the sense that they consist of the explicit discussion of the Constitution found in the records of debates of the federal and state conventions of 1787 and 1788, as well as the commentaries published during the campaign over its ratification. The other two sets of sources can be characterized as *contextual* in that they may enable us—when explicit commentary on particular points seems inadequate—to reconstruct a body of tacit assumptions and concerns that informed the way in which framers and ratifiers thought about the questions they were resolving. On the one hand, there were those broad notions of government that Americans had acquired through their absorption in the political theory of the Enlightenment. But the way in which the political actors of the 1780s thought about the Constitution also reflected their perceptions of what might be called the public-policy issues of their day. Lessons derived from recent experience were arguably as likely to influence their thinking as the maxims and axioms they found in Locke or Montesquieu or Blackstone.

Each of these sources has its virtues and its potential defects. A historical approach to the problem of original meaning has to ask what each contributes to the overall inquiry.

The obvious point of departure must be the records of the Federal Convention itself: the inadequate journal kept by its secretary, William Jackson; Madison's daily notes of debates; and the other notes, memoranda, and speeches preserved by other delegates at Philadelphia. Given the circumstances under which the delegates deliberated, theirs were the only intentions that in any literal sense affected the composition and substance of the Constitution. This was not only because the Convention met in secret but, equally important, because its results ran far beyond what even the most astute observers anticipated or even imagined it would propose. The absence of any accepted agenda prior to the opening of debate in late May 1787 and the fact that the delegates came to Philadelphia essentially uninstructed by their legislative constituents make the internal deliberations of the Convention the first and most salient set of sources for the original meaning of the Constitution.

Tried techniques of historical narration should, in theory, be easy to apply to the task of writing the interior "story" of the Convention. What kind of event could be more susceptible to standard narrative treatment than one involving a limited number of actors (including certifiable "great men") meeting for a brief period and making critical decisions that define the dramatic structure of the entire story? Yet in practice the numerous narrative histories of the Convention have added little of interpretive value to our understanding of the framing of the Constitution. Certain stock themes are so essential to all accounts of the Convention as to defy authors to show a spark of originality. No author can stray far from a heavy reliance on Madison's notes of debates. The central actors must also be cast true to character: Madison, bookish yet politically astute; George Washington, reserved yet charismatic; James Wilson, brilliant but arrogant; Benjamin

Franklin, witty and wise; Luther Martin, inebriated and stultifying yet good for comic relief; Roger Sherman, a crabbed speaker but a dogged parliamentarian; Alexander Hamilton, the candid iconoclast; and Gouverneur Morris, rashly (if apocryphally) draping his arm around Washington's shoulder. And the dramatic structure of the story turns out to be misshapen, since the climactic "great compromise" of July 16 occurred a full two months before Franklin could finally conclude that it was a rising and not a setting sun he had long pondered on the back of Washington's chair.[14]

Even when the literary problems inherent in retelling a familiar, highly stylized story are put aside, the most that any merely narrative approach to the Convention can offer is a dramatic backdrop to the more important analytical questions we want to ask about the making of the Constitution. The dramatic structure of the Convention thus matters far less than the intellectual and political structure of the issues the delegates sought to resolve. For the completed Constitution was not the sum of a series of decisions taken on discrete issues. It is better imagined (to pursue the mathematical metaphor) as the solution to a complex equation with a large number of dependent variables: change the value of one, and the values shift throughout. The central problem thus involves tracing the relation between (or among) individual decisions that often seem to concern discrete issues but were in fact closely connected. Breathless accounts of the changing moods of the delegates or evocations of the heat and humidity of a Philadelphia summer that was, in any case, reasonably mild[15] will not explain why the decision to allow the state legislatures to elect the Senate undermined Madison's proposal to give Congress an absolute veto over all state laws; or how the final tinkering over the mechanics of presidential election was designed to enlarge executive authority in foreign affairs.

The construction of the matrix of these decisions is complicated by the fact that the Convention addressed two distinct types of issues. At the most abstract level, the debates were indeed concerned with such fundamental questions as the nature of representation and executive power, federalism, the separation of powers, and the protection of individual and minority rights. It is evident, too, that the delegates believed that what they did would have lasting implications not only for their constituents but for a larger world. No one dissented when Madison and Hamilton both observed that the decisions of the Convention were destined to "decide for ever the fate of Republican Government."[16]

Yet the debates at Philadelphia also had an intensely pragmatic cast. Much of the Convention was spent on issues that the delegates approached as spokesmen for the particular interests of their constituents.

Here their real challenge did not involve solving theoretical dilemmas posed by Hobbes or Locke or Montesquieu; it instead required efforts to accommodate the conflicting interests of different states and regions on such matters as the apportionment of representation and taxes, the regulation of commerce, and the extension of the slave trade. Rather than view the Convention as an advanced seminar in constitutional theory, historians and many political scientists have preferred to describe it as a cumulative process of bargaining and compromise in which a rigid adherence to principle yielded to the pragmatic tests of reaching agreement and building coalitions.[17] From this perspective, the politics of the Convention resemble that of any legislative body, and its votes become grist for the fine-milling techniques of roll-call analysis that are commonly used to explain decision-making in Congress, state legislatures, or, for that matter, any city council outside Cook County, Illinois. The key to understanding the "great compromise" may thus be found, one political scientist has suggested, through two- or five-factor solutions with the varimax rotation (ortho).[18]*

Ideas or *interests*—these are the classic if hackneyed antinomies upon which much of the debate over the political and intellectual history of the entire Revolutionary era has long been conducted. It is not difficult to see how both affected the deliberations at Philadelphia in 1787. What is elusive is the interplay between them. Some of the arguments the framers advanced were doubtless designed to legitimate positions rooted in calculations of state or regional or class interest. Others carried deeper conviction on their merits, as attempts to resolve issues that were avowedly related to problems of constitutional theory, broadly considered. The true task is thus to find "the middle ground"—a Madisonian metaphor—between the clouded heights of principle and the familiar terrain of specific interests.

Yet precisely because these higher principles often prove difficult to distill from the political maneuvers or elliptical discussions of the Convention, many students of the original meaning of the Constitution prefer to give equal or even greater weight to the commentaries and debates of the ratification campaign. Foremost among these sources are the essays of *The Federalist*, whose sway over modern scholarship begs explanation in its own right. But for all its virtues, *The Federalist* presents only one facet of the wide-ranging debate that erupted with the publication of the Constitution. Nothing like the extraordinary mobilization of public interest the Constitution evoked had been seen since the crisis of independence a full decade earlier. Ratification, it might be argued, created more than a new

---

two- or five-factor solutions . . . : Rakove is making sarcastic use of the technical language of quantitative political science.

framework of national governance. It also demonstrated the possibility of national politics, anticipating the equally noteworthy innovations that enabled Americans, against their expectations, to create effective political parties within a few years.

The records of the ratification campaign are more diverse than those of the Federal Convention. They consist of pamphlets and newspaper essays written to influence public opinion; private letters assessing both the Constitution and the changing state of politics; and the records of debates in the state conventions, whose assent alone gave the Constitution its ultimate legal force. This corpus of material can be put to two general uses.

First, the ratification records occasionally provide useful evidence bearing on the prior deliberations at Philadelphia. Individual framers were often asked to explain why the Convention had acted in one way or declined to act in another; sometimes their responses add significantly to our knowledge of the original debates at Philadelphia. Moreover, the arguments that these framers advanced in support of the Constitution might reflect reliable impressions or summaries of the considerations they felt had prevailed at Philadelphia—and thus attest to the original intentions underlying the text. Certainly some of the respect *The Federalist* commands is due not only to its lucid, comprehensive treatment of the Constitution but also to the privileged position its two principal authors, Madison and Hamilton, held as leading framers.

Far more important, however, is the second use to which the ratification records can be put. Taken as a whole, they provide our best evidence of how the Constitution and its provisions were understood at the moment of adoption. Again, this understanding (or these understandings) cannot be equated with the authorial intentions that gave the Constitution its actual content. It is entirely possible—even probable, indeed almost certain— that the intentions of the framers and the understandings of the ratifiers and their electors diverged in numerous ways, on points both major and minor. Given the highly charged and intensely political character of the ratification campaign, no other outcome was possible. True, the Federalist supporters of the Constitution had a natural incentive to rally around the most effective explanations for particular clauses, and thus to foster a measure of consensus as to their meaning. But their Anti-Federalist opponents could freely credit any objection their imaginations could conjure, no matter how wild. Some of their predictions echoed the hyperbole of eighteenth-century political rhetoric, and Federalists cited this extravagance and the inconsistencies in the Anti-Federalist brief against the Constitution to prove that their opponents were unreasoning and overwrought. Many historians have shared that view.[19] Yet whether extravagant or plausible, Anti-Federalist fears were part of the original understanding of the Constitution, not only in their own right but also because they influenced the arguments that were made in its support.

Our reconstruction of the original understanding(s) of the Constitution, then, cannot be divorced from the political context of the ratification struggle. This does not mean that we should dismiss all statements on either side of the question as so much propaganda, but it does require an evaluation of the expedient needs that particular arguments were made to serve. For both parties, the overriding imperative was to determine whether the Constitution would be adopted, not to formulate definitive interpretations of its individual clauses. Thus while arguments about particular provisions mattered a great deal, in the end, the sole decision the ratifiers took was that of approving the Constitution as proposed or rejecting it. The only understanding we can be entirely confident the majority of ratifiers shared was that they were indeed deciding whether the Constitution would "form a more perfect union" than the Articles of Confederation (even if it no longer claimed, as had the Articles, that this union would be "perpetual").[20]

Our knowledge of what the ratifiers understood they were adopting is further limited by the spotty character of the reporting of the debates at the state conventions and the obscurity of their members. Though a few speeches were reported in more detail than Madison provided in his corresponding efforts at Philadelphia, none of the records of the state conventions, with the possible exception of Virginia, match his notes in quality and breadth.[21] Yet notwithstanding their deficiencies, these records deserve careful scrutiny for one crucial reason that is, however, related more to questions of law than to those of history. Madison stated the key point in 1796, when he argued that questions about the meaning of the Constitution could be answered in the light of the debates over ratification, but *not* by consulting the intentions of the framers at Philadelphia. "Whatever veneration might be entertained for the body of men who formed our Constitution," he told the House of Representatives,

> the sense of that body could never be regarded as the oracular guide in expounding the Constitution. As the instrument came from them it was nothing more than the draft of a plan, nothing but a dead letter, until life and validity were breathed into it by the voice of the people, speaking through the several State Conventions. If we were to look, therefore, for the meaning of the instrument beyond the face of the instrument, we must look for it, not in the General Convention, which proposed, but in the State Conventions, which accepted and ratified the Constitution.[22]

Although Madison had serious problems explaining how the views of the latter were to be ascertained, his position has at least this in its favor: It is fully consistent with the theory of popular sovereignty that was itself one of the great rallying points of Federalist argument in 1787 and 1788. The Constitution became supreme law not because it was proposed by the Federal Convention of 1787 but because it was ratified by the state conventions of 1787–88. By this criterion, the intentions of the framers were legally irrelevant to its interpretation, but the understandings of the ratifiers could provide a legitimate basis for attempting to fix the original meaning of the Constitution.

Even the most intensive examination of the surviving records for the debates of 1787 and 1788 will leave substantial gaps in our knowledge, however. Similarly, the spare language of the Constitution does not make explicit the broader assumptions about government on which it is clearly based. The preamble to the Constitution cannot sustain the close theoretical analysis that has been lavished on the opening paragraphs of the Declaration of Independence.

To fill these gaps in the record and the silences of the Constitution, many scholars have sought to reconstruct the larger intellectual context that shaped the contours of American thought in the late eighteenth century. That thought and the Constitution it produced were expressions of the Enlightenment. There can be no question that the framers and many of their contemporaries were familiar not only with the great works of such luminaries as Locke, Hobbes, Montesquieu, Hume, and Blackstone, but also with the richly polemical literature of seventeenth- and eighteenth-century English politics, the moral philosophy and social science of the Scottish Enlightenment, and the disquisitions on public law of such respected European authorities as Grotius, Pufendorf, and Delolme.* Moreover, it is clear that general historical reading informed the way in which eighteenth-century Americans thought about politics. When they spoke of learning from experience, they did not mean their own so much as that of previous generations, running all the way back to classical antiquity.[23]

All of these writings were somehow part of the intellectual universe the framers inhabited. Yet again, their application to the interpretation of the Constitution poses difficult problems.

Perhaps the most vexatious involves tracing the lines of influence between these authorities and their American audience. At certain points, it is clear, quite specific connections can be made. The way in which Hamilton and Madison both invoke "the celebrated Montesquieu" to introduce their respective discussions of the extended republic and the separation of powers in *The Federalist* (essays 9 and 47) demonstrates the authoritative status that the French baron's treatise *De l'esprit des lois* commanded.[24]

Grotius, Pufendorf, and Delolme: European thinkers whose writings on politics and law were likely to be in American gentlemen's library.

Much has been made, too, of the inspiration that Madison found in David Hume's essay "Idea of a Perfect Commonwealth" as he sought to counter the familiar view that the republican form of government was suitable only for small and homogeneous societies, like the city-states of antiquity.[25] Or again, the Federal Convention's first discussion of executive power on June 1, 1787, presupposes a knowledge of William Blackstone's treatment of royal prerogative in his *Commentaries on the Laws of England.*[26]

Yet it is no easy matter to link specific provisions of the Constitution with the writings of prior authorities. The problem lies in a distinction that Americans at every level of politics understood: that between fundamental *principles* of government, on the one hand, and the actual *forms* that any individual government could take. On the principles of government, a broad consensus reigned. Government existed for the good of the many, and to protect the liberty, property, and equal rights of the citizen. The idea that representation would help the government to determine the common good was commonplace, and so was the belief that separation of powers was essential to the protection of rights. These and other principles were reiterated in all the political writings in which Americans were steeped. Their authority was axiomatic.[27]

Axioms alone, however, do not solve problems; specific calculations are always needed to derive the desired results. In practice, the entire enterprise of constitution making in revolutionary America centered on determining which forms of republican government were best suited to securing the general principles all accepted.[28] Decisions about forms touched such prosaic questions as the respective powers and privileges of the different branches of government or the two houses of a legislature, the basis of representation, terms of office, modes of election, and so on. Though statements by Hume or Montesquieu or Blackstone or Harrington occasionally seemed pertinent to a particular problem, more often a wide number of solutions could be made compatible with the first principles of republicanism. From their reading the framers of the Constitution could extract no simple formulas to determine the exact form the new government should take.

The intellectual world of the Enlightenment, then, provides only a general context within which the Constitution can be located. Though clearly important in its own right, it cannot readily be brought to bear to solve particular puzzles of constitutional meaning.

There is, however, a far broader context within which these writings can be located, and which in turn provides the true framework for recovering what was both original and derivative in the intentions and understandings of 1787–88. For the adoption of the federal Constitution culminated a century and a half of constitutional controversy, contestation, and innovation that gave the American revolutionaries a richly complicated legacy of ideas and practices from which to construct their new republican polity. With a modest risk of oversimplification, this prior history can be divided into four substantial phases.

It is evident, first, that the vocabulary of American constitutional thinking was profoundly shaped by the great disputes between the Stuart monarchs and their opponents (in Parliament and out) which reached a momentous climax in the Glorious Revolution of 1688–89.* On a host of issues—ranging from the great paradigms of mixed government and separation of powers to the "inestimable" right to trial by jury—the contending positions of the Stuart era were still vividly recalled a full century later.

These positions remained vital, in the second place, because the structure of colonial politics gave seventeenth-century arguments a continuing vitality in eighteenth-century America. Colonists naturally regarded their own legislative assemblies as miniatures of the mother Parliament, and the provincial elites who ruled there sought to acquire for these bodies the same rights and privileges that the House of Commons had struggled so long to acquire (or regain, if one clung to the belief that the Norman conquest of 1066 had deprived England of its "ancient constitution" of Gothic liberty). The recurrence in the colonies of these classic quarrels between executive prerogative and legislative privilege made Americans receptive not only to the general principles that Locke had enshrined in his *Second Treatise* but also to the works of more obscure but equally impassioned writers who preserved the radical edge of seventeenth-century polemics amid the complacency of Georgian Britain.

Third, the imperial controversy that began with the Stamp Act[†] of 1765 and ended with the Declaration of Independence sharpened the colonists' understanding of the striking differences between their own political practices and attitudes and those prevailing "at home" in Britain. These differences seemed most conspicuous in the practice of representation, but they were evident as well in the colonists' rejection of monarchy, aristocracy, and much (if not quite all) of the theory of mixed government.

Fourth, and arguably most important, independence necessitated the reconstitution of legal government within all the states (save the corporate colonies of Rhode Island and Connecticut), and it thus gave rise to the "experiment in republicanism" that the past generation of scholars has ex-

---

Glorious Revolution of 1688–89: The upheaval in England in which Parliament expelled the Catholic King James II and called upon his Protestant daughter Mary and her husband, William of Orange (in the Netherlands), to reign instead. The Glorious Revolution is the point at which Parliament established that an English king could not rule on the "absolute" terms that applied in France or Spain.

†*Stamp Act:* The first crisis of the American Revolution, during which Parliament first advanced that its own power over the colonies was absolute.

plored in such detail. The adoption of written constitutions of government in the mid-1770s was in one sense a wonderful accident made possible by the literal-minded way in which the colonists believed the collapse of royal government and the eruption of civil war had reduced them to something like a state of nature. But it also gave them the opportunity to establish new and superior forms of government, more in tune with the conditions of American society and republican principles. And once established, the operations of these state governments in turn provided the most visible examples of what republicanism meant in practice. Their failings not only drove the movement for constitutional reform that brought the framers to Philadelphia in May 1787, they also provided the experimental evidence upon which the Convention drew as it sought to fashion an improved model of republican government.[29] For the convention delegates of 1787–88 came to their task fresh not from research in their studies but from the business of managing a revolution and conducting public affairs at every level of government. Conscious as they were of the fate of other republics and confederacies, ancient and modern, the lessons of the past that they weighed most heavily were drawn from their own experience.

Yet if this decade of constitutional experimentation was the greatest influence on the debates of 1787–88, principles and lessons inculcated over the previous century and a half were not simply sloughed off as the detritus of an irrelevant, pre-Revolutionary ancien régime. Americans were as eclectic in their use of history as they were in their often selective reading of texts and authorities. Reconstructing how they reasoned about the great questions of the late 1780s may therefore require a review—in highly synthesized form—of aspects of Anglo-American politics and political theory that long predate the immediate debates over the Constitution. No simple formula or code can map how these strands of thought came together in 1787–88. Like any other historical effort to explain how texts emerge from contexts, the recovery of original meanings, intentions, and understandings is itself an act of interpretation—but one that can at least be bounded, though not perfected, by canons of scholarship.

Some may object that too great an emphasis on establishing the multiple contexts within which the framers and ratifiers acted risks historicizing the great moment of the Founding, reducing its profound expressions of principle to the prosaic level of mere interest and ideology, and subordinating its transcendent meaning in favor of a time-bound portrait of an eighteenth-century society that remains irretrievably lost and alien.[30] Against these charges, historians can respond in at least two ways. They can plead necessity: The evidence allows no other choice; our knowledge of the complexity of political controversy and debate during this period can sustain no other conclusion. Or they can plead innocence. Far from treating the political thought of the Revolutionary era as the mere product of a fevered ideology, the most important recent historical writing goes to great lengths to describe its originality and creativity. But it does so not by abstracting these creative acts and ideas from the circumstances of their origination but by exploring and explaining the relation between them.

Ultimately, of course, historians, political theorists, and legal scholars diverge in their approaches because they pose different questions and seek different answers. Working historians should have no illusions about their capacity to correct, much less prevent, the errors to which their colleagues seem prone. Nor should historians be surprised when their findings are put to uses they never intended or even contemplated. Surely J. G. A. Pocock, Bernard Bailyn, and Gordon Wood never imagined that their reconstruction of the early modern ideology of republicanism would provide the conceptual foundation upon which an entire school of legal scholars soon launched a "republican revival" of their own, in the process fashioning an originalism of the communitarian left to challenge the originalism of the new (and Republican) right.[31] The forms of historical argumentation employed on both the right and left margins of contemporary scholarship (and politics) are not driven, of course, by the historian's old-fashioned and perhaps naive desire to get the story right for its own sake. They represent, instead, only another chapter in the saga of the American search for a usable past. Historians certainly help this search to go forward, but they may also suggest why its goal is (and should remain) elusive. By taking the problem of "originalism" seriously, by considering the uses and potential misuses of different forms of evidence, it may be possible to advance a debate that is very much about a specific moment in history but is not about history alone.

Notes

1. Madison to William Eustis, July 6, 1819, *Letters and Other Writings of James Madison* (Philadelphia, 1865), III, 140; Max Farrand, ed., *The Records of the Federal Convention of 1787*, rev. ed. (New Haven, 1937), III, 550 (hereafter *Records*).

2. Madison to Edward Everett, March 19, 1823, *Letters*, III, 308–09.

3. J. Allen Smith, *The Spirit of American Government* (New York, 1907); Charles Beard, *An Economic Interpretation of the Constitution* (New York, 1913).

4. James MacGregor Burns, *The Deadlock of Democracy: Four-Party Politics in America* (Englewood Cliffs, N.J., 1963); Robert A. Dahl, *A Preface to Democratic Theory* (Chicago, 1956).

5. For two major statements, see Hadley Arkes, *Beyond the Constitution* (Princeton, 1990), and Walter Berns, *Taking the Constitution Seriously* (New York, 1987).

6. *Records*, III, 551.

7. *Youngstown Sheet & Tube Co.* v. *Sawyer,* 343 U.S. 579, 634–35 (1952).

8. I refer to William Winslow Crosskey, *Politics and the Constitution in the History of the United States,* 2 vols. (Chicago, 1953); a third volume, completed by his student William Jeffrey, Jr., was published in 1980; for the exegesis of the meaning of commerce, see vol. I, part I, "The National Power over Commerce."

9. Gordon S. Wood, "Ideology and the Origins of Liberal America," *William and Mary Quarterly,* 44 (1987), 632–33 (hereafter *WMQ*). Wood here draws on an important article by William E. Nelson, "History and Neutrality in Constitutional Adjudication," *Virginia Law Review,* 72 (1986), 1237–96.

10. By way of example, see the essays by John M. Murrin, "Fundamental Values, the Founding Fathers, and the Constitution," and Isaac Kramnick, "The Discourse of Politics in 1787: The Constitution and Its Critics on Individualism, Community, and the State," in Herman Belz, Ronald Hoffman, and Peter J. Albert, eds., *To Form a More Perfect Union: The Critical Ideas of the Constitution* (Charlottesville, 1992), 1–37, 166–216.

11. Leonard Levy, *Original Intent and the Framers' Constitution* (New York, 1988), 284–398; William E. Nelson, *The Fourteenth Amendment: From Political Principle to Judicial Doctrine* (Cambridge, 1988), 5; and see the earlier but still valuable study, Charles A. Miller, *The Supreme Court and the Uses of History* (Cambridge, 1969). In *The Strange Career of Legal Liberalism* (Yale University Press, 1996), Laura Kalman provides an intellectual history of modern legal scholarship that pays substantial attention to the different versions of originalism which have flourished in the legal precincts of the American academy over the past generation.

12. Amazingly enough, vestiges of that debate are still heard today. See Raoul Berger, *Federalism: The Founders' Design* (Norman, Okla., 1987), 21–76; and H. Jefferson Powell, "The Modern Misunderstanding of Original Intent," *University of Chicago Law Review,* 54 (1987), 1513–44.

13. Gordon S. Wood, *The Creation of the American Republic, 1776–1787* (Chapel Hill, 1969), 483–99; Wood further develops this theme in *The Radicalism of the American Revolution* (New York, 1992).

14. *Records,* III, 85 (Morris); II, 648, (Franklin). The best short narrative account of the Convention is still Max Farrand, *The Framing of the Constitution of the United States* (New Haven and London, 1913); for popular narratives, see Catherine Drinker Bowen, *Miracle at Philadelphia: The Story of the Constitutional Convention* (Boston, 1966); Clinton Rossiter, *1787: The Grand Convention* (New York, 1966); and Christopher Collier and James Collier, *The Constitutional Convention of 1787* (New York, 1986).

15. Hutson, ed., *Supplement,* 325–37.

16. *Records,* I, 423–24.

17. James H. Hutson, "The Creation of the Constitution: Scholarship at a Standstill," *Reviews in American History,* 12 (1984), 463–77; and "Riddles of the Federal Constitutional Convention," *WMQ,* 44 (1987), 411–23, both provide useful short summaries of the state of scholarship. On the duality of concerns operating at Philadelphia, see William E. Nelson, "Reason and Compromise in the Establishment of the Federal Constitution, 1787–1801," ibid., 458–84.

18. Calvin C. Jillson, *Constitution Making: Conflict and Consensus in the Federal Convention of 1787* (New York, 1988), is the most recent and comprehensive of several efforts by political scientists to use roll-call analysis in this way; and see Robert A. McGuire, "Constitution Making: A Rational Choice Model of the Federal Convention of 1787," *American Journal of Political Science,* 32 (1988), 483–522.

19. Thus Leonard Levy: "[M]uch of the Anti-Federalist literature was trash based on hysterical assumptions or on political calculations intended to deceive and incite fear of the Constitution." Levy, *Original Intent*, 4.

20. Kenneth Stampp, *The Imperiled Union: Essays on the Background of the Civil War* (New York, 1980), 3–36.

21. James H. Hutson, "The Creation of the Constitution: The Integrity of the Documentary Record," *Texas Law Review*, 65 (1986–87), 1–39, reprinted in Jack N. Rakove, ed., *Interpreting the Constitution: The Debate over Original Intent* (Boston, 1990), 158–62.

22. *Records*, III, 374.

23. On this point, the classic essay is Douglass Adair, "'Experience Must Be Our Only Guide': History, Democratic Theory, and the United States Constitution," in Trevor Colbourn, ed., *Fame and the Founding Fathers: Essays by Douglass Adair* (Chapel Hill, 1974), 107–23; and more generally, Trevor Colbourn, *The Lamp of Experience: Whig History and the Intellectual Origins of the American Revolution* (Chapel Hill, 1965).

24. *Federalist* 9 and 47, in Merrill Jensen, John Kaminski, and Gaspare Saladino, eds., *The Documentary History of the Ratification of the Constitution* (Madison, Wis., 1976–), XIV, 160–62, XV, 499–501 (hereafter *Doc. Hist.*).

25. Adair, "'That Politics May Be Reduced to a Science': David Hume, James Madison, and the Tenth Federalist," Colbourn, ed., *Fame and the Founding Fathers*, 93–106; the essential point is developed far more elaborately in Garry Wills, *Explaining America: The Federalist* (Garden City, 1981). For a broader examination of the influence of Hume, see Morton White, *Philosophy, The Federalist, and the Constitution* (New York, 1987).

26. *Records*, I, 64–74.

27. On this point, see especially Willi Paul Adams, *The First American Constitutions: Republican Ideology and the Making of the State Constitutions in the Revolutionary Era*, trans. Rita and Robert Kimber (Chapel Hill, 1980), 118–28.

28. John Adams put the key point in his *Thoughts on Government* of 1776. The "animating principle" of all republican government, Adams wrote, was its commitment to "an impartial and exact execution of the laws." But, he added, "Of republics there is an inexhaustible variety, because the possible combinations of the powers of society are capable of innumerable variations." Reprinted in *American Political Writing*, I, 403.

29. That is the great lesson to be learned, I believe, from Gordon Wood's epochal study of republican constitutionalism—rather than the hackneyed and increasingly sterile debate over the respective weight of the republican and liberal strains of American political ideology.

30. For two powerful statements of this theme, see Ralph Lerner, *The Thinking Revolutionary: Principle and Practice in the New Republic* (Ithaca, 1987), 1–38; and Thomas L. Pangle, *The Spirit of Modern Republicanism: The Moral Vision of the American Founders and the Philosophy of Locke* (Chicago, 1988), 28–39.

31. A good place to begin is Cass Sunstein, "Beyond the Republican Revival," *Yale Law Journal*, 97 (1988–1989), 1539–90 (part of a special issue devoted to a Symposium on the Republican Civic Tradition); for a general summary (and post mortem?) on republicanism, see Daniel T. Rodgers, "Republicanism: the Career of a Concept," *Journal of American History*, 79 (1992), 11–38; and see Kalman, *Faith of Our Fathers*, chap. V.

Making Connections

The questions that precede each selection are intended to help students deal with a particular piece of writing. But all the selections here are in dialogue with one another around one larger problem. That problem is how we can best understand the founding moment of the United States, as expressed in the Constitution. As the selections show, there are many possibilities for addressing that problem. They may be mutually exclusive. Or they may complement one another. It is certainly the case that each of these selections makes much more sense if it is read as part of a discussion rather than standing alone. The questions that follow should aid students to realize that the discussion is not finished and that everyone is free to join in.

1. Did the "American people" create the Constitution? Or in some sense did the act of creating the Constitution also create the American people?

2. How did the conflicting "languages" that Kramnick describes intersect with the conflicting social interests that form Patterson's subject?

3. Did the "American science of politics" of which Wood writes offer a means for solving the problems of exclusion that form Lewis's subject?

4. In the light of these selections, is there a social vision hidden within the Constitution? If so, whose was it, and of what did it consist?

5. Again in the light of these selections, which parts of the Constitution seem most directly addressed to the problems American society faced when the document was drafted?

6. Show how both political concepts and social conflict fed into the way the Constitution dealt with the issue of the separate states.

7. Which of the "discourses" that Kramnick discusses seems most helpful to you in understanding the response of Massachusetts Federalists to Shays's Rebellion?

8. The essays by Patterson and Lewis both deal with conflict during the Revolutionary era. How do they differ in their understanding of that problem?

9. Based on your reading of Wood and Rakove, what is your position about taking the Framers' "original meaning" as the best guide to interpreting the Constitution now?

10. Although the arguments about the Constitution were fierce in 1787–88, antifederalism disappeared after its ratification. Use the readings to help you understand why this happened.

11. Did the Constitution's vision of a large society destroy the notion of community in America? Or did it change the terms on which community could exist?

12. Did the Constitution limit the powers of government? Or did it create a government with considerable power?

13. Based on these readings, how would you describe the relationship between the Declaration of Independence and the Constitution?

Suggestions for Further Reading

This volume is not intended to provide a massive bibliography, but any interested student will want to delve into the subject more deeply. For a selection drawn from a book, the best way to start is to go to that book and place the selection within the author's larger argument. Each selection is reproduced with full annotation, as originally published, to allow interested students to go to the author's original sources, study them, and compare their own readings with what the author has made of the same material.

Students may also gain from the studies mentioned in Part Two but not excerpted, including Charles A. Beard, *An Economic Interpretation of the Constitution of the United States* (New York: Macmillan, 1913); Merrill Jensen, *The Articles of Confederation: An Interpretation of the Social-Constitutional History of the American Revolution, 1774–1781* (Madison: University of Wisconsin Press, 1940), and *The New Nation: A History of the United States during the Confederation, 1781–1789* (New York: Knopf, 1950); Conyers Read, ed., *The Constitution Reconsidered* (New York: Columbia University Press, 1938); and Forrest McDonald, *We the People: The Economic Origins of the Constitution* (Chicago: University of Chicago Press, 1958). In addition to McDonald, Beard has generated a minor academic industry. The most thoughtful study of his work is Richard Hofstadter, *The Progressive Historians: Turner, Beard, Parrington* (New York: Knopf, 1968).

The scholarship on republicanism has become enormous. In addition to Gordon S. Wood's *Creation of the Republic,* excerpted here, and his *The Radicalism of the American Revolution* (New York: Knopf, 1992), the absolutely key texts are Joyce Appleby, *Liberalism and Republicanism in the Historical Imagination* (Cambridge: Harvard University Press, 1992); Bernard Bailyn, *The Ideological Origins of the American Revolution* (Cambridge: Harvard University Press, 1967); Drew McCoy, *The Elusive Republic: Political Economy in Jeffersonian America* (Chapel Hill: University of North Carolina Press, 1980); and J. G. A. Pocock, *The Machiavellian Moment: Florentine Political Thought and the Atlantic Republic Tradition* (Princeton: Princeton University Press, 1975). The essays collected in Richard R.

Beeman, et al., eds., *Beyond Confederation: Origins of the Constitution and American National Identity* (Chapel Hill: University of North Carolina Press, 1987), are also helpful. So is Edmund S. Morgan, *Inventing the People: The Rise of Popular Sovereignty in England and America* (New York: Norton, 1988). The most recent explorations of how American political identity developed are Jack N. Rakove, *The Beginnings of National Politics: An Interpretive History of the Continental Congress* (New York: Knopf, 1979), and *Original Meanings,* excerpted here; and David Waldstreicher, *In the Midst of Perpetual Fetes: The Making of American Nationalism, 1776–1820* (Chapel Hill: University of North Carolina Press, 1997). See also Rakove, *Interpreting the Constitution: The Debate over Original Intent* (Boston: Northeastern University Press, 1990). Douglass Adair's essay "'That Politics May Be Reduced to a Science': David Hume, James Madison, and the Tenth *Federalist*" (*Huntington Library Quarterly* 20 [1956–57]: 346–50) remains a classic.

It may be that the debate on republicanism has exhausted itself. That is the conclusion reached by Daniel T. Rodgers in "Republicanism: The Career of a Concept" (*Journal of American History* 79 [1992–93]: 11–38). A possible sign that Rodgers is correct is that the historians' discussion has become mature enough to spill into other disciplines, most notably legal studies. See the special issue of *Yale Law Journal* (97.8 [1988]), given over to a symposium titled "The Republican Civic Tradition."

To develop that point with reference to three key states, see Edward Countryman, *A People in Revolution: The American Revolution and Political Society in New York, 1760–1790* (Baltimore: Johns Hopkins University Press, 1981); Robert A. Gross, *In Debt to Shays,* excerpted here; and Rhys Isaac, *The Transformation of Virginia, 1740–1790* (Chapel Hill: University of North Carolina Press, 1982). The issue of exclusion that Jan Lewis's essay addresses is taken further in two provocative studies: Carroll Smith-Rosenberg, "Dis-Covering the Subject of the 'Great Constitutional Discussion,' 1786–1789" (*Journal of American History* 79 [1992]: 841–73), and Paul Finkleman, "Slavery and the Constitutional Convention: Making a Covenant with Death" (in *Beyond Confederation,* ed. Beeman et al., 188–225). The same problem is discussed at great length in Rogers M. Smith, *Civic Ideals: Conflicting Visions of Citizenship in U.S. History* (New Haven: Yale University Press, 1997). The richest discussion of antifederalism is Herbert J. Storing, ed., *The Complete Anti-Federalist* (Chicago: University of Chicago Press, 1981). Cecilia Kenyon's essay "Men of Little Faith: The Anti-Federalists on the Nature of Republican Government" (*William and Mary Quarterly,* 3rd ser., 12 [1955]: 3–43) remains a very provocative study decades after its publication.

Peter Onuf, "Reflections on the Founding: Constitutional Historiography in Bicentennial Perspective" (*William and Mary Quarterly*, 3rd ser., 46 [1989]: 341–75), explores Constitution historiography more deeply. Michael Kammen, *A Machine That Would Go of Itself: The Constitution in American Culture* (New York: Knopf, 1986), deals with what the Constitution has meant outside the realms of law and academic discussion.